Policing Critical Incidents

Edited by

Laurence Alison and Jonathan Crego

WILLAN
PUBLISHING

Published by

Willan Publishing
Culmcott House
Mill Street, Uffculme
Cullompton, Devon
EX15 3AT, UK
Tel: +44(0)1884 840337
Fax: +44(0)1884 840251
e-mail: info@willanpublishing.co.uk
website: www.willanpublishing.co.uk

Published simultaneously in the USA and Canada by

Willan Publishing
c/o ISBS, 920 NE 58th Ave, Suite 300,
Portland, Oregon 97213-3786, USA
Tel: +001(0)503 287 3093
Fax: +001(0)503 280 8832
e-mail: info@isbs.com
website: www.isbs.com

First published 2008

ISBN 978-1-84392-279-7 paperback

British Library Cataloguing-in-Publication Data

A catalogue record for this book is available from the British Library

Project managed by Deer Park Productions, Tavistock, Devon
Typeset by GCS, Leighton Buzzard, Bedfordshire
Printed and bound by T.J. International Ltd, Padstow, Cornwall

Critical Incidents

Contents

Figures and tables

List of abbreviations

ACPO	Association of Chief Police Officers
CA	Communication Apprehension
CCA	Comparative Case Analysis
CCIR	Centre for Critical Incident Research
CHIS	Covert Human Intelligence Sources
CIA	Community Impact Assessments
CIM	Critical Incident Management
CISD	Critical Incident Stress Debriefing
CPS	Crown Prosecution Service
DJT	Decisions Justification Theory
FLO	Family Liaison Officer
HOLMES 2	Home Office Large Major Enquiry System
IACP	International Association of Chiefs of Police
IMC	Independent Monitoring Commission
IPA	Interpretative Phenomenological Analysis
IPCC	Independent Police Complaints Commission
LOCI	Lexis of Critical Incidents
MIR	Major Incident Room
MIRSAP	Major Incident Room Standard Administration Procedures
MORS	Military Operations Research Society
MPS	Metropolitan Police Service
MRG	Murder Review Group
MWs	Microworlds
NCPE	National Centre for Policing Excellence
NDM	Naturalistic Decision-Making

NFC	Need For Closure Scale
NGO	Non-governmental Organisations
NPIA	National Police Improvement Agency
PACE	Police and Criminal Evidence Act (1984)
PCA	Police Complaints Authority
PCA	Principal Components Analysis
PNC	Police National Computer
RAWFS	Reduction, Assumption-based reasoning, Weighing pros and cons, Forestalling, and Suppression
RPD	Recognition Primed Decision-making
SCT	Self-Categorisation Theory
SEU	Subjective Expected Utility
SIO	Senior Investigating Officer
SOP	Standard Operating Procedures
TDT	Traditional Decision-Making Theory

Acknowledgements

Laurence Alison

The initial passion involved in writing a book is contingent on complete amnesia of the effort that went into the previous one – forget the cramped plane journey and focus on the destination. Having both just seen the proofs for *Policing Critical Incidents* we are (of course) keen to start all over again. Some aspects of the final proof read-through are very satisfying. Others, now, with the benefit of hindsight, could have been significantly improved. But this is our first trip. Next time, we can travel lighter, more effectively and with greater conviction as to the right destination.

Many people have helped us along the way. As ever, Emily, my wife, has shared (endured?) the journey and been a constant source of support. Then, of course, are our co-authors, most of whom are researchers, students or associates of The Centre for Critical Incident Research. Key amongst these is Marie Eyre. She was given the unenviable task of bringing us into line when many other issues perpetually seemed to frustrate our ability to get on with the task. But more than organising the two of us and cajoling us to edit, re-edit and write up, Marie made many intellectual contributions throughout, providing insights and bringing cohesion to a project that was starting to become very large and unwieldy.

Geoff Brown, John Belger, Keith Jones, Carol Foster, Garry Rawlinson and Robbie Stopforth, from SimOps, Merseyside Police regularly welcomed us into the control room on countless occasions. I acknowledge the remarkable work of Jonathan's team and will leave him the opportunity of thanking them fully.

Other practitioners such as Adrian West, Lee Rainbow, Adam and Pippa Gregory, Terri Cole, Paul Lobb, Gary Shaw, Vinny Maitland, Gavin Pue and Sam Harkness (all currently or previously of NPIA) have been constants in our work and many other serving police officers have advised and assisted along the way.

More recently, Ray Groves (West Mercia Constabulary), Sean Cunningham (Metropolitan Police) and Paul Richardson (Merseyside Police) have given us the pleasure of their company in helping us reinvigorate a Masters course for a new breed of police officers. Their contribution, together with our latest intake of practitioner students (Jason Wells and Mark Chambers) is likely to shape the field in a very different direction in the coming years and, in concert with their (only very slightly) more youthful student colleagues, they are likely to bring a vibrant synergy and innovation to contemporary issues relevant to the psychology of policing.

Within the University, I should like to thank our Head of School (Professor Ian Donald) for his continuing support, as well as Dr Louise Almond, Dr Jon Cole and Dr Louise Porter who have all, at various points, engaged with the critical incident work. Jennie Roocroft, Michael Humann and Sam Mullins have also provided significant input. Berni Doran, Matt Long (Kent Police) and Kate Whitfield have made major contributions both to the development of Tactical Decision Game analysis and focus group research respectively. I have no doubt their work will be of great significance in the very near future. Previously, Allison Wright and Clare McLean steered a path through this complex world and Marie Eyre and Lou Almond have continued to cut a swathe through this most difficult of research domains.

Within the Centre for Critical Incident Research at The School of Psychology, I have been unbelievably fortunate in being part of a team that is egalitarian, always ready and never afraid to challenge, fiercely creative and prepared to help each other out at the potential expense of direct individual benefit. This collective, shared mental model of collaboration has been the defining feature of our Centre that I am most grateful for.

Jonathan has (of course) been a complete bl***y nightmare. He never reads anything on time, unceasingly forgets stuff that you have emailed him and asks for absurdly complicated things at the very last minute with no warning. He can't concentrate on the same topic for more than seven minutes and regularly comes out with the most insane ideas that would never work in what he fails to realise is reality. I keep telling myself I will never do another book with him again but I know that is absolutely not going to be the case. You can forgive a lot of a genius. Especially when they are as good a friend as you could hope to wish for.

Finally, my thanks also extend to the hundreds of practitioners that have contributed in sharing their stories and experiences. These include officers of all ranks, experiences and backgrounds, as well as many other emergency services and law enforcement agencies that work so hard for their respective communities. We have been regularly humbled by the accounts given and the efforts made on all our behalves and it has been a pleasure and an honour to capture this knowledge and set of important narratives. We have tried as far as possible (and without compromising anonymity) to retain the stories in the practitioners' own words, rather than superimposition of academic interpretation. Doubtless we have a long way to go in formulating a psychology of critical incident management but surely the first step is to allow our practitioner colleagues to describe the landscape in their own words.

Laurence Alison, January 2008

Jonathan Crego

Well this has really been a journey of love and looking back, the journey was a real adventure, John Grieve introduced me to Shackleton and his 1914 Antarctic Expedition. In Worsley's account there is a touching moment, which for me sums the relationship I have with my fellow explorer Laurence, so poignantly,

> ... we held her north by the stars. While I steered, his arm thrown over my shoulder, we discussed plans and yarned in low tones ...

As for Laurence and myself, I really don't know who we inadequately represent, either Shackleton or Worsley the navigator, I think we changed roles so many times, what I do know is that he is indeed a true friend. I too would like to acknowledge Marie Eyre, who has driven the two of us. She is a formidable woman with great humour and creativity and has platted fog-like material into a wonderful tapestry; I thank the academic team at Liverpool who have breathed life into this book and the continuing research. They are delightfully challenging, intellectually gifted as well as being good fun to be with.

My heartfelt acknowledgement must go to my team, they are the most difficult and loving group of people, they seem to generate more and more crazy exercises with less and less fuss, they live the belief, that 'if it's not right it's completely wrong' and 'immersion is everything'. They work so hard to generate the most deeply immersive exercises that become real; the delegates leave the event with a whole range of emotions from exhaustion to exhilaration but never incredulity. They have, and continue to provide me with immense support both emotionally and professionally and completely blend any traditional distinctions between work and play. My special thanks go to my right hand (and often the left hand too) man, John Jackson and Mick Crick, Geoff Williams, Jim Henson, Andy Lee-Savage, Mark Wilson, Nikki Rogan, Daniel Christian, Chris Higgs, Meryem Cast and with fabulous organisational support from Debbie Brooks, and the most professional event management from Clair Freidrich. Jack Patel, who is always able to pull the rabbit out of the hat with technical wizardry. Helen Schofield from NPIA has worked tirelessly to ensure that this work is imbedded nationally, finally to my good friends John Grieve and Bill Griffiths who have taught me so much about critical incident management.

My continuing respect goes to the people I work with day-to-day who manage sometimes unimaginable complexity, with good humour, stunning leadership and with enormous integrity. It is a continuing privilege to work alongside them and an honour to paint with their colours.

Jonathan Crego, January 2008

Professor Alison's royalties will be donated to a literacy charity in North Wales.

Professor Crego's royalties will be donated to SCOPE.

About the contributors

Professor Laurence Alison BSc, MSc, PhD, is Co-director of the Centre for Critical Incident Research, University of Liverpool where he also holds a Chair in forensic psychology. He is a Chartered Forensic Psychologist and conducts research on investigative decision making and leadership and contributes to national police training programmes. Professor Alison has a track record of publishing on the subject of policing and investigation in leading internationally recognised journals. His core area of interest is social cognition and the processes by which individuals make sense of ambiguous, complex or contradictory information. He has edited and co-authored seven books and is also an accredited behavioural advisor for the National Police Improvement Agency in the UK. His work has attracted attention from many police forces in the UK and abroad and he has contributed to a number of major police enquiries, particularly complex and controversial investigations. He has been a key psychological advisor in several major debriefs, including the 2005 London Bombings.

Louise Almond BSc (Hons), MSc, PhD, is a research associate at the Centre for Critical Incident Research, University of Liverpool. She recently completed a project funded by the Leverhulme Trust, which examined the content of behavioural investigative advice in addition to how such advice is interpreted and used. She graduated with a PhD in Investigative Psychology in 2006. Her PhD thesis investigated the characteristics and behaviour of youths who sexually harm. In 2001, Dr Almond carried out a project commissioned by the Home

Office into arson and arsonists and she has taught research methods and statistics at undergraduate and postgraduate level.

Andrea Caddick holds a BA (Hons) in Psychology and Sociology from the University of Liverpool, and recently completed an MSc in Investigative Psychology at the University of Liverpool. Her research interests include children's social categorisation, domestic violence risk assessment, interviewing techniques, leadership and team co-operation, and intra-group dynamics in gang crime.

Laura Cataudo completed a degree in Psychology at the University of Northumbria in 2004. In the two years following this degree, she worked as a psychological assistant in a Young Offender's Institution in Northumberland. Recently, Laura completed an MSc in Investigative Psychology at the University of Liverpool. Her research interests include violent group crime, leadership and team co-operation, false rape allegations and offenders' forensic awareness in relation to their development and consistency over time.

Professor Jonathan Crego BSc (Hons), PhD, along with William Griffiths and John Grieve, has designed and delivered critical incident training for the last 16 years. His design of the Minerva, Hydra and 10,000 Volt debriefing methodologies incorporated learning from the Taylor Report into Football Community Safety and the Stephen Lawrence inquiry. He generated the strategic management of Critical Incident environments. Jonathan has carried out over 90 debriefing sessions dealing with 9/11, the 2004 tsunami, London bombings, multi-agency perspectives on child protection and murder reviews both pre- and post-charge. He holds a research Chair and is Co-director of the Centre for Critical Incident Research at the School of Psychology, University of Liverpool. His Hydra and Minerva methodologies are now operating at 31 locations internationally; he has generated a community where ideas are created and shared.

Marie Eyre is a research associate working with Professor Laurence Alison in the Centre for Critical Incident Research, University of Liverpool. She is currently working on projects examining leadership and decision making in critical incidents. She is specifically interested in the relationships between broad cultural/organisational contexts and the ways in which they influence the cognitive processes of individuals in the dynamic environment of critical incidents. With a professional background in teaching and a commitment to research that has applied value, she supports Professor Alison's work in advising the police service on the role of psychology in decision making and helps to deliver training to practitioners in the field.

Alasdair M. Goodwill BSc (Hons), MSc, PhD, C.Psychol, is a lecturer in forensic psychology in the Centre for Forensic and Family Psychology, Birmingham University. His main research interests are in offender profiling, in particular developing, analysing and delivering pragmatic methods for suspect prioritisation in serious and violent criminal investigations. His research includes work on profiling stranger rapists by victim choice consistencies, geographical profiling and comparative analyses of profiling approaches. He has contributed psychological analysis of suspects and provided profiling advice on several high profile sexual offences across the UK. Dr Goodwill has been involved in research to promote ethical and considered guidelines to providing investigative advice to law enforcement agencies. Currently, he is investigating advanced methods of decision making to develop investigative decision support tools for stranger sex offences.

Professor John Grieve CBE, QPM, BA (Hons), Mphil, served in every rank as a detective, was the first Director of Intelligence for the Metropolitan Police and managed the Metropolitan Police's intelligence project. He led the anti-terrorist squad and was National Co-ordinator for Counter Terrorism during the 1996–98 bombing campaigns. He created and was the first Director of the Racial and Violent Crime Task Force (CO24) in response to the Stephen Lawrence public inquiry. Retiring in 2002, he is Chair of the Centre for Policing and Community Safety and Professor Emeritus at London Metropolitan University, Senior Research Fellow at Portsmouth University and a Commissioner for the Northern Ireland peace process following the Good Friday Agreement. With Jonathan Crego and William Griffiths, he helped create critical incident immersive learning and helped to pioneer the use of independent advisors and family liaison officers as fully engaged members of an investigation.

William Griffiths BEM, QPM, joined the Metropolitan Police Service as a 20 year old in 1967 and retired as Deputy Assistant Commissioner in 2005 having served mainly as a detective. Finally as Director of Operations and Tasking, he was responsible for all serious and specialist crime investigations ranging from homicide to armed robbery, kidnap and fraud. He was the Metropolitan Police's lead on learning from the Victoria Climbié and Damilola Taylor public inquires. He now leads the Commissioner's Development Initiative as Director of the Metropolitan Police Leadership academy. With John Grieve and Jonathan Crego, he helped design Critical Incident Leadership Training programme and has been the Director of Critical Incident Leadership Training for the last eight years. He has driven learning from these critical events into organisational learning and change

Clare McLean is a research assistant at the Centre for Critical Incident Research, the School of Psychology, University of Liverpool. Clare has examined multi-agency collaboration in complex inquiries, decision errors and decision inertia. She has worked on a variety of operational debriefs in major inquiries and has provided internal reports for several police forces in the UK.

Sam Mullins received an MA in Psychology from the University of Glasgow in 1999. This was followed by a brief period working in the addictions field before studying for the MSc in Investigative Psychology at the University of Liverpool, in which he received a distinction. His interests include the psychology of policing and the social psychology of terrorism.

Jennie Roocroft completed her BSc (Hons) in Psychology at the University of Liverpool in 2005. The following year, she completed her MSc in Investigative Psychology for which she was awarded a distinction. Her dissertation entitled 'Understanding counter terrorism: from recognition and metacognition to organisational identification' provided a qualitative analysis of a HYDRA simulation, which was followed by a quantitative study into organisational identification and lethal force decisions. Since her masters, Jennie has been employed as a Strategic Improvement Officer with Northamptonshire Police Service and has recently joined Westminster City Council, Crime and Disorder Reduction Team as a Performance Officer.

Kate Whitfield is a PhD student at the Centre for Critical Incident Research. Under the supervision of Professor Laurence Alison and Dr Louise Porter, her work focuses on leadership, teamwork and organisational identity within critical incident management. She holds a BA (Psychology and English) and a BA Honours with distinction (Psychology) from Rhodes University, South Africa, as well as a MSc in Investigative Psychology from the University of Liverpool. She has attended a number of critical incident training simulations run by the Metropolitan and Merseyside Police (including firearms, abduction, and multi-agency child protection exercises), and has subsequently written reports for both Merseyside Police and the National Centre for Applied Learning Technologies.

Allison Wright BSc, MSc, PhD, completed her first degree at McMaster University in Canada. She received her MSc in Investigative Psychology from the University of Liverpool and went on to complete a PhD in forensic psychology at Kent University. She was formerly a lecturer at the Institute of Criminal Justice Studies at Portsmouth University. Her research interests range from police leadership to methods for improving ways of interviewing older or vulnerable eyewitnesses who may be easily intimidated. Dr Wright has also explored perceptions of human rights among minority groups within criminal investigations.

Foreword

A conversation that mattered

William Griffiths BEM QPM
Director of Leadership Development,
Metropolitan Police Service

In April 1998, I found myself at Simpson Hall on the Hendon Training Estate addressing the 120 most senior detectives of the Metropolitan Police Service (MPS or Met). This 'gig', that I still remember vividly, was not for the faint-hearted on two counts. First, they were a massively experienced group of investigators, analytical by training if not entirely by practice, and notoriously sceptical by culture. 'Grim-faced' and 'hard-nosed' would have been the adjectives describing the collective noun from the crime reporters' lexicon for the group of detectives assembled that day.

Second, I was delivering a difficult and unpalatable message: that the Met had failed in the most privileged of our duties – to investigate the death of a fellow human being – in the conduct of the investigation into the racist murder of Stephen Lawrence in April 1993. Following an investigation by Kent Police into complaints from the Lawrence family, the Police Complaints Authority (PCA) had concluded that no fewer than 11 lines of inquiry had been missed in the original investigation and the review that had been undertaken was hopelessly flawed.

As we now know, Home Secretary Jack Straw wasted little time in announcing the Stephen Lawrence Public Inquiry, with full powers under the Tribunals Act, that played out in the summer of 1998 and published its findings in February 1999. Subsequently, my stark message to colleagues was more than justified when Sir William Macpherson's Inquiry published its conclusions about the investigation:

There is no doubt but that there were fundamental errors. The investigation was marred by a combination of professional incompetence, institutional racism and a failure of leadership by senior officers. A flawed MPS review failed to expose these inadequacies. The second investigation could not salvage the faults of the first investigation.

As an Area Commander, then Deputy Assistant Commissioner, with responsibility for crime matters in south-east London, I had some involvement with the second investigation; indeed, had worked with the Lawrence family and their lawyers on their private prosecution attempt at the Old Bailey, and had been the liaison officer to support the Kent investigation. No surprise, therefore, that I found myself at Simpson Hall that day spelling out the implications of the PCA Report for homicide investigation in London and the actions that I would now lead from an office at New Scotland Yard.

And that is the day that I had a 'conversation that mattered' with Dr (now Professor) Jonathan Crego that went something like this:

Jonathan: Bill, having heard about the problems you face, I think I can help you.

Bill (*gladly*): Thank you.

I knew Jonathan from when I had supported the hostage negotiator training from time to time, where he had designed an immersive learning environment for us known as Minerva. There we could train and prepare negotiators for real situations. As a non-academic practitioner myself, I fondly regarded him as an eccentric 'boffin' type who was slightly mad (as in, I didn't really understand his thinking) even before he became a professor.

From that conversation we formed an informal partnership to initiate the essential work that was needed just to begin the journey that would flow – and still runs eight years later – directly from the Stephen Lawrence Inquiry, even though we could not have foreseen at that stage the profound consequences for the MPS and, indeed, UK policing, arising from the Inquiry.

But, through our respective small teams of practitioners that were assembled, we could, and did, begin to focus on the core issue of critical decision-making. This is where I started to learn from Jonathan's study of emotions within decision-making.

What emerged, before the report was published, was Hydra – immersive learning, designed by Jonathan, with a 'remote control' to pause, rewind or fast forward events to support the experiential learning process. Moreover, Hydra enabled teams managing the same set of circumstances both to elicit more information to inform their decision-making and to give direction to virtual resources, thereby influencing the way in which the incident or investigation unfolded for them and allowing them to 'live' with the consequences, which could be highlighted in a facilitated discussion.

In the world of policing, this is the nearest thing to a 'flight simulator' I have encountered and I have enjoyed my small role in sometimes facilitating the learning that takes place in Hydra. I am glad that investigators can spend an entire week in Hydra with their investigation, secure in the knowledge that they can safely push at the envelope of learning in order to prepare themselves for some of the greatest challenges and accountabilities in policing.

Then came '10,000 Volts'(10kV), a liberating debriefing tool designed by Jonathan Crego that could capture the learning from participants within the Hydra environment and, significantly for the body of research reported in this book, from those colleagues and partners involved in real incidents and investigations around the world.

Here was a system that allowed those involved to 'tell it how it was', without fear or favour, expressing (or not – their choice) the emotions that they had experienced and the leadership they had observed, all the while knowing that they could celebrate success as well as point to how improvements could be made.

What a breakthrough! No more meaningless flip charts; no more Post-it notes and no more conversations (including those unspoken) left in the room. Hard data; actual phrases and sentences from the people who were there, who have permission as well as the facility to 'speak out'; not some sterile interpretation of a bullet point.[1]

As a detective, trained to work on evidence, not hunches, this material has great appeal to me. It takes research to a new, more credible and pragmatic level and I commend it to academics, practitioners, students and 'wannabe' detectives alike. It has particular relevance to the understanding of leadership under the pressure of events, which, from a personal perspective, fits neatly with my current job with the Met and, even after 40 years' experience, I have learned a great deal more from the analysis that is presented here in this book.

The journey continues, with a partnership that has, through adversity, become a true friendship. The tragedy that was the killing of Stephen Lawrence in 1993 has, as with all painful human experience, somehow produced a dividend. The capability of investigators is at an unprecedented level of professionalism that actually delivers upon the needs of families and communities as never before.

Its practitioners are proud to be engaged in a continuum of learning, courtesy of Professor Jonathan Crego and his (slightly mad) ideas.

So, continuing the conversation that matters:

Jonathan: Bill, having heard about the problems you face, I think I can help you.

Bill (*gladly*): Thank you. Keep going!

Note

1 Both Hydra and 10kV are fully explained in Chapter 3.

Preface

Understanding critical event learning and leadership: Hydra/10kV immersive learning, debriefing and other tools

John Grieve CBE QPM

A policing renaissance may be more useful than policing reform. Policing is learning. The police have relearned a considerable amount since 1999 about critical events, their prevention, minimising dysfunctional consequences of actions, ethics committees and challenge groups, administrative systems, compliance reviews, and evidential, investigative opportunity scenario-building from reviews. They are just beginning to learn a new lexicon from the detailed analysis of creative reviews. This is what the 10kV system now helps to achieve. Policing has always involved comparative case analysis but is now about beginning to build a register of near-miss critical events. A policing renaissance would recover learning, add to it and develop new concepts and a lexicon to describe the complicated world it now inhabits. This is achieved partly by collecting other people's accidents, both virtual and real, and writing the lexicon of how to describe decisions made and the reasons for making them. This volume contains an account of that detailed analysis. It avoids the climate of blame and concentrates on learning and the recovery and rearticulation of learning from the past.

I owe the following account in part to many conversations and reviews with Jonathan. This is a start at building the lexicon, using his descriptions. The debriefs and reviews have enabled a closer scrutiny of the relevance and synthesis of naturalistic versus classical decision-making in the complex post-modern world of twenty-first-century policing.

The naturalistic model moves away from mechanistic check-lists, away from systems where someone must be found to be a scapegoat, where 'The computer says no!' is the solution; away from the 'Let us change the manual' way of solving problems. It looks at the related interactive roles of both emotion and logic. It considers prejudice, bias, information overload, confusion, ambiguity, uncertainty, dynamic changes, shifting/blurred goals, boundaries and concepts which are ill defined and ill structured, the pressures of time, resource limitations, multiple decisions by multiple actors with different values or organisational perspectives. Each person brings their own worries and anxieties when making decisions or choosing between consequences.

The classic model retains the notion of decision error, bias and frameworks of interpretation that enable us to examine individual decisions. The approach that Laurence and Jonathan have adopted – namely, practitioners describe their experiences – allows policing to begin to understand better the relevance of these different paradigms within specific contexts. The approach emphasises Jonathan's comments that both naturalistic and classical approaches to decision-making make a valuable contribution. Thus, the 10kV system has been the initial step in building a lexicon of knowledge around anyone's previous critical experiences, with a view to informing subsequent practice.

As part of learning from the past I am interested in building up both individual and organisational near-miss registers for intelligent critical incident management (CIM). This builds on previous work in, for example, the anti-terrorist branch in the late 1990s. That is part of the renaissance work we have been doing with Jonathan and Bill, and also with and based upon other academics' work (see, for example, Flin (1996) on critical incident management, Fricker (2002) on epistemic imbalance and injustice and Grant (1981) on assessments). Using risk analysis as a CIM tool, I have also been pursuing a general thesis to 'make police intelligence non-threatening to communities' again. This intelligence project is concerned with, for example, Community Impact Assessments (CIA), which involves informed community consent, educated customers of intelligence, and intelligence as education. This is not unrelated to the long-term police activity of looking for tension indicators as a means of assessing or problem-solving certain kinds of critical incidents or significant events. Tension indicators are concerned with unusual assaults on officers, weapons, hostility, a rise in racist attacks, other local incidents, inter-group (particularly youth) hostility. A rise in graffiti, internet or other published activity (e.g. leaflets, free press), a rise in the activity of extremist politicians or in support for them can also indicate a rise in tensions and, hence, risk. But there is more to risk and CIA than assessing tensions.

Lessons learned from Irish issues are especially relevant. This is an arena in which I now work as a Commissioner for Independent Monitoring of some risks generated by activity in respect of both the closing down of paramilitary organisations and security normalisation as part of the peace process. Jake Chapman (2004) describes the risk that one set of values of these multiple players can have a dysfunctional impact on another set working within the same organisation and lead to system failure. Risk models and analysis are therefore at the heart of these simulated exercises and practical debriefing of real operations. The following are six of the most useful tools we have been using:

1 CCA (Comparative Case Analysis), which has been at the heart of my intelligence work for over 40 years and originally derived from work I was undertaking in the field of CHIS (covert human intelligence sources) management – then called participating informants – a descriptive phrase that identifies more clearly for a lexicon the risks involved.
2 PLAN BI (Proportionate, Legal, Accountable, Necessary acting on Best Information) – the human rights assessment for activity that interferes with anyone's rights.
3 EEP (experience, evidence, potential) – another means of analysing a risky decision.
4 SAFCORM (Situation, Aims, Factors involved, Choices, Options, preferred Risk and Monitoring) is a briefing and preparatory model borrowed from the military. STEEPLES (below) forms part of the SAFCORM model and comes into play under the Factors element.
5 STEEPLES (Social, Technical, Environmental, Economic, Political, Legal, Ethical, Safety and health) – the well-known scanning model that considers pertinent Factors that, when unpacked or combined with other variables such as impact/likelihood, consequence/ reputation, temporal/urgency/importance, vulnerability or financial details, gives a capability that enables officers to reach the next stage outlined below.
6 RARARA (Record, Analyse, Remove, Accept, Reduce, Avoid – Averse) as a way of arriving at methods to deal with possible consequences/outcomes, whether functional or dysfunctional.

We have been using these six tools while involved with critical incident management (CIM) and leadership training for the past eight years. As the chapters here indicate, CIM is a complex element of twenty-first-century policing and investigations. As a direct result of the Stephen Lawrence Public Inquiry (1999), family liaison, community impact and engagement assessment, and independent advice were combined with an intelligence-led approach that helped record in detail the decision-making processes and the rationale behind policing. Hydra was devised as the vehicle for delivering immersive learning and many people contributed to the creation of exercises, debriefing and learning (for an inadequate list of those who contributed, see Grieve, Griffiths and Crego, 2007).

I have heard it argued that complexity is overemphasised in describing policing. However, in one investigation/operation I used law, medicine, nursing, public health, politics, administration, finance/accountancy, banking, civil service, local, regional and national government, public sector, education, social sciences and services, philosophy, logic, ethics, chemistry, metallurgy, biology, sociobiology, geography, demographics, public duty, voluntary sector, military doctrine, military logistics, forensic science, fingerprints, DNA, fibres and intelligence led-policing. Each of these disciplines has variations or unique systems of reasoning. However, as the chapters that analyse the 10kV critical incident debriefs demonstrate, those disciplines and their reasoning processes are but the tip of the iceberg where there are more disciplines that can contribute to our thinking.

Critical incidents are also about risk, threat, hazard, concerns, worries, anxieties, consequences, likelihood and analysis. They are about proximate, distal and/or cumulative impact, sometimes aggregate risks that need tactical, operational and strategic assessments by police leaders in partnership with many other agencies. Policing critical incidents can often be leadership within hearing of the click of the handcuffs and the antagonistic aspects of a criminal justice system.

Risk assessments as a tool for avoiding critical incidents – and for CIM when they do arise – are a Human Rights Act requirement. They need records; and recording the rationale and decision-making is itself a form of risk, gap or threat analysis. They need to be ethical, transparent, inclusive, evidence- and intelligence-based, wide-ranging and based primarily on existing contacts in the local community together with prior arrangements for the exchange of information about concerns. But they also need creativity to help explain a complex decision-making environment that contains anomalies and ambiguities and where it is not always possible to supply the very specific types of evidence required by the criminal justice system. Risk assessments require something closer to a rationale that describes,

'We are persuaded that ... in the absence of any further evidence to the contrary ... in spite of ...'

If we stop to consider the reasoning behind such assessments, my recent experience in facing the CIM of legal challenges in Northern Ireland led us to conclude that the Independent Monitoring Commission (IMC) must apply some defined criterion or evidential threshold for the purposes of fact-finding – namely, one of 'confidence'. A key passage from the IMC Fifth Report (2005), which was favourably cited in the High Court hearing, stated: 'We will not say anything, or draw any conclusion, unless we have confidence in it.' That criterion, if properly applied with appropriate rationale, is an appropriate one and gives rise to no procedural unfairness on the part of the IMC. In the First IMC Report (2004), for example, the language repeatedly used was that of belief rather than confidence. On the other hand, when it comes to the findings of fact about a crime in the Fourth Report (2005), the language used was more emphatic. Looking at the reports as a whole, the Court saw no reason to reject the IMC's clear statements that the commissioners will not say anything or draw any conclusion unless they have confidence in it. The process by which I achieved 'confidence' was of the sort outlined in these chapters.

CIM for my work in Ireland is also about intelligence and Douglas Hofstadter (1980), in a book about artificial intelligence, gives a helpful contribution to a broader view of intelligence and one that is closer to its role in what is described here. He lists eight criteria or abilities to be instantiated in using the word 'intelligence':

- Respond to situations very flexibly;
- Take advantage of fortuitous circumstances;
- Make sense of the ambiguous or contradictory;
- Recognise relative importance of different elements;
- Find similarities between situations despite differing elements;
- Draw distinctions despite similarities;
- Synthesise new concepts from old, put together in new ways;
- Come up with ideas that are novel.

This last criterion or ability – 'ideas that are novel' – is about creativity. Christopher Ross has written about creativity as 'a space in the mind to sift for truth, ever alert for subtleties and gradations of meaning or even fuzziness, the apparent contradiction of opposites being simultaneously true' (2000: 153).

The poet John Keats (quoted by the novelist Philip Pullman (1997: 92)) described a creative state of mind as 'capable of being in uncertainties, mysteries, doubts without any irritable reaching after fact and reason' and, although Keats was referring to literary greats, the qualities of being able comfortably to remain open and receptive to information may be applied to critical incident management. Laurence and his team are making strides in exploring such constructs. One of the ways in which they utilise Hydra simulations is to examine individuals' degrees of success as critical incident managers in relation to Webster and Kruglanski's (1994) need for closure (NFC) scale.

I am arguing that these chapters analysing the Hydra/10kV debriefs that have followed both simulated and real critical incidents demonstrate the creative, analytic, emotional and rational practices of the different disciplines involved. The reasoning processes go far beyond that. I am also arguing that the processes that go on in policing during critical incidents, Hydra/10kV debriefs and the analysis in the chapters that follow are examples of consilient thinking – the very best kind of creative group problem-solving.

In *The Ghost Map*, Steven Johnson (2007) argues that the great step forward for London's public health protection in 1855 was due to consilient thinking when mapping cholera in Broad Street, Soho. Three men from different disciplines came together: Dr John Snow of St George's Hospital, an anaesthetist; the Reverend Henry Whitehead, a Soho clergyman; and William Farr, the London Registrar General. Johnson writes: 'The most impressive thing about his [Snow's] research was not the levels of social class that he traversed but rather the intellectual strata, the different scales of experience that his mind crossed so effortlessly' (2006: 67). Snow was a truly consilient thinker, in the sense of the term as it was originally formulated by the Cambridge philosopher William Whewell in the 1840s (and recently popularised by the Harvard biologist E.O. Wilson). 'The Consilience of Inductions,' Whewell wrote, 'takes place when an induction, obtained from one class of facts, coincides with an induction obtained from another different class. Thus consilience is a test of the truth of the theory in which it occurs.' This consilient thinking is what is going on in Hydra/10kV, in the following chapters of this book and in all the intelligence-led responses to critical incidents in policing that continue the learning as part of a policing renaissance.

References

Chapman, J. (2003) *System Failure*. London: Demos.
Flin, R. (1996) *Sitting in the Hot Seat*: *Leaders and Teams in Critical Incident Management*. Chichester: Wiley.

Fricker, M. (2002) 'Power, knowledge and injustice', in J. Baggini and J. Stangroom (eds), *New British Philosophy*. London: Routledge.

Grant, I. (1981) *Units 26 and 27 U202 Inquiry*. Buckingham: Open University Press.

Grieve, J., Griffiths, W. and Crego, J. (2007) 'Critical incident management', in T. Newburn, T. Williamson and A. Wright (eds), *Handbook of Criminal Investigation*. Cullompton: Willan Publishing.

Independent Monitoring Commission Reports Numbers 1–15 (2004–2007) London and Dublin: Stationery Offices.

Hofstadter, D.F. (1980) *Gödel, Escher, Bach: An Eternal Golden Braid*. London: Penquin Books.

Johnson, S. (2006) *The Ghost Map*. London: Allen Lane.

Pullman, P. (1997) *The Subtle Knife*. London. Scholastic.

Ross, C. (2001) *Tunnel Visions*. London: Fourth Estate.

Savage, S., Poyser, S. and Grieve, J. (2007) 'Putting wrongs to right', *Criminology and Criminal Justice*, 7: 83–105.

Webster, D.M. and Kruglanski, A.W. (1994) 'Individual differences in need for cognitive closure', *Journal of Personality and Social Psychology*, 67: 1049–62.

Laurence Alison

To family, friends and colleagues
(Many of whom fall into all three categories)

Jonathan Crego

To Adam, Robert and Jessica, and my ever caring Sharon
And all who give me my sense of purpose

Laurence and Jonathan

To all officers who have served their commanders with
great integrity and in the face of considerable adversity

Chapter 1

Introduction

Laurence Alison

In the 1969 Presidential address to the American Psychological Association, George A. Miller outlined how psychologists were responsible for fostering accounts of human behaviour that did not connect with, nor could be easily understood by, the public. He argued that an exclusive club of self-styled 'experts' had emerged in which an 'elite canon of knowledge' had been constructed. The canon was to convert this previously soft science into a hard science more in line with physics and chemistry than philosophy and literature. Miller suggested that this exclusivity had led to a general mistrust of the discipline and, subsequently, to psychology falling short of its potential.

Despite tying themselves to experimental laboratory-based research and, firstly, the principles of reductionism (that complexity can be explained by simple fundamentals); secondly, determinism (that events are predictable and can be explained through causal chains); and, thirdly, control and the compartmentalisation of behaviour without reference to context, psychology had repeatedly failed to generate a grand theory of human behaviour. This focus on lab-based research was compounded by psychologists' concern with describing and analysing behaviour in order to manipulate it. Miller argued that the way forward was for psychology to re-evaluate its role as an agent of social control. Instead of *telling* people how to lead their lives, psychologists must find a way of allowing non-psychologists to practise psychology so that they could best judge how it could be employed within their own particular domain. The 'giving away' of psychology to non-psychologists for the purpose of assisting in solving specific problems has become known as a 'pragmatic approach'.

In this book we have aligned ourselves with many of the central principles of pragmatism – especially the requirement that research should be guided by the need to address particular problems faced by practitioners. In our case, this involves identifying key issues that are of direct concern to police officers. This book reflects one particular aspect of our recent work – specifically, our careful documentation of critical incident debriefs conducted over the last five years. The intention is to retain and preserve the central themes relevant to critical incidents in the words of the individuals involved in those debriefs, simulations and inquiries. In parallel, we draw upon the extant literature on decision-making and leadership that helps inform and contextualise those comments.

Some of the central themes that have emerged from those observations and which are referred to throughout the rest of the book include:

(i) *Complexity, ambiguity, sensitivity.* Perhaps more than any other field, the investigation and management of critical incidents involves practitioners working in high-stakes environments with complex, ambiguous, sometimes politically sensitive and nearly always multi-agenda, multi-agency information. Although systematic lab-based traditional decision-making paradigms will doubtless prove very fruitful, we should not be under the illusion that effective decision-making is wholly defined by comprehensive search for evidence and logical inferences drawn from that evidence. Rather, it occurs within a highly litigious, complex organisational, cultural context, subject to public reviews, intensive media scrutiny and in high-pressure environments.

(ii) *Individual perceptions.* The unique background and experiences (professional, personal and trait-based) of the different practitioners who must work with this information appears to shape the way in which complex, competing, contradictory and ambiguous material is interpreted. These various interpretations, which are converted into 'working/situational models' or 'investigative narratives' influence the particular lines of inquiry that are adopted. We have formed the view that an examination of individual differences may prove very productive. Specifically, intelligence, conscientiousness, tolerance for ambiguity and a variety of emotional/interpersonal measures are likely to prove worthy of research.

(iii) *The impact of context.* Context exerts a powerful influence on these investigative narratives and thus on styles of leadership and critical decisions. Context needs to be defined and described so that we have a better understanding of its influence.

(iv) *Context defined.* Context is multilayered and multifaceted. Unlike several other fields of decision-making, policing critical incidents involves many layers of decision makers, at different ranks, across different constabularies, different agencies and all within the very public eye of the community that it serves. In seeking to respond to all these agendas (some of which are competing and/or contradictory) it is extremely difficult to develop criteria for an 'optimal decision'. It is, therefore, more useful to examine the *processes* by which any given decision was arrived at rather than the product. There is an urgent need to look beyond public reviews, and not simply at those inquiries that 'went wrong'. Instead, one needs to examine 'near misses' and 'successes' since all potentially yield useful information on process as well as product.

(v) *Decision inertia.* Because of the powerful influence of context and the very serious repercussions of decisions (even those that were taken in good faith, with the best intentions and based on careful examination of the information available at the time) a frequent problem for decision-makers and leaders is failure to make decisions (decision inertia) rather than making the wrong decision (decision error).

(vi) *Emotional decision-making.* Underpinning many critical incident decisions are emotional responses – both in terms of anticipatory emotions (for example, anticipating regret or blame for a decision and thus seeking to *avoid* those aversive consequences by avoiding the decision) as well as consequential emotions (for example, the satisfaction and *esprit des corps* generated by groups pulling together in the face of adversity). Simply regarding decision-making within a rational framework fails to capture the richness and complexity of decisions that affect lives and careers.

(vii) *'Healthy' organisations.* Leaders and managers within organisations may be able to reduce inertia and error by providing a framework and culture within which creativity, challenge, critical thinking, sensitivity and support are clearly articulated and transparent across all strata of that organisation. Decision-makers who

3

feel hamstrung by having to accept all the responsibility and knowing that they will get no support if the 'product' of the decision is wrong (even if the process was right) will be far less inclined to commit to the 'right process' and will be disinclined to make any decision at all. Instead, the preference may be to pass the responsibility (or diffuse it) among other individuals or organisations.

(viii) *Operational preparedness*. Returning to individual perceptions: decisions and strategies for leading (as well as following) are strongly influenced by individuals' perception of the organisations that they belong to. Often, this perception appears to be influenced by the organisation's response or lack thereof to some basic needs. These include developing mechanisms that ensure officers do not work absurd numbers of hours during an inquiry, that the catering is adequate, that basic resources (methods for communication) work effectively and that senior managers care about their staff. Although some of these may seem banal in the extreme, an inability to provide a hot cup of coffee for an officer called out to a hostage negotiation incident for 19 hours has a profound influence on that officer's perception of the organisation and his/her subsequent feelings about wanting to do his/her best. This organisational attitude to the basics can have profound short- and long-term consequences for running an inquiry as well as for the legacy that the critical incident has on the organisation and the community that it serves.

So, our initial remit in writing this book was to set out a range of issues/questions/ideas connected to leadership and decision-making that had emerged from concepts generated in operational debriefs of major investigations. The idea was to establish whether (and to what extent) the issues that practitioners talked about were consistent with (or different from) the research literature. In establishing this overlap/discrepancy, we intended either to bridge gaps, suggest other avenues of research or synthesise previous models of decision-making/leadership. In a field where barely any literature exists it was important to establish, as a starting point, those issues that practitioners felt were relevant and merited further exploration. Since the initial impetus for this book, Jonathan has conducted debriefs of the Sharm El Sheikh bombings, the Metropolitan Police response to the tsunami, the abduction and murder of Holly Wells and Jessica

Chapman, the London bombings, the investigation of the M25 rapist, the Hackney siege, the Buncefield fire, the poisoning of Alexander Litvenenko and the recent murders in Ipswich, as well as 40 other high-profile murders, rapes, hostage negotiations, responses to natural disasters and public order incidents. Much of this book draws upon the observations of practitioners from those debriefs and, as such, is very much in line with the starting-point principles of pragmatism; that is, we endeavoured to begin by 'listening' to practitioners' experiences, successes, problems, goals and aims rather than appearing as some supposedly omniscient, didactic expert of the type criticised by Miller. We will hint at how these debriefs are beginning to generate a more systematic research agenda, with attendant questions around training, selection, stress and stress inoculation and, of course, methods to enhance decision-making and leadership skills.

Just to illustrate further the range and frequency of the types of investigations that the police and related services must deal with, one need look no further than the daily newspaper. For example, at the time of writing, today's top stories in *The Independent* include letter bombings and the arrest of school caretaker Miles Cooper; the arrest of nine men as part of an alleged plot to kidnap a Muslim soldier, and the speeches of Omar Bakri Mohammed as suspected of inspiring the alleged plot, and the conviction and sentencing of Kimberly Harte, 23, and Samuel Duncan, 27, jailed for a total of 22 years yesterday for systematically torturing their four- year-old-disabled daughter.

In each of these cases there will have been issues connected with family liaison; community pressures; handling the media; appropriately and effectively assigning roles and duties within the team, as well as maintaining morale; careful consideration of policy and the need to establish its 'fit' with the individual case; working with other agencies; and, of course, dealing with complex, ambiguous material in which judgements must be made about the sense, relevance and need to act upon (or not) certain aspects of the information. Thus, we begin with a brief overview of those aspects that relate to interpretation of complexity.

Interpretive frameworks

There are differences between individuals in the way they might interpret the same piece of information. Differences also exist between groups of individuals; in other words, the interpretive framework a group adopts will have an influence, and one of the first publications that I undertook, conducted under the supervision of Adrian Furnham (one of the central figures in occupational psychology) was a study in which we compared a group of police officers with a group of offenders. Both groups were acting in a mock role as jurors. Perhaps unsurprisingly, we discovered that social role, experience and position all have a powerful impact on the way in which individuals respond to neutral and ambiguous information.

The study focused on the phenomenon of juror bias – the extent to which an individual will interpret neutral or ambiguous statements in favour of either a prosecution or a defence, even though that information is redundant and legally irrelevant (Alison and Furnham 1994). So, irrespective of its legal relevance or the extent to which statements had anything to do with the argument at hand, individuals used redundant information to defend their prior beliefs about the guilt or innocence of the suspect. Additionally, these redundant pieces of information were used by the 'jurors' to rationalise the lenience or severity of a particular punishment, as well as to justify their personal view on how an individual had come to commit a given offence. Police officers tend to interpret ambiguous statements as indicative of a suspect's guilt. They are also more inclined to view criminal behaviour as emerging from some genetic or immutable defect that differentiates offenders from the rest of society (a 'consensus' view). Finally, they are in favour of more extreme punishment. In contrast, the offender 'jurors' tend to rely on redundant information to bolster a belief in a suspect's innocence; they tend to see crime as emerging from social exclusion and oppression and are less in favour of punishment (unless, of course, the individual under consideration is a sex offender – in which case offenders are even more punitive than police officers).

As a phenomenon, differences in interpretive frameworks are not confined to police officers and offenders acting as jurors. Many other studies of social perception have shown that there is an apparent predisposition for individuals to generate an immediate and seemingly involuntary cognitive response in which they try to make sense of information – *any information* – however complex, redundant, ambiguous or meaningless it is. This has been well documented in studies of visual perception and in much the same way that we all see faces in clouds or dancers in the flames of fires, individuals read patterns, stories and meaning into information – even when that information is random and senseless. Further, the way in which that information is interpreted is shaped by prior experience. So, a police officer may be more likely to see the face of a villain in the patterns of the wallpaper and a nurse may be more likely to see a patient. In studies of visual perception this is known as the *priming effect* and can be demonstrated by the 'duck/rabbit' illusion (see Figure 1.1).

With not too much effort we can 'leap' back and forth to see a duck or rabbit in the image. If prior to seeing the image one presents participants with several images of real ducks, one can increase the number of respondents who initially report seeing *this* image as a duck. However, if one subjects participants to a series of rabbit images prior to viewing the illusion one can increase the number of respondents who initially see the image as a rabbit. Of course, there are many other ambiguous illusions like these – the old/young woman or the face/saxophonist – and immediate prior experience and longer-term influences appear to shape how individuals see the images. Interestingly, as well as one's individual framework and experience, another powerful influence on what one sees is context (see Figure 1.2). So, if the same illusion appears among 'stimuli' that look more 'duck'-like, it will be seen as a duck, and where it appears among 'rabbit'-like stimuli it will appear as a rabbit.

The central point for our purposes is this: although some research has tried to pigeonhole human behaviour into neat categories, human action is dynamic and strongly affected by its surroundings. Contemporary trait psychology reveals that this is because interactions between individuals and the situations that they find themselves in are important determinants of behaviour. This applies whether someone has merely been primed with pictures of ducks or rabbits in a benign experiment or whether he or she is leading a murder investigation under the media spotlight, keenly aware that a predecessor's efforts culminated in a public inquiry. In other words,

Figure 1.1 The 'duck/rabbit' illusion

Figure 1.2 The 'duck/rabbit illusion in context

context exerts a powerful influence on investigative narratives and on the decisions that are made as a consequence. We reflect on these themes throughout the book. However, a taxonomic classification of critical incident context has yet to be established but, in Chapter 7, consideration is given to the many layers that impact upon individual decisions (including the decision environment, the influence of teams, groups and hierarchies, as well as multi-agency collaboration, and the various forms of decision: their reversibility, the person taking responsibility, their urgency, and how much evidence supports the decision).

Context also appears to influence leadership style and follower behaviour. In the behavioural analysis of two teams of four officers making decisions in the investigation of a kidnap and rape simulation discussed in Chapter 6, it is clear that directive and participative leadership styles partly emerge in response to the decision environment, with directive behaviour emerging at information bursts and participative styles during review stages. Further, the simple dichotomy of participative and directive and their relative influences on follower behaviour is rather subtle, with some individuals using directive behaviours effectively through careful and sensitive interpersonally appropriate dialogue and others presenting a more autocratic and less sensitive framework. Unsurprisingly, the latter is ineffective at propelling followers into action.

Chapter 5 on directive and supportive leadership also makes a compelling point about how even the most charismatic and effective leaders may find that their opportunity to shine can be compromised by an organisation's lack of initial planning and failure to build an infrastructure that supports such inquiries. Thus, an ill-prepared organisational context negatively impacts upon the best decision-makers and the best leaders, disabling in turn their own capacity for drawing upon skilled decision-makers and leaders. In that chapter, we argue that one way of ensuring preparedness is to develop scenarios that test the limits of what can be prepared for. This can and, indeed, is being achieved, throughout the UK, in part through the Hydra system. We discuss simulations and Hydra specifically in Chapter 3, and indicate that those simulations can have a direct impact on recommendations for the organisation.

Naturally, the organisation is not the only influence on decision-making that obtains beyond specific incidents or investigations and in Chapter 8, we review briefly some of the literature in relation to empirically well-established heuristics and biases that can affect decision-making processes. Notwithstanding the emphasis on contextual factors, it is important not to minimise the influence of individual styles and differences between various leaders and decision-makers and it is also clear that different officers have quite different responses. Needless to say, this book does not argue for an entirely situational model. Indeed, any basic flirtation with studies of personality and social cognition reveals a quite natural relationship to the wider, contextual issues. A line from Allport reflects this idea: 'Within the individual [we can] find the behaviour mechanisms and the consciousness which are fundamental in the interactions between individuals' (Allport 1924: v).

Indeed, it is perhaps significant that Allport, who was a firm proponent of studying the individual, also studied economic control, leadership, social movements and industrial conflict. The work presented in this volume is sympathetic to this perspective and, as we have emphasised, it is important to retain a basic understanding of individual perceptions and how they emerge when conducting research on social interactions and team and organisational behaviour in managing critical incidents. So, although we have failed to find any relationships between the Big Five indicators (openness, agreeableness, conscientiousness, extroversion and neuroticism) (McCrae and Costa 1990) and, for example, what elements of critical incident management individuals report they are best/worst at (family liaison, community relations, dealing with the media, creating a positive team atmosphere, assigning roles and responsibilities etc.), our more recent studies are beginning to illustrate that certain constructs do have an impact on decision-making and leadership styles.

Throughout the qualitative material from the debriefs there are distinct differences of opinion, as well as many examples where individuals concur. Some debriefs generated heated debates between delegates. These included disagreements about the utility and relevance of skills acquired by individuals who had previously managed natural disasters and the transferability of those skills to dealing with counter-terrorist operations. Other examples included different perceptions (sometimes even definitions) of risk.

Even within individual inquiries there were differences of opinion in the inner workings of an investigation. As long as the emotional fallout of these robust challenges does not bleed into other areas of the inquiry, such disagreements and tensions can be very productive; they can lead to greater scrutiny of individual decisions as well as fostering an environment in which challenge, examination of points of conflict and observations of inconsistencies are more clearly highlighted than where there is consensus. A real danger exists when one side of the argument is beaten down into submission. Thus, lively debates need to be encouraged and thoroughly explored. A cult of personality and the assertive power of an autocratic environment do no one any favours in major investigations.

It is worth pausing here for a concrete illustration of how investigative decision-making can go awry. This case also happens to be the one that consolidated my academic interest in perception and the interpretation of complex information – the investigation of the murder of Rachel Nickell on Wimbledon Common. This inquiry, perhaps more than any other since, is a prime example of how the way in which information is perceived and understood is so contingent on individual factors, the agenda and roles of the relevant perceiver as well as social/community and media context. Rachel Nickell was murdered mid-morning on Wimbledon Common in July 1992 while walking with her son Alex and their dog, Molly. Paul Britton was the psychologist asked to provide an offender profile, as well as other forms of guidance on the case, including the provision of a report on the potential sexual fantasies of the offender, and input into the initiation and development of an undercover operation with the key suspect, Colin Stagg.

Subsequent to detectives' suspicions, based probably, in part, on inconsistencies in Stagg's account, on the witness statements of a number of people who claimed to have seen Stagg near the murder scene that morning, and on the profile generated by Britton, the investigating team (again under the direction of the psychologist) decided to set up a covert operation known as 'Operation Edzell'. This involved an undercover officer with the pseudonym 'Lizzie James' 'befriending' the suspect, firstly through letters, then phone calls and finally in a set of meetings.

Broadly speaking, the letters began in a rather benign fashion – with exchanges involving discussion of mutual interests, expressions of loneliness and flirting. However, before long, sexual elements began to dominate the letters, with 'Lizzie' referring to her 'chequered past'. Though at first these were oblique references, Lizzie eventually disclosed that she was involved in some bizarre cult rituals involving group sex, human sacrifice and drinking blood. This was revealed to Stagg in a meeting.

Stagg, who was a 30 year old virgin at the time, was desperate for an intimate relationship with a woman and, in an effort to impress her, he wrote increasingly violent sexual fantasies that culminated in a reference to an attractive blonde woman being teased with a knife so that blood was drawn. This scenario, among previous violent fantasies, which was set in the open air near a tree, was enough to convince the inquiry team that Stagg's fantasies were increasingly approximating core features of the murder of Nickell. Moreover, to Britton and the investigation team, he fitted the profile they allegedly originally constructed at the beginning of the inquiry.

In a report that I prepared with David Canter (also now at the School of Psychology, University of Liverpool) we highlighted the inadequacies of the profile, as well as the entirely inappropriate methods for conducting the covert operation. We demonstrated that it was the operation itself that had guided much of Stagg's response, rather than its having emerged spontaneously and without prompting, as Paul Britton had argued.

What strikes one about this case, as well as the issues relevant to the inappropriate use of profiles, was the extent to which the case represented some apparently fundamentally flawed decision-making on the part of the inquiry team. These investigative decisions appeared to exemplify the cognitive short cuts known as 'heuristics', which were identified by Daniel Kahneman and Amos Tversky (1973).[1] Could it really be the case that officers had directed so much attention at Stagg, and neglected to pursue other lines of inquiry? Had they committed classic confirmation bias errors by failing to look for evidence to *discount* Stagg (for example, the fact that he gave an incorrect description of the position of the body and indeed of the offence) and considered only information that appeared to fit (that he introduced the topic of a knife in one of the fantasy letters)?

Were they using what is known in the literature as the representativeness heuristic, a cognitive short cut in which one draws upon a stereotype view to inform a decision rather than examining the attendant base rate information? And were they reframing Britton's ambiguous, Barnum-type 'profile' to lend extra credibility to a view that Stagg was their man? The Stagg case appeared to suggest that there was an abundance of these sorts of decision errors.

The Stagg case consolidated my interest in the area but as I gained increasing knowledge and access to the decisions in other major cases, Gary Klein and Eduardo Salas's work also resonated (see e.g., Klein and Salas 2001). Their work takes on board some of the complexity of real world decisions and the fact that there is rarely such a thing as an 'optimal decision'. Further, there is rarely all the information available to make a decision. Their argument is that effective decision-making is not simply about an adequate search for information and the generation of appropriate inferences on the basis of that information. Indeed, Crego and Spinks (1997) present a strong argument for the view that both naturalistic and traditional methods make a contribution (see Chapter 3 for a brief discussion of the two methods) and that their relevance is partly dictated by timing, with the faster, time-compressed decisions being better examined under the naturalistic umbrella and the slower burn aspects better captured under the traditional framework. This notion of timing and the evolution of the inquiry is a theme also picked up in Chapter 7.

Although both traditional and naturalistic approaches allow for a fuller appreciation of what went wrong in the Stagg inquiry, more recently we have argued that neither of these theories, nor any other in the decision-making literature, offers an adequate explanation of effective investigative decisions, errors in policing and, perhaps most importantly of all (because of its hugely destructive effects), decision inertia – i.e., the failure to make a decision at all.

Decision inertia

As we noted earlier, it has become clear that events that emerge within Hydra, as well as the views within the increasing corpus of debriefs, have led us to argue that a common shortcoming of both Traditional Decision-Making (TDT) and Naturalistic Decision-Making (NDM) approaches is a neglect of organisational context. Previous theories do not give a great deal of attention to how qualities of the organisation directly influence the way in which decisions are made. Multi agency debriefs and simulations in particular (where the police have to work alongside paramedics, child protection services, education, health and social services, as well as firefighters, hospitals and community-based organisations) have demonstrated that any decision considered by any one individual is always filtered through an organisational lens. This has a profound impact on decision-making. As pointed out in Chapter 10, the requisite conditions for successful search and inference (for example, being in possession of all relevant information and so forth) are not always sufficient to make individuals commit to and take responsibility for difficult decisions.

Decision inertia emerges from the impact of organisational structures that may constrain practitioners in their day-to-day decision-making. This volume argues that existing theories of decision-making do not fully represent these relationships in policing critical incidents. As such, anticipated regret and blame are key factors in decision-making, and these in turn are influenced by other processes and situational factors. In our studies of multi-agency work, we have noted how organisational structure and climate are overwhelmingly significant situational factors that warrant further extension and elaboration of rational–emotional models of decision-making.

These observations (discussed at length in Chapter 10) have emerged from a close examination of practitioners' experiences, which are treated as central in developing and informing the research programme and deriving general principles. Ultimately, we aim to collate, archive, analyse and evaluate material both from Hydra and 10kV to formulate what we have recently termed a 'Lexis of Critical Incidents', with the intention of: (i) supporting the extraction of themes, enabling researchers to develop targeted pieces of more traditional empirical research and to derive robust and replicable psychological models of decision making, stress and emotion; and (ii) informing practitioners and assisting in subsequent, similarly difficult cases.

In light of the former, our more recent work with Hydra Merseyside has enabled us to examine how decisions are formulated in the face of complex and ambiguous information; establish the extent to which officers are able to hold several situational models in mind simultaneously so that the range of lines of inquiry does not become too restricted; and examine the negative impact of strict organisationally constraining parameters in inhibiting effective decision-making. As well as identifying the key features of organisations that can encourage poor decisions or decision inertia, we have found some preliminary evidence for underlying dispositions as having some impact on poor decision-making – notably the so-called 'need for closure scale' (NFC), developed by Webster and Kruglanski (1994). Individuals who score high on NFC are uncomfortable with ambiguous situations, and prefer order and predictability. Our work with the UK, Hong Kong,

Indian and Dutch police suggests that discomfort with ambiguity appears to be an indicator of less effective decision-making; those individuals who are able to tolerate ambiguity well are more likely to develop multiple situational models to explain the information they are being presented with and, being better equipped to systematically challenge these views, they cling to them less dearly when they are failing to reap results.

Similarly, in our work on police interviewing, individuals who score high on discomfort with ambiguity appear to be more prone to resort to emotionally coercive interviewing strategies with a concomitant potential for the abuse of human rights; perhaps because they hold a very focused single view of the information, and anything that fails to support this view elicits frustration and further discomfort. However, one should caution against too generic a statement about the relevance of this work with the caveat that, in more time-pressured decisions, it may be important to narrow down the range of possibilities rather rapidly. Further, there is some emerging evidence that other factors (both personality-based and situational) may be important in either reducing or increasing stress responses to managing such incidents and therefore compromising effective decision-making. Specifically, we have begun to identify how features of the organisation itself can either enhance or inhibit effective decision-making.

Certainly, in the work I conducted with Detective Sergeant Ross Leonard from the New South Wales Police, as well as in observations based on debriefs of several critical incidents, the organisation's response to dealing with stressed officers had a powerful effect on decision-making. Specifically, our study investigated appraisal and coping behaviours, and symptom and expectation outcomes following shooting incidents (Leonard and Alison 1999). Recent events have thrown this study into sharp relief again, with the shooting of PCs Sharon Beshenivsky and Rachael Bown, in Yorkshire and Nottingham respectively.

Our studies of Australian police officers compared groups that had been offered Critical Incident Stress Debriefing (CISD) against those that had not. The group that had been offered CISD showed a significant reduction in anger levels and greater use of specific adaptive coping strategies. However, we argued strongly against the idea that the intervention in and of itself was the factor that had an impact on post-symptom outcome. What emerged was the fact that the simple *offer* of providing psychological intervention improved outcome. Indeed, those who were offered CISD but refused it fared rather better than officers who were offered and accepted it. Again, this work forces one to reflect on the significance of perception on human behaviour. Those officers perceived that the organisation, by offering therapeutic intervention, was clearly validating and responding to the fact that they had been through tough times. Similarly, the organisation's recognition of the seriousness of the incident also helped others within the service, as well as family and friends, appreciate the trauma that these officers had been through. In stark parallel, where the organisation had neglected to offer any help, and instead loaded officers with more paperwork and forms to fill in, it had failed to signifiy to those officers and the supportive network that would otherwise have surrounded them, the seriousness of the incident. This exacerbated anxiety, depression and anger, with the latter emotion frequently directed specifically at the organisation.

Subsequent studies, conducted some five years later, more clearly identified what we had hinted at and CISD has been largely discredited since. Our work again flagged up the important organisational landscape that featured so heavily in officers' lives and which had a direct impact upon the outcome responses to such incidents.

Forensic psychology: prison or forum?

The pragmatic approach with which this volume is closely aligned reflects the forum-based approach that initially defined the word 'forensic' and in which a range of individuals is consulted, both in the actual applied world of policing and in the other emergency services. Of course, there are inherent dangers in aligning oneself so closely as an advisor to industry, the police, the Government and the military. At the start of this introduction, I mentioned George Miller's 1969 address; his talk was delivered during a period of upheaval in defining and reviewing the role of psychology. So-called radical psychologists accused their pragmatic colleagues of reinforcing the power of the state, rejecting theory and supporting behaviourism and social engineering. Pragmatists were considered cynical and lacking in passion, concerned only with short-range solutions and unconcerned with moral and political questions associated with their work. Pragmatists were also told that financial dependence led to academic and intellectual servility.

In a book that argues for the significance of the influence of organisational context, it would be foolish to reject outright the difficulties inherent in financial dependence on any body. In other respects, times have changed since the 1960s. Moral and political questions associated with the work of academics and the police service alike are very much in the foreground – consider the impact of the Stephen Lawrence Inquiry, the immediate consequences of which Bill Griffiths offers some insight into in the Foreword to this volume. Indeed, it has been my experience of working with the police service and, more specifically, on this volume on critical incident management that, increasingly, there is a passion for learning from mistakes, and embracing a scientific outlook. Further, the police service is no stranger to detailed scrutiny, with many major cases open for painful public review, and where cases that have been resolved effectively are never held up for public applause.

Finally, I would argue that there is little doubt that many of the key theoretical concepts of relevance to forensic psychology that have emerged in the past 40 years have come as a direct result of psychologists having to respond to social problems. Authoritarianism, prediction of risk, compliance, social influence, group dynamics, leadership, stress and cognitive dissonance have all emerged partly as a response to pragmatic concerns with how we lead our lives.

Notes

1 Kahneman and Tversky conducted seminal decision-making research and helped form some early views on the contribution that psychology might make to enhancing police decision-making; see Chapter 8 for further discussion.

References

Alison, L. and Canter, D. (2005) 'Rhetorical shaping in an undercover operation: the investigation of Colin Stagg in the Rachel Nickell murder enquiry', in L. Alison (ed.), *The Forensic Psychologist's Casebook: Psychological Profiling and Criminal Investigation*. Cullompton: Willan Publishing.

Allport, F.H. (1924) 'Social psychology as a science of individual behavior and consciousness', *Social psychology*. Boston: Houghton Mifflin.

Crego, J., and Spinks, T. (1997) 'Critical incident management simulation', in R. Flin, E. Salas, M. Strub and L. Martin (eds), *Decision making under stress: emerging themes and applications*. Aldershot: Ashgate.

Furnham, A., and Alison, L. (1994) 'Theories of crime, attitudes to punishment and juror bias amongst police, offenders and the general public', *Personality and Individual Differences*, 17: 35–48.

Kahneman, D. and Tversky, A. (1973) *Judgement under uncertainty: heuristics and biases*. Cambridge: Cambridge University Press.

Klein, G. and Salas, E. (2001) *Linking expertise and naturalistic decision making: research and applications series*. Mahwah, NJ: Lawrence Erlbaum Associates.

Leonard, R. and Alison. L. (1999) 'Critical incident stress debriefing and its effects on coping strategies and anger in a sample of Australian police officers involved in shooting incidents', *Work and Stress,* 13: 144–161.

Lipshitz, R., Klein, G., Orasanu, J. and Salas, E. (2001) 'Taking stock of naturalistic decision making', *Journal of Behavioural Decision Making*, 14: 331–52.

McCrae, R.R. and Costa, P.T. (1990) *Personality in Adulthood.* New York: The Guildford Press.

Miller, G.A. (1969) 'Psychology as a means of promoting human welfare', *American Psychologist,* 24: 1063–75.

Murphy, J., John, M. and Brown, H. (1984) *Dialogues and Debates in Social Psychology.* London: Lawrence Erlbaum Associates.

Webster, D.M. and Kruglanski, A.W. (1994) 'Individual differences in need for cognitive closure', *Journal of Personality and Social Psychology,* 67: 1049–62.

Chapter 2

The journey

Jonathan Crego

'Now, you've answered all my questions very fairly, sir, and here's just one more. If you were me, what question would you ask of the Consul of the Witches?'

For the first time Dr. Lanselius smiled.

'I would ask where I could obtain the services of an armoured bear.'

Philip Pullman, Northern Lights

This book chronicles a journey, an adventure; and, as with all adventures, there are moments of danger, excitement and fear. Journeys usually start with a destination in mind but, sadly, reaching the destination can sometimes be a disappointment; however, the journey for me has always been exciting. Some years ago I met a fellow traveller, Laurence Alison. We immediately got into a conversation about pragmatic psychology. This was a term I had never heard before. Laurence appeared to be taking a different approach; one that seemed to me to be exactly right. It was like a bridge between the world I was observing and participating in and a world of dusty, lofty academics whose theoretical descriptions in no way described the complex world of emotion, stress, flair and commitment that the police, allied professionals and I experience every day. Laurence – through his experience with high-profile investigations – was a pragmatist, someone who could help make sense of my world of critical incident management.

All the theory suggested that the psychology behind decision-making was straightforward, easily defined, measurable and predictable. During my own PhD research experience, I had fought strongly against the strait-jackets of control of meaningless variables, control groups and the ubiquitous triangulation of research methodologies when clearly only one would be appropriate. Aided by my teacher, Professor James Powell, I was able to describe the early thinking behind Hydra, Minerva and 10kV debriefing. Since that time, much of what I had read from the academic world merely extrapolated these meaningless results to generate predictive models in an attempt to describe what would (or indeed should) occur in a similar situation.

My argument that the management of critical incidents could not be reduced to a scientific predictive model, that it relied on the complex relationships between teams and their environment, either fell on deaf ears, generated scornful critical review or otherwise met with derision from academia. I would argue that the problems facing decision-makers in critical incidents were, as Horst Rittel (1972) put it, 'wicked'. He suggests that 'A wicked problem is one for which each attempt to create a solution changes the understanding of the problem.' The team-based problems of multi-agency management were clearly relevant to his suggestion that 'Wicked problems always occur in a social context – the wickedness of the problem reflects the diversity among the stakeholders in the problem.' At last I had a context that started to make sense; it reflected the world that I was observing. So, as I was looking for the services of an armoured bear, I found an extremely cunning and intelligent bear in Laurence Alison, someone whom I admire greatly and consider to be a very close friend. Laurence and I created the International Centre of the Study of Critical Incident Decision-making (www.incscid.org).

The chapters in this book really do describe the evolution of the thinking on the journey of Hydra and 10kV development. They demonstrate consilient thinking – a term introduced to me by my friend John Grieve, a man who is hugely creative, has mentored me over the past 17 years and who has latterly been an Independent Monitoring Commissioner for the Good Friday Agreement in Northern Ireland. He describes consilient thinking as a 'jumping together of ideas' from often disparate and parallel worlds. He has taught me to recognise that questions need to be considered creatively and the answers will evolve.

The quotation at the start of this chapter has a wonderful poignancy. By turning the question back to Dr Lanselius, heroine, Lyra, can continue her journey. 'If you were me, what question would you ask?' is exactly the type of question that John Grieve has taught me to ask. During his counter-terrorism days, he would search not for remains of explosives, but for the extruded aluminium that housed the bombs themselves. This example illustrates precisely the sort of creativity needed when managing critical incidents.

There have been others on the way who have made the research unique and it would be inexcusable if I did not spend some time looking at the practitioners directly. I have carried out over 70 debriefing sessions and hundreds of Hydra/Minerva exercises and what has struck me is that the people who make the decisions are unbelievably committed, creative, emotional and effective. Assistant Chief Constable Simon Parr from Hertfordshire Police (Gold Commander at the Buncefield oil storage depot fire) challenged the whole notion of decision-making as a passive description of reality. He coined the term 'consequence choosing', suggesting that it is an active act of choosing between a number of considered outcomes and, in the final analysis, as the decision-maker is likely to be held highly accountable, outcomes are a very public matter. Terms like the 'least worst option' begin to help to describe the reality.

Nowhere is this clearer than in contending with the advent of suicide bombers, which is the new reality in the West. The 'least worst option' may be to hope to save the lives of many civilians by killing one suspected suicide bomber. Training for making such firearms decisions requires that we ask radically different questions. Officers cannot react to an emerging sequence of events, relying on the fact that a suspect will want to escape or surrender. For suicide terrorists, 'the choice of death over surrender has already been made and malice is intended towards any third party including (perhaps particularly) the police' (ACPO 2006: 8).

In these new decision-making environments, the danger may be unclear yet absolutely present. There is certainty in someone wildly waving a gun and shouting threats to all and sundry in public. Any fool can decide that such an individual is dangerous. Proactively shooting an individual who looks as innocuous as all the other bystanders in a crowded public place requires profound trust in the senior officer who makes the decision and in the months of planning and intelligence-gathering on which that decision is based.

Given that the world of policing is examined in detail, especially by institutions such as the Independent Police Complaints Commission (IPCC), the 24/7 media, victims and their communities, in addition to the protectionism of other agencies, consequence choosing is clearly a scary place to find yourself though Hydra is proving instrumental in helping to prepare officers for a reality where only 'least worst options' might be available.

Chapter 9 on Emotions in Policing looks at the realities of emotion-driven decision-making and the counter-cultural language that is used to describe it. Emotional intelligence, while alive and well, kicking and screaming, has to compete with a blame culture that is all-consuming, both internally and externally; a performance-driven environment where only things that are measurable count and those that are difficult to measure just don't get measured.

When I debriefed Victoria Climbié's murder or the murders of Jessica and Holly in Soham, I identified the enormity of the unspoken influence of emotion on the performance of the teams that were formed from groups of strangers, often within the white heat of a critical incident. On our journey Laurence and I did not always travel through deserts and deserted plains. Sometimes we found a fabulous oasis of emotional awareness and acceptance that the way teams work is hugely dependent on their abilities to show these emotions and to share a common language that enables the team to express a shared mental model of the problem.

Debriefing the body recovery team deployed to Sharm El Sheikh or the nine debriefs of the London bombings on 7 July 2005 was a humbling experience. John Grieve once asked me the question, 'Who debriefs the debriefer?'

How do teams operate in these most difficult of environments? How can their learning drive the next generation of consequence choosers? What does success really look like? Finally, how can one capture this experience 'like footprints in eternity'? The environment of policing and allied disciplines is not good at celebrating success. Sir Hugh Orde, the Chief Constable of the Police Service of Northern Ireland, said at the Future of Policing Conference 2007, 'We do failure very, very well here.' I have been careful to look at learning from success as the main driver from the debriefing methodology I have developed. I will leave the disgraceful hunger for failure to others. The findings from the London Resilience Forum 'Looking Back, Moving Forward' are a distasteful example of disproportionate energies being expended into failure. In another example, the BBC report of 30 April 2007 'Five get life over UK bomb plot' gives a paragraph describing the successful convictions before it moves into a blame culture, asking: 'Could the July bombings have been stopped?' The lessons from this successful prosecution are being taken forward through this research to the police community, albeit behind the scenes.

Decision-making means teams and teams need good leaders. Bill Griffiths, the Director of Scotland Yard's Leadership Academy, has been instrumental in embedding into the service the learning from the murders of Stephen Lawrence, Damilola Taylor and Victoria Climbié. Bill is a guru in the world of murder investigation, leading on hostage negotiation, serious and organised crime, and is a great believer in learning from success. Bill has facilitated countless Hydra events and has become a great personal friend.

The 10kV and Hydra methodologies have driven the analysis and this analysis provides the evidence behind the wisdom of the writings in this book. The material has been carefully considered by a most lovely, bright and difficult team of academics at our centre at the School of Psychology at the University of Liverpool and another difficult, unmanageable creative team led by Detective Inspector John Jackson at the Hydra Operations Centre at the Metropolitan Police Leadership Centre. Laurence and I created the Centre to act as an academic hub to provide the bridge between the practitioners and the academic world in order to make the research applied and pragmatic.

Where now? The research continues. The 35 sites running Hydra, Minerva and 10kV methodologies are licensed into a community of ideas originating from the United Nations, the Red Cross, policing, fire ground commanders, civil contingencies and the new National Police Improvement Agency. Part of the licence ensures that all these agencies share the research.

The future looks like a new journey, another one where the destination is unclear, but built on our experiences up to now. With the 2010 Winter Olympic Games to be held in Canada, and the 2012 Games in London, my catchphrase of 'Ten minutes before the ball is not the time to learn to dance' has a very particular resonance.

References

ACPO (2006) *The UK Police Service Response to the Threat Posed by Suicide Terrorism: Review by the Association of Chief Police Officers Use of Firearms Committee.* Retrieved 22 November 2006, from http://www/acpo.police. uk/asp/policies/Data/ACPO%20(TAM)%20(PUF)%20Review.doc

Klein, G. and Crandall, B. (1990) *Recognition-Primed Decision Strategies: First-Year Interim Report.* ARI Research Note 90-91. Alexandria, VA: US Army Research Institute for Behavioral and Social Sciences. Maxwell AFB, AL: Air University Library. Document No. M-U 31716-29 no. 90–91.

Rittel, H. (1972) *On the Planning Crisis: Systems Analysis of the 'First and Second Generations'*. Bedriftsøkonomen, Nr. 8. Also Reprint No. 107, The Institute of Urban and Regional Development, University of California, Berkeley, CA.

Chapter 3

Electronic debriefs and simulations as descriptive methods for defining the critical incident landscape

Marie Eyre, Jonathan Crego and Laurence Alison

Introduction

Existing research provides only a partial explanation of leadership and decision-making in law enforcement and, in particular, there has been little exploration of police management of critical incidents. Major events in the past five years – from terrorist attacks such as September 11 and the London bombings, to natural disasters like the 2004 Boxing Day tsunami – have intensified the need to identify and understand the factors that shape the police response to such events. Although there have been significant advances made within particular paradigms, there has been little integration or synthesis of the various methods that would help to generate a holistic picture of critical incident management.

In this chapter, we introduce two unique and innovative methods for researching critical incident decision-making in the domain of law enforcement. The first is 10,000 Volts (10kV), which is an electronic focus group method. Named 10kV because the impact of a critical incident has been likened to experiencing a 10,000-volt shock, this tool is used primarily to debrief practitioners following their response to a critical incident. It has been used for over 70 debriefs and this book has relied heavily on the method for capturing the views of practitioners. The second method is Hydra, which is an immersive simulation system used both for research and for training practitioners in preparation for the real-life emergencies they will face as professionals. Hydra, Minerva and 10kV methodologies have been developed by Jonathan Crego over 20 years. Working from Scotland

Yard in London, Crego has evolved critical incident environments to meet the operational, research and debriefing needs of critical incident management in police, fire and humanitarian arenas. Hydra simulation exercises typically operate in real time over several hours or days and provide practitioners with a high-fidelity replication of the complexity and decision-making challenges posed by critical incidents. Hydra sites now exist around the UK and there is also a Hydra suite in Canada and Australia. One of the newest installations and the only academic site now operational is located at the Centre for Critical Incident Research within the School of Psychology at the University of Liverpool.

Although 10kV and Hydra were developed for debriefing and training respectively, both methods have provided a wealth of new opportunities for research. Specially devised for use within a policing context, they enable researchers to capture and preserve the experiences of highly specialised 'real-life' practitioners (and transcend the often contrived setting of a lab study). How and why most of us make decisions most days of our lives is of interest, of course, but such choices are rarely life-or-death decisions and generic research based on Traditional Decision-Making Theory (TDT) will likely miss the atypical or even unique features of critical incidents. Naturalistic Decision Making (NDM) methodologies have extended the decision-making literature by focusing on the decision-making, teamworking and leadership skills that professionals actually use in their working lives. We argue here that 10kV and Hydra can help to synthesise these previously disparate areas of TDT and NDM and, as such, they represent a significant advance in setting out some interesting avenues of research and, at these earliest stages of exploring leadership and decision making in critical incidents, are effective methods for comprehensively describing some of the key issues.

The data captured by these methods are dense and richly textured precisely because 10kV and Hydra are not decontextualised exercises. Because participants are experienced practitioners, they bring to the exercises all their knowledge and experience of the organisational context within which they work. For example, in their daily professional lives, police officers are subjected to a vast array of political, legislative, hierarchical, policy and procedural constraints and these factors would be impossible to induce in a student participant in a lab study. Hence, the vital critical incident context that affects decision-making is captured.

The denseness of 10kV and Hydra data offers an enormously

versatile research tool; to that end, we are currently using the data to develop the Lexis of Critical Incidents (LOCI). LOCI will eventually form a comprehensive archive of critical incident debriefs. When fully developed, LOCI will form an integrated, synthesised and rich database that can be accessed by security-cleared professionals for research and training purposes (see below for details).

In this chapter, we shall first outline traditional, naturalistic and pragmatic methods, then introduce 10kV and Hydra as a backdrop to some of the later chapters in the book that focus in more detail on the key issues that have emerged from research utilising the two methods. The strengths and weaknesses of each are discussed.

Existing methods in decision-making research

Traditional decision-making theory (TDT)

TDT (Bernoulli 1738; Savage 1954) is rooted in the rational choice assumption that individuals aim to do what is best for them, and sets out norms that proponents argue decision-makers should follow to achieve this goal. Research methods of this school are predominantly laboratory-based, the most common being 'the gamble'. In this method participants, gathered in a laboratory, are presented with a choice between the status quo and an alternative that could, with some uncertainty, result in either an outcome that is better than the status quo or an outcome that is worse (Beach and Lipshitz 1995). Participants are thought to weigh up and compare the relative values of all the options available (referred to as the subjective expected utility or SEU).

TDT posits that the option with the highest SEU will be chosen; thus, if the SEU of the gamble is regarded as greater than the SEU of the status quo option, people will take the gamble. For example, retaining the status quo by keeping your old car on the road will save you the expense of a new purchase (i.e., this option has the highest SEU). However, if it is costing you more and more money in repairs, you might decide that purchasing a new car is the best option (i.e., the reliability of a new one will have the highest SEU). You take the gamble that, in the long run, a new car will cost less money than maintaining the old one.

TDT models have contributed a good deal to our understanding of the cognitive processes in individuals' decision-making, albeit the early notion of entirely rational human beings has been revised as research has moved on. Heuristics and biases affect an individual's decision making and these findings are empirically well established (Kahneman and Tversky 1973); moreover, many of these findings are applicable to decision-making in critical incidents.

For example, confirmation bias (when a decision-maker seeks only to confirm his/her tentative hypothesis and fails to consider alternative information that might disconfirm it) contributed to decision errors in the incident at Three Mile Island, a nuclear power plant in the USA (Chien Wei Chia 2005). Operators at the plant were alerted by warning signals that the nuclear reactor was overheating. In fact, a valve had stuck open and the reactor was losing the water supply needed to keep it cool, but the system did not tell operators about water levels. It told them of pressure levels. Knowing that pressure was high in the reactor, they formed *a tentative hypothesis* that the high pressure was due to excessive levels of water. Operators could have used other instruments to disconfirm this hypothesis but, as decision-makers, they did not behave in the entirely rational manner predicted by SEU theory (that is, they did not consider *all* available information and options). Instead, having hypothesised that excess coolant was the problem, their confirmation bias meant that they ignored other crucial information; this led to the disastrous decision to override the emergency back-up system that would have automatically pumped more water in to cool the reactor. The result was a partial meltdown of the nuclear reactor core and the worst disaster in the history of the US nuclear industry.

TDT, then, has been revised over the years and research has added knowledge about heuristics and biases such as confirmation bias. However, the TDT approach still has several limitations. Firstly, as Shafer (1986) points out, the analogy between the choice of the decision-maker and the choice of the gambler is not always cogent, since decision-makers usually have a degree of control over events, whereas the gambler has little or none. Furthermore, in real-life decisions, subjective probabilities and utilities are rarely independent (Slovic 1966) and, in unique decisions, the theory that choice should be based on the expected values of alternatives may not be appropriate (Lopes 1981). Finally, many studies have found that 'even real gamblers fail to conceive of real gambles' in the way TDT prescribes (Beach and Lipshitz 1995: 28; see also e.g., Keren and Wagenaar 1987; Wagenaar and Keren 1988).

Ultimately, the essential failing of 'the gamble' and other laboratory-based TDT studies lies in their non-dynamic, decontextualised character. They fail to incorporate the wealth of contextual factors that are in play in real-life decision situations, and therefore have little utility as methods for researching decision-making in complex environments. In other words, TDT does not consider the chaotic pace and complexity of the critical incident environment. It does not consider the backdrop of competing teams, agendas, egos, frenetic media demands or political interference; neither do university lab studies generally take place amidst flashing lights, warning alarms and the intense stress engendered by the imminent prospect of a nuclear explosion.

Nonetheless, limited does not mean invalid and we must be careful not to reject the contributions made by TDT. Some factors in decision-making will transfer into the critical incident domain and can occur despite highly specialist skills and training required for such jobs. Using our example above, confirmation biases can affect individuals whether they are professionals within the nuclear industry, police officers or someone making an everyday seemingly simplistic decision. In summary, despite its limitations, generic decision-making research and TDT, in particular, has helped us to understand the role of many factors that influence the decision-making process.

Naturalistic Decision-Making (NDM)

NDM (Klein, Orasanu, Calderwood and Zsambok 1993) challenges the TDT approach, defining itself as 'an attempt to understand how people make decisions in real-world contexts that are meaningful and familiar to them' (Lipshitz, Klein, Orasanu and Salas 2001: 332). NDM, then, recognises the very significant impact of context on decision-making and the dynamic nature of decision tasks. Research methods within the NDM paradigm are primarily field based, although lab studies and Microworld simulations (discussed below) are also used (Lipshitz *et al.* 2001). NDM research has shown that the decision-making strategies that are actually used in dynamic, 'high stakes' real-life situations are significantly different from the decision-making strategies revealed by TDT studies. In this respect, NDM research has offered novel and valuable contributions to the decision-making literature.

A key technique of NDM research is The Critical Decision Method. This method is a form of cognitive task analysis and was used by Klein, Calderwood and MacGregor (1989) to develop the Recognition Primed Decision (RPD) model of decision-making (see below). Principally, the Critical Decision Method involves gathering retrospective data from experts about what they actually did when making decisions in critical incidents. Common ways to collect such data include:

1   Event recall and probe question-based interviews (see e.g. Klein *et al.* 1989). These can involve both: (a) domain-specific probe questions, where the interviewer conducts some prior analysis of the domain and prepares a fixed set of questions about it; and (b) generic probe questions, which are not necessarily specific to the domain of interest. Generic probe questions are generally used to validate, refine and extend previously elicited knowledge (Hoffman, Shadbolt, Burton and Klein 1995).

2   Retrospective verbal reports of the problem-solving process. In this approach, experts provide a commentary after the incident and explain what they had been thinking at various points during the event (Woods 1995).

3   Cued retrospective verbal reports, where a record of experts' behaviour during the incident is used to cue their post-incident commentaries: for example, flight recorder transcripts, post-incident interviews and video recordings of task performance (see e.g. Omodei and Wearing 1994, 1995; Woods 1995). Using this approach, Omodei and colleagues developed the Own-Point-of-View Video Cued Recall technique (McLennan, Omodei and Wearing 1996; Omodei, Wearing and McLennan 1997); this involves head-mounted video recording, where participants wear lightweight cameras on their heads during incidents, followed by a two-stage debriefing procedure, where participants watch the video replay of their behaviour and provide a verbal commentary on it.

4   Expert drawing of domain maps, where experts create graphical representations of the domain, focusing on the links between domain elements (Hoffman *et al.* 1995).

NDM researchers have not relied solely on retrospective techniques; they have also used methods designed to gather data about decision-making as incidents unfold. These include:

1   Think-aloud protocols, where experts are instructed to verbalise their thought processes (i.e. to think aloud) as they work on problems.

2 Limited information techniques. In one version of this approach, experts are asked to solve problems given incomplete information (Hoffman *et al.* 1995); the theory is that selective withholding of information can reveal experts' reasoning processes (see e.g. Hoffman 1987) and thus provide insights into how experts make decisions in the uncertain conditions that are typical in a time-pressured environment.

3 Field observation of task performance. As Lipshitz *et al.* (2001) report, researchers may work *in situ* with experts, and critical features of task environments can be varied to reveal experts' thought processes.

4 Commentaries on experts' behaviour made by other domain knowledgeable observers (Woods 1995).

While each of these NDM approaches is significantly more advanced (in terms of the appreciation of complexity) than the classic TDT laboratory experiments, in terms of recognising and examining the effects of context on decision-making, we have found that this approach is also limited in terms of critical incident management within the police. NDM has been criticised for being relatively atheoretical. Field observation is limited by the potential for distortion caused by the fact that a researcher is present, while think-aloud protocols require caution with regard to differences in the verbal expressiveness of participants (Hoffman *et al.* 1995).

Retrospectively-based methodologies are also open to criticism. The use of retrospective methods to generate models of decision-making in critical incidents is predicated on two assumptions and existing research indicates that both assumptions are unwarranted (e.g., Loftus and Zanni 1975; Mather, Shafir, and Johnson 2000; Nisbett and Wilson 1977). The first assumption is that during high-stress, high-time-pressure events, experts have good introspective access to their decision-making processes and the factors influencing their decisions; the second assumption is that experts' memories of their decisions are available and intact (LeBoeuf and Shafir 2001). Although Omodei and colleagues' (1997) Own-Point-of-View Video Cued Recall technique was developed in an attempt to enhance the validity of retrospective reports, potential methodological weaknesses remain; for example, wearing cameras might have an impact on participants' behaviour and there has been little detailed exploration of this area. The general point here is that memories are fallible so retrospective accounts can pose problems for researchers. As Woods points out, 'Any reconstruction is a fictional story' (1995: 237).

Recognition Primed Decision-Making (RPD) is described as the 'prototypical NDM model' (Lipshitz *et al.* 2001: 335). According to RPD, decision-makers decide on an action by pattern matching the current decision situation to one they have previously experienced, using '*If*' > '*Then*' rules in much the same way as computer programs do: '*If* situation S' > '*Then*' action A'. The problem is that critical incidents, by definition, are atypical or even unique events and attempts to 'pattern match' may be as unsuccessful as Cinderella's stepsisters trying to squeeze into a petite glass slipper. One size does not fit all.

Minerva simulation technology was born as a response to recommendations from Lord Taylor's public enquiry into the Hillsborough tragedy where 96 football fans were crushed to death in overcrowded pens. If we apply the RPD process to police officers' decision-making during the Hillsborough incident, we may consider that officers were *primed* from past experience to *recognise* the unfolding situation (of fans trying to escape on to the pitch) as a public order problem; by pattern matching, we can see the decision process thus: '*If* situation S' (Public order problem) > '*Then*' action A' (Contain the crowd) when, with the benefit of hindsight, of course, the situation should have been assessed as an issue of public safety not of public order. This example shows the potential for tragic decision consequences when pattern matching plays a part in the decision-making process but the RPD model itself is also limited in that it does not adequately address atypical situations. It argues that where the situation is unclear, the decision-maker utilises a story-building strategy (e.g. Pennington and Hastie 1997) – that is, they aim to enhance the clarity of the situation by mentally simulating the events leading up to it. However, the implicit assumption is that this storytelling process will identify the situation as a particular typical case, and from there a decision can be made through pattern matching.

The third variation of the model, which describes how decision-makers can evaluate options without comparing them to alternatives by mentally simulating their implementation, also makes this problematic assumption. It begins with the decision-maker having a range of options to choose from – however, in the absence of an alternative explanation as to how these options were generated, it can only be concluded that the situation is assumed to be typical, and that potential courses of action have been identified through pattern matching.

In summary, RPD gives us valuable insight into individuals' decisions in the real world, how those decisions can be made quickly and also explains how reliance on pattern matching can cause decision 'errors' in atypical events. Indeed, in a recent analysis of several complex simulated responses to terrorist threats, we found Cohen, Freeman and Wolf's (1996) RPD model to be a very good match to the process incident commanders engaged in during their generation of hypotheses and assessment of the situation (Alison, Roocroft, Crego, Eyre and Cole, Internal Report). Notwithstanding, individuals can and do make successful, creative decisions in atypical or unique events in the real world despite the fact that no pattern exists, and the RPD model does not adequately account for these decision processes.

Another concern with NDM generally is that research has been confined to highly specialised domains and, thus, findings may not be generalisable. NDM has focused on military and, more recently, fire-fighting decision-making. In concentrating on narrow aspects of these two domains, NDM research has overlooked a wealth of contextual issues with potentially high impacts on critical incident decision-making. For example, factors such as media intrusion, positive and negative event reporting, community feedback and family liaison, shape and partially define the environment of incident commanders, and are therefore likely to play a significant role in the decisions they make. The high stakes within their work may well include personal career risk, organisational reputation, team expectations and victim needs. We have found that this is particularly true of the law enforcement environment and, thus, any method for investigating police decision making in critical incidents must accommodate and explore these salient features.

Lord and Hall (2005) argue that expert knowledge should not be expected to transfer to domains that do not build on the same principles. Likewise, the context that influences expert decision-making does not transfer. Put simply, some of the issues that apply in the working world of fire-fighters and the military may not apply to nuclear power plant operators or to a policing context and vice versa. Hence, we argue that limited generalisability may be a spurious criticism of NDM. Decision-making in specialist domains requires specialist decision-making models if they are to capture the role of context on decision-making processes. Of course, some features are domain general so a balance needs to be struck between identifying generic influences on decision-making (e.g. biases and heuristics common to us all in all situations) and those that obtain in specialist and very specific environments such as critical incidents (e.g. stress, time pressure, uncertainty, organisational constraints).

Pragmatism

10kV and Hydra were developed under the umbrella of pragmatism and they adhere to pragmatic principles. As a paradigm, pragmatism has its roots in the social psychology of the US led by William James at the turn of the 20th century (Leahy 2004). It is a paradigm that has seen renewed interest in recent times (Fishman 1999). We mentioned at the beginning of this chapter that there is an urgent need to provide a more integrated and holistic picture of decision-making in the specific context of critical incidents and a major paradigmatic strength of pragmatism is its eclectic approach and focus on case-specific material. Pragmatism can combine several aspects of the 'best of both worlds' offered by TDT and NDM research though it also carries some of their weaknesses. The pragmatist principle of utility prescribes that end goals take precedence over theory building. Research should, therefore, be guided by the need to address particular problems faced by practitioners, in this case recognising key issues that are of direct concern to police officers (here drawing on NDM strengths). Notably, pragmatism does not eschew theory and model-building completely. Once a research agenda has been established, more targeted traditional experimental studies can be undertaken with a view to developing robust and replicable models (here embracing TDT strengths).

A specialist domain: understanding the landscape of policing

In accordance with pragmatic principles, then, the first step in exploring decision-making in law enforcement is to define the research environment; that is, to develop an understanding of the social, organisational, cultural and political contexts in which policing decisions are made. This in turn will aid an appreciation of the complexity and challenges of the policing and multi-agency worlds of critical incident management. One particularly effective way of achieving this goal is to build a detailed archive of critical incident management cases.

Analysis of existing 10kV debriefs that have been conducted with experienced law enforcement professionals has allowed us to identify key issues that regularly emerge in critical incident management, and has progressed our understanding of the complex landscape of policing. This knowledge has, in turn, shaped the development of a methodology with the unique ability to capture the complex, dynamic character of critical incident decision-making: the Hydra Immersive Simulation System. Both 10kV and Hydra retain some aspects of the context of policing and we are currently using Hydra to observe and analyse the environment in which investigative decisions are made. Our particular focus is on the factors that shape decision-making in critical incidents, the specific impact of those factors, and the ways in which they interact. By involving professionals as participants 10kV can assist us in identifying the impact of organisational context. In the next two sections, we shall discuss each method separately.

10kV

Development and delivery of 10kV

10kV was originally developed as a debriefing tool for police officers involved in critical incidents, either real or simulated (Crego 2002). It was devised at the request of the chair of the British Association of Chief Police Officers (ACPO) (Crego and Alison 2004a). Recently, it has also been used to debrief education, health and social service professionals following participation in multi-agency simulations and to prebrief police teams prior to operations. The procedure has seven stages as follows:[1]

1 Generation of unstructured accounts

Essentially, this stage of 10kV creates an electronic focus group. Each participant (aka delegate) has a laptop computer and is asked to reflect on and record their experiences of managing a specific critical incident (either real or Hydra-simulated). They are also asked to identify the issues that they felt contributed significantly to the outcome. The laptops are connected together with collaborative software such that as each individual logs this information, it is simultaneously but anonymously distributed to all participants. Participants can comment on statements and add suggestions, questions and further information to the already logged comments, thereby facilitating more detailed exposition of particular points. *Example statements:*

> *'Having to fight continuously* [sic] *for staff or running an inquiry on a shoestring and often being blamed for the force's performance against targets' (2004a: 13).*

'Time and volume of work is not an excuse the family or the media will accept' (2004a: 14).

2 Theme building
Participants are split into groups to review the collective data held on the system and to generate a list of themes that they collectively feel summarises the large corpus of free narrative statements collected at Stage 1.

3 Plenary
The generated themes are discussed and agreed.

4 First sort
The group organises all the items generated at Stage 1 into agreed themes. *Example themes: Media, Culture, Family Liaison.*

5 Summation
These themes are synthesised into key statements.

6 Prioritisation
Participants are asked to score the issues against different criteria. *Example: 10 point scales were devised for each of two criteria. The criteria were: Ease of Implementation and Impact. The respective scales ranged from 10 = huge impact to 1 = very low impact and 1 = very easy to get right and 10 = very difficult (e.g. 'Managing the media' may score highly because it has a huge impact on the inquiry in terms of staff time, morale and so on and is also rated as very difficult to get right).*

7 Feedback and development
General comments are sought from participants in terms of developments, feedback and recommendations. *Example: 'The management of politicians, Police Authority, local community and local council have to be carried out and these take trust and long-term work. These skills in these areas are seriously underdeveloped and need considering alongside critical incident training'* (2004a: 12).

Evolution of 10kV

10kV has undergone regular development and revision since its inception in 2002. The system can now be used remotely and international debriefs involving more than 250 delegates (offering simultaneous contributions) have taken place, giving it enormous flexibility and potential. In the absence of a real live person, a virtual facilitator has been incorporated. Instructions to delegates can appear as 'pop-ups' (e.g. 'Thank you; I would now like us to focus on the emerging discussion under the heading of "tensions and how I overcame them"') and messages can also flow across screens in the form of 'tickertape' banners, much as 'Breaking News' items run across the bottom of the screen on television programmes.

Discussion threads can be formed so that delegates can respond in a reciprocal fashion to the comments of others (and thus, the analyst knows afterwards which comments relate to which others). The groups can also be re-categorised as the facilitator wishes. For example, it is possible to select delegates within the same agency so that police officers share the same discussion group and paramedics form a separate discussion group or, alternatively, one may wish to group all delegates in the same country together in order to conduct cross-cultural analyses. Significantly, within these sub-groups, the individuals can be isolated from each other, allowing them to enter their comments without being contaminated by issues such as 'groupthink'. This control can also be removed to allow for challenge or for additional comments to be added.

10kV's facility for non-attributable comments is responsible for the very candid responses that are elicited. However, this preservation of anonymity led to an early difficulty in identifying whether the total number of comments (raw or percentage) – and the subsequent themes that emerged therefrom – actually comprised a disproportionate contribution from a small number of vociferous delegates; in other words, some people have much more to say than others. Revisions to the system mean that comments can now be matched to other comments from the same delegate (while retaining anonymity) and tracked throughout. Although confidentiality is still maintained, the possibility of skewing the data (through not knowing, for example, whether negative comments represent the group or just one participating 'vociferous' delegate) has been eliminated.

Comments are now also time-coded, so shifts in emphasis or discussion topics can be monitored throughout the debrief. Time-coding also provides an opportunity to conduct sequence analyses; that is, to explore any patterns by looking at the way discussions develop as the session unfolds over time. For example, anecdotal evidence suggests that delegates find 10kV debriefs cathartic. It is possible that this occurs immediately (as the first statements are written) as a result of being able to 'ventilate'. These debriefs have sometimes been the first opportunity for individuals to tell the story of the traumatic experiences entailed in, say, investigating the murder of a child; alternatively, it may be after group discussion has revealed that distress is common to others and thus a delegate might be helped by feeling that his/her response is a normal reaction.

As outlined earlier, post-discussion, delegates distil the initial flood of comments into the core essence of issues they deem to be most relevant, and agree on constructs they think ought to be measured. The facility to generate questionnaire items (where delegates also devise scales) is an enhancement of the original system. Recall that in Crego and Alison's (2004a) debrief, delegates highlighted 'Impact' and 'Ease of Implementation' as two central constructs and generated items they wanted to measure across the two constructs.

The system can now also run a Principal Components Analysis (PCA) whereby statements that have been generated (e.g. 'Manage the media effectively', 'Leading and supporting the investigative team', 'Developing diplomatic political skills') can be represented visually in a two-dimensional or three dimensional space where contiguity indicates strength of effect and relatedness of statements. An analogy may help here. If we imagine a bird's eye view of a school playground, we would look down on a 'picture' of children clustered in different friendship groups. The stronger the relationship (e.g. best friend), the nearer the children will be to each other. Conversely, the 'enemy' who pulled your hair yesterday is likely to be on the opposite side of the playground.

Returning to the model, then, it makes intuitive sense that the statements 'Manage the media effectively' and 'Developing diplomatic skills' would be related; if so, one can see the effect immediately as the model would show the two close together in the visual representation on screen. The system will even advise whether a 2D or 3D model is the best structure and is, thus, an invaluable aid to researchers.

Utility of the 10kV method

First we shall discuss the advantages of 10kV over traditional focus group methods. The anonymity afforded by 10kV's use of a non-attributable reporting system eases the main causes of situational Communication Apprehension (CA), namely subordinate status, conspicuousness, degree of attention, and fear of retribution from others (see e.g. Clapper and Massey 1996; Easton, Easton and Belch 2003). Furthermore, anonymity has also been found to reduce inhibitions in electronic focus groups similar to 10kV (see e.g. DeSanctis and Gallupe 1987). These are particularly pertinent issues when conducting research with law enforcement personnel, among whom awareness of rank and the potential repercussions of admitting to errors or uncertainty could otherwise inhibit frank and candid discussion. 10kV's distinct advantages are summarised below:

1 Participants are able to express their views openly without fear of consequences (see e.g. Clapper and Massey 1996; Crego and Alison 2004a); the effects of interpersonal differences are also lessened (see e.g. Montoya-Weiss, Massey and Clapper 1998).

2 Controversial, sensitive or ethical issues are more easily explored (see e.g. Clapper and Massey 1996);

3 Individual participation rates tend to be higher (see e.g. Easton *et al.* 2003; Nunamaker Jr, Briggs, Mittleman, Vogel and Balthazard 1996/1997), and so the 'quiet voices' in the group are also heard (e.g. see Kitzinger 1994; Montoya-Weiss *et al.* 1998; Robinson 1999; Sullivan 2001). Notably, participation also tends to be more evenly distributed (e.g. see Easton *et al.* 2003; Nunamaker Jr *et al.* 1996/1997; Parent, Gallupe, Salisbury and Handelman 2000).

4 Ideas are 'weighted on their merits rather than on their source' (Nunamaker Jr *et al.* 1996/1997: 7/28), helping to eliminate possible deference to superior ranks.

5 A substantial amount of data can be collected in a relatively short space of time (e.g. see Krueger 1994; Robinson 1999; Robson 2002; Sullivan 2001). For example, in the first 10kV session (run by Crego, November 2002) 28 senior police officers generated over 250 statements in just over 20 minutes and developed 15 key themes by the end of the session (Crego and Alison 2004a). To date, researchers have rarely been able to capture in-depth views of individuals at this level of seniority within the police service; as their time is extremely precious, they are reluctant to engage with demanding and resource-intensive methods such as individual interviews. The efficiency of 10kV makes it a highly appealing alternative.

Benefits common to 10kV and other focus group methods

The 10kV approach has further strengths, which it shares with the traditional focus group method:

1 The experience is empowering, stimulating and dynamic. As Morgan (1988: 12) points out, the hallmark of focus groups is 'the explicit use of the group interaction to produce data and insights that would [otherwise] be less accessible'. Having a voice empowers participants (e.g. see Bryman 2004; Howitt and Cramer 2005) and the interaction can motivate and stimulate individuals (e.g. see Howitt and Cramer 2005).

2 The group dynamic can help create a focus on the most important topics that participants perceive to be significant (Robinson 1999; Bryman 2004) and issues are formulated in participants' terms. Kitzinger (1994: 108) notes: 'Group work ensures that priority is given to the respondents' hierarchy of importance, *their* language and concepts, *their* frameworks for understanding the world.'

3 Linked to point 2, in drawing out these key issues, pertinent research questions can be framed. In other words, it is a valuable starting point for further validation studies – for example, the use of questionnaires, interviews and simulations to examine in-depth factors that participants themselves regard as highly significant.

4 Participants can probe each other's reasons for holding certain views, thereby enabling the researcher to develop an understanding about *why* people feel the way they do (Bryman 2004; Morgan 1988).

5 Participants may become aware of perspectives that they may not otherwise have thought of (Bryman 2004). Thus, as Kitzinger (1994: 112) argues, 'Being with other people who share similar experiences encourages participants to express, clarify or even to develop particular perspectives.'

6 The material generated facilitates the extraction of general, abstract themes in law enforcement, while preserving the rich detail that embellishes and provides further subtle shades of those themes.

Ultimately, the success of a focus group is 'dependent on the creation of a *non-inhibiting, synergistic* [italics added] environment in which *group members feel comfortable sharing ideas* [italics added]' (Montoya-Weiss *et al.* 1998: 714). The anonymity inherent in and the interaction generated by, the 10kV method, creates just such an environment. The process is flexible, dynamic, cost-effective and encourages candid and open views of participants. It is thus particularly suited to research with law enforcement personnel, where time is precious, and among whom issues of rank, and the fear of consequences of admitting to error and uncertainty, may be especially prominent. In summary 10kV is a valuable method through which we can further our knowledge of complex decision-making, which in turn will have many practical benefits for professionals involved in critical incident management.

Developing a 'Lexis of Critical Incidents' (LOCI)

We have begun using 10kV to develop a 'Lexis of Critical Incidents' (LOCI) (see also Alison, Barrett and Crego 2006). To date, we have successfully collected detailed information on a range of major cases, including child abduction (Crego and Alison 2004a), hijack (Crego 2004), murder, and race and diversity issues in policing (Crego and Alison 2004b).

We are currently archiving this material in a similar format to that found in electronic databases, such as the Lexis or Westlaw computerised database systems used in legal research to 'look up' what happened in earlier cases and deduce generic transferable principles (Hibbets 1997; Fishman 2003). Ultimately, the 'Lexis of Critical Incidents' will:

(i) inform and assist police officers in managing subsequent, similarly difficult critical incidents;
(ii) support the extraction of key themes that transfer across a range of critical incidents.

Complemented by subsequent empirical support, models and theories derived should prove more robust and as generic as it is possible to be within specialist domains. In other words, we will be better placed to strike the optimal balance between the specialist and the general.

Hydra

The Hydra Immersive Simulation System

The Hydra Immersive Simulation System (hereafter Hydra) is a unique, high-fidelity learning environment that enables the monitoring of real-time leadership and decision-making in critical incidents (for example, terrorist attacks, murders, abductions). The system evolved from an original system called Minerva (Newland, Creed and Crego 1997) which was principally designed to support team-based decision-making in the management of football and other public order incidents (See Taylor 1990). After the Stephen Lawrence murder, a new approach was needed to develop the strategic and critical decision-making skills of SIOs (Crego and Harris 2002); more recent exercises have also involved education, health and social services professionals in simulated multi-agency incidents (for example, child protection inquiries) and non-governmental organisations (NGOs) (for example, hostage recovery) in the humanitarian world. In light of the terrorist context, the multi-agency response to terrorist incidents has gripped the latest developments of the methodology.

In each simulation, participants are split into teams typically comprising four to seven members; in multi-agency exercises, participants can either be assigned to teams comprised of either several agencies or of single agencies. Each team operates within a separate 'pod' which functions as a microworld (Senge 1990); they are monitored via CCTV and boundary microphones, and equipped with the Hydra computer screens, keyboards and printers. A team of directing staff comprised of Hydra learning experts and subject matter experts runs the exercise from a central control room. A facilitator also observes the behaviours and requests from the microworld participants. The facilitators can see and hear teams at all times via CCTV and everything entered on the teams' computers is also displayed in the control room. Hydra exercises use preconstructed case scenarios. For example, participants might begin with an initial report of an abduction and rape on day one and, by day three, they have successfully (or otherwise) identified and arrested the suspect.

The incidents unfold in real time, continually moving between 'slow-burn' tasks (e.g. analysis of witness statements, examination of forensic evidence) and 'fast-burn' tasks (e.g. highly volatile family liaison, press attention) (Crego and Harris 2002). The Hydra system has a comprehensive and sophisticated multi-media store of information that can be communicated to teams at any point. It includes 'paper feed' written information (such as records of criminal convictions or eyewitness statements that might constitute an alibi for a suspect; faxes; criminal records; and other analytical product) and visual information (such as photofits of suspects or video clips of actors conveying information, telephone calls, radio traffic etc.).

Facilitators can 'fire off' pre-stored triggers as and when they feel it appropriate, based on the time-line of the incident and the actions of the syndicate teams; this would include the appropriate timing of press conferences or briefings with senior officers or members of other agencies, Gold groups etc. As with reality, these triggers are either slow or fast burners, and the subsequent activities from, say, a press conference may well lead to some of the participants being selected for a live press conference that will take place in a television studio. Such features strengthen immersion and participants feel a great sense of 'Presence' (where Presence is defined as the subjective experience of being in one place or environment, even when one is physically situated in another (Witmer and Singer 1997)). It is through this feeling of Presence that the selected delegates can attend role-play events and fully immerse themselves in the problem. Many of them report how incredibly real it felt for them and how valuable they found the experience.

Of course, communication must be reciprocal and the teams are by no means passively receiving information. Teams agree decisions and submit them to the control room via computer. They might submit: a) straightforward requests for information and/or b) instructions to 'virtual' staff on their inquiry team. The facilitators in the control room then respond to teams' decisions and actions.

Indeed, the significant difference between this approach and other scenario-based exercises is that the team occupying the Hydra microworld is free to manage the incident any way it wishes; there are no pre-selected menus of action. The teams are able to command the incident and are not constrained, so anything goes! This is hugely important; as Crego and Harris (2002) were clear to point out, immersion into critical incident management is about living with complexity, uncertainty, short time-scales for action and so forth, so it is essential that the decision-makers feel that, not only are they free to operate in this environment without constraint, but also the outcomes of the incident are closely coupled to their decisions and situational awareness of the incident. Also, by receiving this feedback through Hydra, decision-makers are able to modify their approach in light of either expected or unforeseen consequences of their action.

Thus, the exercise could begin (and, hence, the simulated investigation be launched) with an allegation of kidnap and rape where the complainant describes the offenders' car. Armed with this information, a team might ask for a PNC[2] check of all cars of that description registered in the area. The control room would feed back a shortlist of, say 10 such cars with details of registered owners. In response, a team might decide to instruct the control room to send (virtual) officers to interview all 10 owners.

Facilitators can, at any point, play a video clip (of an actor in role as a police officer) reporting the outcome of the interviews with the car owners. The facilitators' ability to control the timing of feedback means that they can replicate real world conditions; that is, even a virtual officer may take several hours to conduct 10 interviews with car owners. Thus, information becomes available in an incremental manner. Decisions are also recorded in a decision log, along with the rationale supporting them. Entries in decision logs are displayed on control room screens throughout the exercise so that facilitators can monitor teams' decisions, actions and justifications. They are also stored by the system. The data gathered during Hydra simulations comprise:

1 decision logs, which enable researchers to examine and track decisions throughout the simulation, and to explore the factors that shape those decisions;
2 communication logs, which serve as an important record of the information requested by teams during the exercise.

Furthermore, with the system it is possible for participants to complete research questionnaires at regular intervals throughout the simulation, and to be interviewed immediately post incident. Cumulatively, this material constitutes unique, rich, previously unexploited material for research into decision-making.

Microworlds methods

Simulations attempt to reproduce the essential elements of real-world situations within the confines of a relatively controlled environment, thereby representing 'a half-way house between the decontextualized artificiality of the laboratory setting and the sometimes intractable and inaccessible real world setting' (Robson 2002: 363). Microworlds (MWs) are one of the most common forms of simulation in decision-making research. These are dynamic, complex, computer-generated environments within which participants must (typically) act repeatedly over time (DiFonzo, Hantula and Bordia 1998). 'Fire Chief' (Omodei and Wearing 1993), in which participants take on the role of commander to forest fire-fighting teams, is arguably the most well-known of the Microworld generating programs.

Benefits common to Hydra and other simulation methods

This time we shall discuss first the strengths shared by Hydra and other simulation methods (i.e. Microworlds (MWs)). Albeit each method is used in different specialist domains (with Hydra, of course, examining complex decision-making in law enforcement), they share some methodological strengths:

1 They offer high levels of experimental realism (participant involvement), which, in turn, increases internal validity (DiFonzo *et al.* 1998). DiFonzo *et al.* suggest three reasons for this high experimental realism, stemming primarily from the dynamic nature of such simulations:

(a) they involve participants' physical and temporal senses;
(b) they require active participation; and
(c) they present challenging tasks, which often mirror real-world goals viewed as significant by participants.

2 In reproducing key dynamic features of real-world situations, they offer higher levels of mundane realism than non-dynamic laboratory experiments (and, hence, correspond with the field experience) (DiFonzo *et al.* 1998).

3 They capture and store a substantial amount of high-quality data in a rapid, inexpensive manner (DiFonzo *et al.* 1998)

Utility of the Hydra method

Hydra goes much further than traditional MWs in reproducing the critical incident decision-making environment.

1 Whereas MWs are limited to participants working separately, interacting solely with a computer program, Hydra involves participant interaction in teams and utilises a wide range of media, such as telephones, fax machines, video footage and audio recordings. Experimental realism is therefore much higher. For example, Crego (1996) found similar heart rate patterns among participants in Minerva simulations (the predecessor to Hydra) and police commanders in real-world critical incidents.

2 Variables of interest can be much more readily controlled in Hydra simulations; for example, facilitators can alter a range of factors including:

(a) level and nature (positive or negative) of interaction with others outside the police force such as media intrusion, community response, and family liaison interactions;
(b) time pressure;
(c) amount and ambiguity of information; and
(d) competing demands.

3 Hydra allows for participants to complete research questionnaires at intervals throughout the simulation, and to be interviewed immediately post-incident.

4 The Hydra system videos decisions and the team context in which they are made in real time.

Contributions of 10kV and Hydra

10kV and Hydra can make significant contributions in furthering academic research into critical incidents, and the development of the Lexis of Critical Incidents (LOCI), in particular, promises to be a significant step forward in aiding research in this underexplored area. Given the pragmatic paradigm that underpins 10kV and Hydra, we can also make a valuable and comparatively rare contribution to professional practice. Recall that pragmatism's principle of utility ensures that research findings will be guided by applied goals rather than theory for theory's sake. We have already identified skills that are crucial to successful critical incident management. We have also enhanced our knowledge of the challenges such incidents pose. Both are key issues relevant to training needs, employee recruitment and selection. Our commitment to the delivery of research findings to practitioners in the field will enhance effective practice and, importantly, ensure that future practice is evidence based. Vigorous research is ongoing to supplement and enhance the valuable data that are already in our archives.

These two methods are successful in identifying skills and challenges at all levels, ranging from the cognitive processes in individuals, through issues relating to teamwork, up to the broadest level of the challenges faced by organisations and the communities and political culture in which they operate. Illustrated by our earlier example, Crego and Alison's (2004a) 10kV debrief, the way in which the police service would be perceived by the community, and how best to respond to media demands, emerged as the two most difficult aspects of an inquiry to manage. A typical comment was: '[The difficulty of] satisfying the insatiable appetite of the media and preventing their intrusion' (2004a: 11). Thus, due to the richness of the 10kV data, it emerged that legacy, control and accountability were prominent issues for practitioners, not only on an individual level but also at a broader level, with respect to the organisation.

Accountability was also a major concern for public sector professionals who took part in a multi-agency Hydra exercise that simulated a child abuse inquiry – again, a concern with ramifications at the individual and organisational level. Decision avoidance was also prominent in this simulation (See Chapter 10 for discussion of McClean and Alison's 2005 study). Assessment of child protection concerns was conducted proficiently but little effective action followed thereafter. McClean and Alison highlighted barriers to effective multi-agency co-operation in the form of a readiness to blame others. Sample comments were:

'Police and Social Services did not carry through the decision to do a home visit.'

'Why did health not follow through decisions of strategy meeting?' (2005: 12).

Using 10kV data, we have categorised specific leadership skills required in critical incident management along cognitive and interpersonal dimensions (See Chapter 5 for discussion of participative and directive leadership). In Chapter 9, we discuss the 10kV-borne finding that frustration and disappointment were the two emotions most commonly experienced by police officers investigating murder. With evidence that police officers find discussion of emotion a taboo subject (Pogrebin and Poole 1991), the anonymity of 10kV may have provided the shield that yielded these insights. Doran and Alison's (2005) study into stress has furthered stress research by refocusing the emphasis away from separate explorations of stressors and stress responses towards the relationships between moderators and augmenters of stress, providing a more synthesised approach.

10kV and Hydra have enabled researchers to develop models that will assist in understanding cognitive and social psychological processes in critical incidents, ways to understand the decision environment that obtains, ways to establish chains of causality that lead to decision errors or decision avoidance; thus, we can devise practical ways to transcend the challenges faced (e.g. Crego and Alison's (2005) management pyramid, discussed in Chapter 4, or the taxonomy of decision-making, in Chapter 7).

Potential criticisms

Naturalistic decision-making (NDM) research has been criticised for being relatively atheoretical. A further criticism of NDM is that there is a danger of relegating itself to the 'merely' descriptive (Lipshitz, Klein, Orasanu and Salas 2001). 10kV and Hydra *are* allied to NDM in that they take practitioners in the field as a starting point for research; that is, they investigate what is done rather than what ought to be done.

However, Hydra and 10kV were devised under the auspices of pragmatism and you may recall that the eclecticism of this paradigm offers ways to overcome the limitations of NDM. Specifically, we argued that pragmatism does not reject theory completely; it simply prioritises end goals. Findings can, at any point, be supplemented by existing or developing meta-theory. Neither do pragmatic methods such as 10kV and Hydra confine themselves to description. 10kV and Hydra are initially qualitative methods; empirical support for initial findings emerging from 10kV and Hydra data can be sought using more traditional experimental methods, thus embracing the strengths of traditional decision-making theory (TDT).

Earlier, we mentioned existing research, which indicates that a central NDM assumption is unwarranted (i.e. that experts' memories are available and intact for retrospective record). This criticism is doubtless a weakness of the 10kV method. However 10kV is very much a real-time group endeavour and fellow participants may provide cues and prompts that aid recall. Moreover, several sessions have involved prebriefs or 'hot' debriefs, shortly *before* engaging in an incident or *during* an incident. The former provides a context in which we can capture the thinking prior to officers becoming fully immersed in the incident itself, and the latter allows us to capture the thinking as an incident unfolds.

'Groupthink' (Janis 1972) might pose a difficulty in large samples. Our ability to block sections of the 10kV event can inhibit this to some extent but the potential problem of a 'collective mind' remains. On the other hand, the anonymous nature of the sessions assists delegates in challenging views that they might otherwise fail to criticise. Certainly, comparative studies of the methods introduced here against other NDM or Microworld methods would be an interesting area for future research and are to be welcomed.

Despite potential weaknesses, the two methods have a valuable synergy. 10kV data elicited from debriefs of real-life or simulated critical incidents can help to establish a research agenda and subsequently enable us to identify influences on decision-making. Based on 10kV findings, we can thereafter construct Hydra scenarios that are eminently controllable. These scenarios can be as varied and wide ranging as a researcher's imagination.

Conclusion

In this chapter, we have discussed how previous approaches to examining decision-making have, in our view, not yet captured the full complexity and dynamic nature of critical incidents in law enforcement. The laboratory-based methods of TDT, for example, have explored only relatively static decisions and, furthermore, have not generally considered the contexts in which these are made. They cannot, therefore, provide a complete understanding of decision-making in real-world environments. NDM research, on the other hand, is specifically aimed at understanding these phenomena, and has developed methods that capture the dynamic nature of decision tasks in some highly challenging incidents.

However, the focus on military and fire-fighting decisions and, specifically, the relatively narrow range of contextual factors considered, limits NDM approaches at the current time in relation to law enforcement scenarios. Factors such as media coverage, community relations, and family liaison, are salient features of law enforcement environments; in hitherto excluding them from consideration, NDM precludes an understanding of the specialist domain of police decision-making in critical incidents.

This chapter has introduced two unique research methods, specifically designed for researching critical incident management in law enforcement. As well as embracing the strengths of NDM and TDT, these methods complement one another. Through 10kV, we can understand the multifaceted domain of policing, identify the key issues in managing critical incidents, and develop pertinent questions for research. Through Hydra, we can then explore these areas in greater depth, design simulations, manipulate factors, and observe and analyse the exercises.

The process is evolving – through post-simulation 10kV debriefs we can explore these areas even further, as well as any new issues that might have arisen during the simulation. Research therefore constantly evolves, shaping, exploring and redefining the research area. Combined, 10kV and Hydra constitute a comprehensive package for developing and executing a research programme to build an understanding of critical incident management. Of course, there are practical, theoretical and ethical limitations with all these methods but triangulation of method and development of the research across different types of inquiry will enable greater precision in modelling criticality in such investigations (Crego and Alison 2004a).

By comparison with other generic decision-making literature, research into critical incidents is in its infancy and, clearly, further development is required; each theme in its own right requires further elaboration and investigation. However, this chapter provides a starting point for further work and enables us to delve deeper into the experience-based knowledge of critical incident management.

Finally, we should remain cognisant of the fact that these are early days. Critical incident decision-making and leadership have hitherto been relatively underexplored. Thus we have to be modest in our expectations of what is possible to validate empirically in terms of selection, training and prediction. The important first steps lie in describing the complexity of the phenomena that we wish to study. This book is an effort to draw together some descriptions from major incidents of the past five years – sieges, kidnaps, murder inquiries and disaster and terrorist responses – in the voices of those who were there. We are fortunate and honoured to have been able to capture these views from the coalface – from the individuals who are helping to shape the research agenda and first steps forward in this challenging arena.

Notes

1 The appendix lists the debriefs we have conducted at the time of writing.
2 The examples throughout this section refer to Alison and Crego's (2004a) 10kV debrief of senior investigating officers (SIOs) who had led investigations ranging from sieges to child murders.
3 Police National Computer.

References

Alison, L., Barrett, E. and Crego, J. (2006) 'Challenges to expertise in criminal investigative decision making: context and process', in R. Hoffman, (ed.),

Naturalistic decision making conference No. 7, edited book of reading. New York: Lawrence Earlbaum.

Alison, L., Roocroft, J., Crego, J., Eyre, M. and Cole, J. (in press). 'Recognition, metacognition and time-contingent judgements in counter terrorism operations', Internal Report, Metropolitan Police Service.

Beach, L.R. and Lipshitz, R. (1995) 'Why classical decision theory is an inappropriate standard for evaluating and aiding most human decision making', in G.A. Klein, J. Orasanu, R. Calderwood and C.E. Zsambok (eds), *Decision making in action: models and methods* (pp. 21–35). Norwood, NJ: Ablex.

Bernoulli, D. (1738) 'Specimen theoriae novae de mensura sortis' [exposition of a new theory of the measurement of risk], in *Commentarii Academiae Scientrum Imperialis Petropolitanae*, 5: 175–192.

Bryman, A. (2004) 'Focus groups', in A. Bryman, *Social research methods* (2nd edn, pp, 345–362). Oxford: Oxford University Press.

Chien Wei Chia (2005) 'Countering the confirmation biases in command teams: an experiment with different interventions.' Paper presented at 10th International Command and Control Research and Technical Symposium: The Future of C2. Retrieved 5 April 2006, from http://www/dodccrp.org/events/2005/10th/CDpapers/169.pdf

Clapper, D.L. and Massey, A.P. (1996) 'Electronic focus groups: a framework for exploration', *Information and Management*, 30: 43–50.

Cohen, M.S., Freeman, J.T. and Wolf, S. (1996) 'Meta-recognition in time-stressed decision making: recognising, critiquing and correcting', *Journal of the Human Factors and Ergonomics*, 38: 206–19.

Crego, J. (1996) *Critical incident management: engendering experience through simulation.* Salford: PhD thesis.

Crego, J. (2002) '10,000 volts for critical incident managers', Police Training College, England, November 2002.

Crego, J. (2004) *Metropolitan Police New Scotland Yard: Hydra debrief – Athens hijack: 6 April 2004.* Athens: Foreign and Commonwealth Office.

Crego, J. and Alison, L.J. (2004a) 'Control and legacy as functions of perceived criticality in major incidents', *Journal of Investigative Psychology and Offender Profiling*, 1: 207–225.

Crego, J. and Alison, L. (2004b) *Identification of key issues for best practice post 'The Secret Policeman' documentary: results from an electronic focus group.* Metropolitan Police Service: internal document.

Crego, J. and Alison, L. (2005) *Celebrating success, learning from experience.* Briefing report for the North Yorkshire Police.

Crego, J. and Harris, C. (2002) 'Training decision-making by team based simulation', in R. Flin and K. Arbuthnot (eds), *Incident command: tales from the hot seat* (pp. 258–269). Aldershot: Ashgate.

Crego, J. and Spinks, T. (1997) 'Critical incident management simulation', in R. Flin, E. Salas, M. Strub and L. Martin (eds), *Decision-making under stress: emerging themes and applications* (pp. 85–94). Aldershot: Ashgate.

DeSanctis, G. and Gallupe, R.B. (1987) 'A foundation for the study of group decision support systems', *Management Science*, 33(5): 589–609.

DiFonzo, N., Hantula, D.A. and Bordia, P. (1998) 'Microworlds for experimental research: having your (control and collection) cake, and realism too', *Behavior Research Methods, Instruments and Computers*, 30(2): 278–86.

Doran, B. and Alison, L. (December 2005) 'Stressors and stress moderators in critical incident management.' Paper presented at 8th International Investigative Psychology Conference, London, UK.

Easton, G., Easton, A. and Belch, M. (2003) 'An experimental investigation of electronic focus groups', *Information and Management*, 40: 717–27.

Fishman, D.B. (1999) *The case for pragmatic psychology.* New York, NY: New York University Press.

Fishman, D.B. (2003) 'Background on the "psycholegal lexis proposal": exploring the potential of a systematic case study database in forensic psychology', *Psychology, Public Policy and Law*, 9: 267–74.

Hibbets, B.J. (1997) *Last writes? Re-assessing the law review in the age of cyberspace.* Retrieved April 12 2006, from http://www.law.pitt.edu/hibbets/lastrev.html

Hoffman, R.R. (1987) 'The problem of extracting the knowledge of experts from the perspective of experimental psychology', *The AI Magazine*, 8: 53–66.

Hoffman, R.R., Shadbolt, N.R., Burton, A.M. and Klein, G. (1995) 'Eliciting knowledge from experts: a methodological analysis', *Organizational Behavior and Human Decision Processes*, 62(2): 129–58.

Howitt, D. and Cramer, D. (2005) *Introduction to research methods in psychology.* Harlow: Pearson Education Ltd.

Janis, I.L. (1972) *Victims of groupthink.* Boston, MA: Houghton Mifflin.

Kahneman, D. and Tversky, A. (1973) *Judgement under uncertainty: heuristics and biases.* Cambridge: Cambridge University Press.

Keren, G. and Wagenaar, W.A. (1987) 'Violation of utility theory in unique and repeated gambles', *Journal of Experimental Psychology: Learning, Memory and Cognition*, 13(3): 155–80.

Kitzinger, J. (1994) 'The methodology of focus groups: the importance of interaction between research participants', *Sociology of Health and Illness*, 16(1): 103–21.

Klein, G.A., Calderwood, R. and MacGregor, D. (1989) 'Critical decision method for eliciting knowledge', *IEEE Transactions on Systems, Man, and Cybernetics*, 19: 462–72.

Klein, G.A., Orasanu, J., Calderwood, R. and Zsambok, C.E. (eds) (1993) *Decision making in action: models and methods.* Norwood, CT: Ablex.

Krueger, R.A. (1994) *Focus groups: a practical guide for applied research* (2nd edn). Thousand Oaks, CA: Sage.

Leahy, T.H. (2004) *A history of psychology: main currents in psychological thought.* London: Prentice Hall.

LeBoeuf, R.A. and Shafir, E. (2001). 'Problems and methods in naturalistic decision-making research', *Journal of Behavioural Decision Making*, 14: 373–75.

Lipshitz, R., Klein, G., Orasanu, J. and Salas, E. (2001) 'Taking stock of naturalistic decision making', *Journal of Behavioural Decision Making*, 14: 331–52.

Loftus, E.F. and Zanni, G. (1975) 'Eyewitness testimony: the influence of the wording of a question', *Bulletin of the Psychonomic Society*, 5: 86–88.

Lopes, L.L. (1981) 'Decision making in the short run', *Journal of Experimental Psychology: Human, Learning and Memory*, 7: 377–85.

Lord, R.G. and Hall, R.J. (2005) Identity, deep structure and the development of leadership skill, *The Leadership Quarterly*, 16: 591–615.

Mather, M., Shafir, E. and Johnson, M.K. (2000) 'Misremembrance of options past: source monitoring and choice', *Psychological Science*, 11: 132–8.

McLean, C. and Alison, L. (2005) *Difficulties and decision-making in multi-agency child abuse enquiries.* London: Metropolitan Police Service internal working report.

McLennan, J., Omodei, M. and Wearing, A. (November 1996) 'A new methodology for naturalistic decision making research: investigating fire officers' decisions.' Paper presented at the Judgment and Decision Making Society Annual Meeting, Chicago.

Montoya-Weiss, M.M., Massey, A.P. and Clapper, D.L. (1998) 'Online focus groups: conceptual issues and a research tool', *European Journal of Marketing*, 32(7/8): 713–23.

Morgan, D.L. (1988). *Focus groups as qualitative research.* Newbury Park, CA: Sage.

Newland, P., Creed, C. and Crego, J. (July 1997) 'Consciousness reframed – art and consciousness in the post-biological era.' Paper in the proceedings of the 1st International CAiiA Research Conference, Newport: University of Wales College.

Nunamaker Jr, J.F., Briggs, R.O., Mittleman, D.D., Vogel, D.R. and Balthazard, P.A. (1996/1997) 'Lessons from a dozen years of group support systems research: a discussion of lab and field findings', *Journal of Management Information Systems*, 13(3): 163–208.

Omodei, M.M. and Wearing, A.J. (1993) *Fire Chief* (Version 2.2) [Computer Program]. Melbourne: University of Melbourne, Department of Psychology.

Omodei, M. and Wearing, A. (1994) 'Perceived difficulty and motivated cognitive effort in a computer-simulated forest firefighting task', *Perceptual and Motor Skills*, 79: 115–27.

Omodei, M. and Wearing, A. (1995) 'The Fire Chief microworld generating program: an illustration of computer-simulated Microworlds as an experimental paradigm for studying complex decision making behaviour', *Behavior Research Methods, Instruments and Computers*, 27: 303–16.

Omodei, M., Wearing, A. and McLennan, J. (1997) 'Head-mounted video recording: a methodology for studying naturalistic decision making', in

R. Flin, E. Salas, M. Strub and L. Martin (eds), *Decision-making under stress: emerging themes and applications* (pp. 137–46). Aldershot: Ashgate.

Parent, M., Gallupe, R.B., Salisbury, W.D., Handelman, J.M. (2000) 'Knowledge creation in focus groups: can group technologies help?', *Information and Management*, 38(1): 47–58.

Pogrebin, M. and Poole, E.D. (1991) 'Police and tragic events: the management of emotions', *Journal of Criminal Justice*, 19: 395–403.

Robinson, N. (1999) 'The use of focus group methodology – with selected examples from sexual health research', *Journal of Advanced Nursing*, 29(4): 905–13.

Robson, C. (2002) *Real world research: a resource for social scientists and practitioner-researchers* (2nd edn, pp. 284–9). Oxford: Blackwell Publishing.

Savage, L.J. (1954) *The foundations of statistics*. New York: Wiley.

Senge, P.M. (1990) *The fifth discipline: the art and practice of the learning organization*. New York: Doubleday.

Shafer, G. (1986) 'The combination of evidence', *International Journal of Intelligence Systems*, 1: 155–80.

Slovic, P. (1966) 'Value as a determiner of subjective probability', *IEEE Transactions on Human Factors in Electronics*, 7: 22–8.

Sullivan, T.J. (2001) *Methods of social research*. Orlando: Harcourt College Publishers.

Taylor, P., Lord Justice (1990) *Inquiry into the Hillsborough stadium disaster: final report*. London: HMSO.

Wagenaar, W.A. and Keren, G. (1988) 'Chance and luck are not the same', *Journal of Behavioral Decision Making*, 1: 65–75.

Bob, G., Witmer, B.G. and Singer, M.J. (1997) 'Measuring presence in virtual environments: a presence questionnaire.' Retrieved 13 March 2007, from http://www.mitpressjournals.org/doi/abs/10.1162/105474698565686?journalCode=pres

Woods, D.D. (1995) 'Process-tracing methods for the study of cognition outside of the experimental psychology laboratory', in G.A. Klein, J. Orasanu, R. Calderwood and C.E. Zsambok (eds). *Decision making in action: models and methods* (pp. 228–251). Norwood, NJ: Ablex.

Chapter 4

The current state of police leadership research

Allison Wright, Laurence Alison and Jonathan Crego

Leading critical incidents

According to the Home Office (2001), there is a growing need for enhanced training, leadership and professionalism at all levels of the police service. For example, in the next five years only 20 per cent of English and Welsh officers will have more than five years of experience at managing critical incident inquiries (Police Skills and Standards Organisation 2002). Various initiatives have recently been instigated to help improve police leadership in the UK, such as the creation of a Police Leadership Development Board in 2001, whose role is to facilitate the recruitment and promotion of individuals who have the potential to reach senior positions.

In the past, the management practices of police departments have tended to be evaluated only *after* a crisis or performance breakdown, when public or governmental pressures force supervisory policies to be re-examined (Crego and Alison 2005; Hansen 1991; Murray 2004). This reactive approach can be quite damaging for the police, as it may create unnecessary costs and disruptions, undermine public confidence in the police as an organisation, and cause discord and stress among police officers and other officials (Hansen 1991; Murray 2004).

This chapter examines the issue of police leadership from a more proactive perspective, by reviewing the academic, professional and police administration literature. Specifically, it integrates and critically evaluates existing literature in order to increase our understanding about the psychological features that may determine supervisory effectiveness. The current challenges faced by today's police organisations, and how these may alter the structure of police leadership, will also be considered. Finally, recent efforts to examine police leadership during critical incidents, and future areas of critical incident leadership research, will be addressed.

Leadership and management – definitional issues

Leadership is a complex, abstract idea that is defined in many different ways by many different people (Bolden 2004; Murphy and Drodge 2004; Osborn, Hunt and Jauch 2002). Some consider it to be a personal trait or inherent quality (i.e. a characteristic that one possesses) and others perceive it to be a set of behaviours and actions (i.e. what one does) (Bass 1990; Yukl 1989). In part, such definitional inconsistencies exist because researchers have used many different methods for studying leadership and have failed to co-ordinate their efforts or integrate their findings (Yukl 1989).

Adding further complexity are debates about the distinction between 'leadership' and 'management', where, in general, leadership is defined as people-/process-oriented (i.e. concerned with inspiring and rewarding others, team building and development, creative planning, and innovation) and managerial behaviours are defined as task-/result-oriented (i.e. concerned with decision-making, policy implementation, procedure specification, and the preservation of organisational infrastructures). Although most researchers acknowledge that leadership and management represent two separate ideas, little consensus has been reached about the degree of overlap between them (Yukl 1989). Some argue that one cannot be both leader and manager, since managers focus on accomplishing tasks, whereas leaders focus on motivating and strengthening teams (Bennis and Nanus 1985; Zaleznik 1977). Others claim that leadership and management are highly related processes that are performed in conjunction with one another and are both directed at achieving similar results (e.g. House and Aditya 1997). Thus, management without leadership lacks humanity, adaptability and creativity. This results in inefficient practice and poor staff performance. Conversely, leadership in the absence of management creates practical complications that make goals difficult to achieve (Bolden 2004; Gosling and Murphy 2004).

Interestingly, those who agree that leadership and management are overlapping concepts often still disagree about the extent and nature of this overlap. For example, some maintain that leadership is an aspect of management (e.g. Chemers 2000) while others consider management to be a component of leadership (e.g. Goldsmith 2001). Still others indicate that the relative importance of management and leadership activities differs depending on the situation (e.g. Petrillo and Delbagno 2001; Rosberg, Kuykendall and Novak 2002).

Why are effective leaders important?

Most researchers agree that effective leaders are integral in improving employees' productivity, enhancing their commitment to an organisation's goals and values (Brewer 1995; Dobby *et al.* 2004; Goldsmith 2001; Hansen 1991; Wigfield 1996; Wigfield, Burton, Aitchison and Knill 1998), increasing their motivation (Berson, Shamir, Avolio and Popper 2001), and instilling in them a sense of group identity (Conger, Kanungo and Menon 2000). In addition, the police literature suggests that effective police supervisors are instrumental in communicating organisational changes to employees (Deszca 1988), preventing ethical misconduct (Goldsmith 2001; Muir 1977), and enhancing public perceptions of the police (Stevens 2001).

'In the same way that there is debate about definitions of 'leadership', disagreements also abound with regard to the precise meaning of '*effective* leadership'. In the past, leadership effectiveness has been determined by: measuring the actual performance of a team or individual (e.g. Komaki, Desselles and Bowman 1989; Silverthorn and Wang 2001); determining employees' attitudes towards, and level of satisfaction with, their job or supervisor (e.g. Brewer, Wilson and Beck 1994; Dobby *et al.* 2004; Putti and Tong 1992; Scandur and Williams 2004; Zaccaro, Craig and Quinn 1991); examining superior managers' assessments of leader behaviour (e.g. Densten 2003; Krimmel and Lindenmuth 2001; Pearce and Sims 2002); considering the amount of extra effort employees exert (e.g. Densten 2003); and gauging the rate of employee absenteeism and turnover (e.g. Silverthorn and Wang 2001). Although greater value may be placed on evaluations that utilise several indicators of efficiency, in practice, research has rarely examined multiple criteria (Brewer 1995).

Major approaches to studying police leadership

Research about police leadership is generally categorised according to trait, skills, behaviours/style, situational, transformational and power-influence approaches.

Trait approach

This approach assumes that certain people are born with specific traits or characteristics that make them effective leaders (Bass 1990). For example, early research considered whether physical characteristics (e.g. height, weight, age or appearance), cognitive ability (e.g. intelligence) and social characteristics (e.g. assertiveness, sensitivity) were related to effective leadership (e.g. Flemming 1935; Lindgren 1973).

Police leadership research in this area has focused primarily on individual differences, specifically cognitive ability and personality. Price (1974), for instance, used the Dynamic Personality Inventory to measure the personality characteristics of 227 male and 26 female supervising officers in three American police departments. Females were more self-confident, flexible, liberal and creative. In a later study of 49 recently recruited Maryland State police officers, Mills and Bohannon (1980) found that those who were the most tolerant, self-motivated and intelligent were also considered to be the best leaders by their supervisors.

The trait approach assumes that standardised testing can identify individuals who possess a set of predefined desirable 'leader' characteristics (e.g. a certain personality type or intelligence level) and such tests have been used extensively in police hiring and promotion procedures (Ash, Slora and Britton 1990; Gowan and Gatewood 1995). However, although leader effectiveness is weakly associated with characteristics such as motivation, stress tolerance, energy and self-confidence (Fraser 1978; also see Yukl 1989), most research indicates that traits do not reliably predict effective leadership (Bolden 2004; Brewer 1995) and nor are they useful in distinguishing between leaders and non-leaders (Roberg *et al.* 2002). This relative lack of success may be due, in part, to the fact that the trait approach fails to consider how different situations (e.g. stressful versus routine) can influence leadership (Northouse 2004). Thus, a challenge for the trait approach may be to: a) identify requisite skills; and b) define the range of situations within which those skills might be required. Work at the Centre for Critical Incident Research (CCIR) is beginning to explore, for example, whether certain personality indicators are associated with making difficult decisions outside of policy (Alison 2007).

Skills approach

This approach maintains that leaders possess certain skills and abilities that set them apart from others, suggesting that such skills can be learned and developed over time (i.e. they are not innate and immutable). For example, Katz (1955) argued that an effective leader has advanced technical skills (knowledge about the work being conducted), human skills (ability to work with other employees) and conceptual skills (ability to work with ideas).

More recently, Mumford, Zaccaro, Harding, Jacobs and Fleishman (2000) used data collected from over 1,800 army officers to outline a skills-based model that attempts to define the relationship between a leader's knowledge and skills (i.e. competencies) and his/her performance efficacy. The model is composed of five different parts: Individual Attributes (including general cognitive ability, personality, and motivation); Competencies (i.e. problem-solving skills, social judgement skills and knowledge); Leadership Outcomes (i.e. effectiveness and performance); Previous Career Experiences; and Environmental Influences (which include any factors beyond the leader's control). Although this model claims not to be a trait approach, it is sometimes criticised for the fact that its Individual Attributes component is highly trait-driven (Northouse 2004).

Wigfield (1996; Wigfield *et al.* 1998) asked Sussex police officers about the skills that were important for officers of each rank to possess. They found that officers at different hierarchical positions possessed rank-related skills. For example, higher-level officers (e.g. superintendents), but not sergeants, were expected to possess numerical skills, whereas the ability to evaluate information accurately was more important for sergeants.

In a more recent study, Krimmel and Lindenmuth (2001) examined supervisors' ratings of Pennsylvanian police chiefs (N = 205) and found that the chiefs who were better educated, had attended the Federal Bureau of Investigation's training academy, and who had been promoted from within, rather than from outside, their own department were rated as being the most effective leaders. On the other hand, Stevens (2001) found that officers (N = 145) from 20 different American police agencies described 'excellent' police leaders to be tough and decisive (76 per cent), action-oriented (91 per cent) and to have integrity (62 per cent).

According to the skills approach, it should be possible to develop a check-list of the skills that effective leaders possess. This could then be used to assess officers' competencies, or to develop training programmes to improve certain skills. However, the skills approach is criticised for being too broad and for failing to explain properly certain phenomena. For example, it does not describe how variations in a person's skills influence his/her leadership performance. Like the trait approach, this paradigm fails to account for changes in a leader's situational circumstances (Northouse 2004).

Behaviour/style approach

Unlike the trait and skills approaches, which emphasises personal characteristics and abilities, behavioural approaches examine the particular *actions* that are associated with leadership. Such approaches often involve classifying leaders into groups based on their behavioural type or style. For example, several researchers (e.g. Hemphill and Coons 1957; Judge, Piccolo and Remis 2004; Lok and Crawford 2004) distinguish between leaders who are:

- *Task-oriented*: concerned with accomplishing an organisation's goals (e.g. by defining employee responsibilities, organising resources and tasks); and

- *Socio-emotional- (or team-) oriented*: concerned with developing and maintaining team relationships (e.g. by ensuring that employees are comfortable with each other, themselves and the work environment).

Others consider different *combinations* of task (concern for results) and socio-emotional (concern for people) behaviours. For example, Blake and Mouton's (1964, 1985) Managerial Grid model describes five different leadership styles:

- *Authority-compliance management*: low concern for people, high concern for results – such leaders are results-driven and regard people as tools to accomplish a goal;

- *Country club management:* high concern for people, low concern for results – such leaders ensure that the personal and social needs of employees are met and de-emphasise production;

- *Impoverished management:* low concern for people, low concern for production – such leaders are indifferent, uninvolved and resigned;

- *Middle-of-the-road management*: intermediate concern for both people and production – such leaders are expedient, avoid conflict and make compromises between employee needs and production; and

- *Team management:* strong emphasis on people and production – such leaders promote participation and teamwork and motivate employees to be committed to their work.

Other researchers (e.g. Eagly and Johnson 1990) categorise leaders according to how much leader–employee interaction they allow, such that:

- *Democratic/participative leaders* enable employees to participate in decision-making activities; and

- *Autocratic/directive leaders* discourage employee contributions.

Most contemporary police leadership research is based on the behavioural approach. For example, Reichman *et al.* (1977) found that Canadian police supervisors tended to be primarily task-oriented, although they preferred leadership styles that were high in both task and socio-emotional orientation. Glogow (1979) found that American deputy sheriffs also preferred this style of leadership.

Applying the Managerial Grid model to police supervisors who attended workshops in the south-eastern United States (N = 104), Swanson and Territo (1982) found that the team style of leadership was used most frequently (38 per cent), followed by the task style (25 per cent). Kuykendall (1985) found that 255 police supervisors from 165 American law enforcement agencies used all five Managerial Grid styles, with the Team, Middle-of-the-Road and Authority-Compliance being the most frequently employed styles. Kuykendall (1985) also found that supervisors' styles changed depending on the type of activity they performed. Specifically, the planning stages of an operation tended to be characterised by the use of Team or Middle-of-the-Road approaches, whereas the actual implementation or evaluation of a plan was associated with Authority-Compliance or Country Club management.

Bruns and Shuman (1988) found that American sergeants and lieutenants (N = 365) who were enrolled in managerial training programmes described the leadership practices in their department as being predominantly Autocratic (i.e. little interaction between supervisors and employees, condescending supervisors and decision-making processes being mostly concentrated among management, with some delegation to employees). Most officers also said that they would prefer leadership systems that were more Democratic/Participative. Witte *et al.* (1990) and Wycoff and Skogan (1994) also found that officers favoured the use of Democratic/Participative leadership. Wycoff and Skogan (1994), for example, found that increases in Democratic/Participative leadership were related to increased employee satisfaction with work, supervision, and the department as a whole. Officers who believed that their supervisors were more Democratic/Participative also tended to consider their work to be more important than before and were more receptive to change within the department. Conversely, a survey conducted at a US police department (Reams, Kuykendall and Burns 1975) found that officers did not believe that Democratic/Participative leadership was possible in a police context, since officers regularly encounter circumstances (e.g. crises) that benefit from the use of authoritarian leadership.

Many of the studies that claim to test the behavioural approach tend to 'pigeon-hole' police leaders into different types without considering whether some styles of leadership are more effective than others (Bruns and Shuman 1988; Engel 2001; Krimmel and Lindenmuth 2001). Of the research that *does* address this issue, a strong link between leadership style and effectiveness has not been found (Bryman 1992; Chemers 2000). Indeed, the only consistent relationship that has been found between leadership style and effectiveness is that employees who have considerate (i.e. socio-emotional-oriented) leaders are generally more satisfied than those who have task-oriented leaders (Yukl 1994).

In addition, the behavioural approach does not consider whether different leadership styles are effective across different circumstances (Northouse 2004). As Engel (2001) notes, methodological weaknesses also limit the validity of many behavioural leadership studies. For example, most of these studies rely heavily on lower-ranking officers' perceptions of leader effectiveness, rather than incorporating information about supervisors' self-perceptions and actual behaviours. Many studies are also unclear about whether lower-ranking officers answered questions about one specific leader, several leaders, or about leadership in general. Such issues are especially relevant when studying the police, since employees work several different shifts and are generally supervised by multiple leaders (Engel 2001).

Although there are problems with the behavioural approach, it does still hold value. By evaluating their leadership style, supervisors can determine how they are being perceived by others and can use this feedback to try and improve their behaviours (Northouse 2004).

Situational approaches

Situational approaches emphasise that different kinds of leadership are useful depending on the situation (e.g. the task to be accomplished, the characteristics of employees, the resources available). Several situational approaches exist. For example:

Situational Leadership Theory (Hersey and Blanchard 1988) identifies four leadership styles:

- *Directing/Telling:* the leader displays many directive behaviours (explicit direction, setting time lines and defining employees' roles) and few supportive ones (asking for input, providing social and emotional support to employees).
- *Coaching/Selling:* the leader is both very directive and very supportive.
- *Supporting/Participating*: the leader is not directive but is very supportive.
- *Delegating:* the leader displays few directive or supportive behaviours.

According to this theory, effective leaders are able to determine the developmental stage of their employees and adapt their leadership styles to suit. Four categories of employee developmental levels are described:

- D1 employees display low skills and high commitment (e.g. are excited about a new task but are unfamiliar with it);
- D2 employees have some competence but low commitment;
- D3 employees have high competence but lack commitment;
- D4 employees have both the skills and motivation needed to successfully accomplish a task.

This approach suggests that as employees' skill and maturity increases, leaders should become less directing and coaching.

Path-Goal Theory (House 1971) argues that an effective leader motivates employees and encourages them to see that performance at work can lead to the achievement of personal goals. Like Situational Leadership Theory, it assumes that the *nature of a leader's employees* (e.g. their social needs and preference for structure) affects how a leader's behaviours influence employee performance. In addition, however, Path-Goal Theory argues that the *nature of the task* (e.g. how clear or repetitive it is) also affects leadership performance. Path-Goal Theory describes four main types of leader behaviours:

- *Directive:* e.g. sets clear job roles, performance standards and rules – most effective when subordinates are inflexible and tasks are unclear.

- *Supportive:* e.g. approachable, attends to the well-being of others – most effective when tasks are structured but unsatisfying.

- *Participative:* e.g. consults with subordinates during decision-making, facilitates learning – most effective when employees believe that they are in charge of the events that occur in their lives and when a task is ambiguous.

- *Achievement-oriented:* e.g. challenges subordinates to perform to the best of their ability, seeks continual improvement, and expresses high degree of confidence in employees – most effective when a task is ambiguous.

Kuykendall and Usinger (1982) examined American police supervisors' (N = 155) leadership styles as defined by Situational Leadership Theory, and found that supervisors either had no dominant leadership style (45 per cent) or used the Coaching/Selling style most often (51 per cent). Only 25 per cent of the managers were effective at adapting their leadership behaviours to suit employees' developmental needs.

In the only study to examine police leadership using Path-Goal Theory, Jermier and Berkes (1979) found that when tasks were unpredictable, American police officers (N = 158) were more satisfied with, and committed to, their jobs when their supervisors used Directive and Participative leadership behaviours. However, when tasks were predictable, Supportive leadership behaviours resulted in greater employee satisfaction.

Few studies have tested Situational Leadership Theory, and some of the findings are contradictory (e.g. Fernandez and Vecchio 1997; Vecchio 1987). Situational Leadership Theory fails to define clearly employees' developmental levels (e.g. the definition of 'employee commitment' is not specific) and does not explain how employees can move from one developmental level to the next (Northouse 2004).

Path-Goal Theory is criticised for failing to explain the relationship between employee motivation and a leader's behaviour, and for failing to account for the possibility that subordinates can also influence leaders (Northouse 2004). In addition, Path-Goal Theory has received only partial empirical support, and does not provide as much information about Participative and Achievement-oriented leadership as it does about Directive and Supportive leadership (Northouse 2004).

Transformational approach

The transformational approach (developed by Burns 1978; Bass 1985) is currently one of the most popular theories of leadership. It considers the leader's role in making work situations meaningful for employees, as well as how leaders and followers influence each other, rather than focusing exclusively on how leaders alter the behaviour of followers (Deluga and Souza 1991; Yukl 1999). The transformational approach identifies three types of leaders:

- *Transactional:* uses rewards (e.g. money bonuses, job security) to motivate employees, and may use negative feedback to correct employees' behaviour.

- *Transformational:* engages with employees to create motivation that is felt equally among the leader and employees, raises employees' consciousness by appealing to their higher ideals and values, and convinces employees to go beyond their own self-interests for the good of the team. Transformational leaders act as good role models for employees, by encouraging creative problem-solving, and coaching/advising employees.

- *Laissez-faire:* adopts a 'hands-off' approach, by delaying decisions, avoiding responsibility, and providing little feedback to employees.

Several studies have examined police leadership using the transformational approach. For example, Singer and Singer (1990) found that New Zealand police officers (N = 60) were more satisfied when their supervisors used transformational leadership behaviours. In addition, officers reported that their supervisors generally displayed more transformational than transactional behaviours, and were particularly efficient at creating a supportive team environment. Similarly, through interviews with 28 Royal Canadian Mounted Police officers from diverse ranks, Murphy and Drodge (2004) found that the most valued supervisors were those who used transformational leadership.

In a larger UK-based study, Dobby, Anscombe and Tuffin (2004) interviewed 150 police officers, and surveyed another 1,066 about the type of leadership they received on a daily basis. Officers were also asked about their perceptions of effective leadership. Most of the effective leader behaviours identified by participants were transformational (e.g. valuing and developing staff). Employee job satisfaction, commitment and self-confidence were found to be greater among individuals who stated that their leader was transformational. However, participants reported that a third of their line-managers were not having such a positive influence.

Thus, there is some fairly compelling evidence that transformational leadership is related to employee satisfaction, motivation and performance (Yukl 1999). However, the reliability of the tests used to determine whether a leader is transformational, transactional, or laissez-faire has been criticised (Northouse 2004; Yukl 1999).

Power-influence approach

This approach examines how leaders exert their influence to shape employees' behaviours, as well as how employees can alter a leader's behaviour. Three major types of influencing behaviours have been described (e.g. Kipnis and Schmidt 1985):

- *Forcing behaviours (Hard):* pressure is exerted to make employees comply with a leader's wishes, or vice versa (e.g. job security is threatened, threats are made to notify an external agency if an individual fails to comply).

- *Non-forcing behaviours (Soft):* motivates an individual by using flattery, praise and helpful behaviour or by appealing to his/her sense of loyalty and friendship. Many soft, non-forcing behaviours are similar to transformational behaviour.

- *Non-forcing behaviours (Rational):* motivates an individual by offering rewards (e.g. money bonuses). Rational non-forcing behaviours are similar to transactional leadership behaviours.

In the general academic literature, soft and rational non-forcing behaviours have been found to be the most effective at influencing an individual's attitudes and behaviours. In particular, the soft non-forcing approach appears to be more successful than the rational approach (e.g. Emans, Munduate, Klaver and Van de Vliert 2003; Yukl, Kim and Flabe 1996).

In Emans *et al.* (2003), Spanish police officers (N = 145) stated that when their supervisors relied exclusively on forcing techniques, employees were much less likely to comply. However, when forcing and non-forcing styles were used together, employee compliance was high. Interestingly, Girodo (1998) found that the types of behaviours used by police supervisors differed depending on the situation. Specifically, a survey of 197 police officers from North America, Western Europe and Australia suggested that soft non-forcing behaviours were used the most frequently by supervisors who were involved in training and community-oriented policing initiatives. Rational non-forcing and manipulative behaviours were associated with supervisors in administrative positions.

Summary – the state of police leadership research

Although each of the aforementioned leadership theories provides some useful insight into police leadership, none sufficiently addresses the myriad of contexts within which police leaders must operate. A diverse range of factors influence a police leader's impact on organisational outcomes such as subordinate productivity and satisfaction, though there is little information about how these factors can be co-ordinated to best exploit leader effectiveness (Brewer 1995). Indeed, most studies simply describe different traits, skills and behaviours of police supervisors, rather than linking these to supervisory performance (e.g. Auten 1985; Mills and Bohannon 1980; Swanson and Territo 1982).

The lack of specific, clear theories and consistent evidence about different leadership styles and techniques means that there are no universally accepted benchmarks against which to compare police practice (Dobby, Anscombe and Tuffin 2004; McCallin 2003). This is especially problematic when a police force attempts to create leadership-training programmes, specify standardised leadership guidelines, or investigate concerns about leader performance. Indeed, as noted in the recent report *Strengthening Leadership in the Public Sector* (Cabinet Office 2001),

There is little shared understanding of the qualities required for effective leadership in today's public services [with many] conflicting interpretations ... Fundamental to improved leadership is a clearer shared understanding of what leadership behaviours work in delivering today's public services. (2001: 5)

The operant approach – a means to reduce ambiguity?

In an effort to identify specific recommendations that leaders could use to enhance their effectiveness and to promote optimal employee behaviour, Komaki and colleagues (e.g. Komaki 1986; Komaki 1998; Komaki *et al*. 1989; Komaki, Hyttinen and Immonen 1991) developed the operant model of effective supervision. Its principles are grounded in the well-established field of operant conditioning (Skinner 1974). According to the operant perspective, the consequences of an individual's performance (e.g. the feedback he/she receives) strongly influence his/her subsequent behaviour. Operant leadership theories suggest that effective supervisors are more likely to identify clear expectations (i.e. provide appropriate antecedents to help structure employee behaviour) and to ensure that the consequences they administer accurately reflect employee performance (i.e. employee performance should be carefully monitored to guarantee that positive consequences are given for positive performance and negative consequences are given for poor performance). These claims are extensively supported by empirical research (e.g. Hackman and Walton 1986; Komaki, Coombs and Schepman 1991).

Komaki and colleagues developed an instrument (Operant Supervisory Taxonomy and Index, OSTI; see Table 4.1) that can be used to objectively categorise supervisory behaviours (Brewer *et al*. 1994). Several other versions of the OSTI have been developed subsequently but all share the same basic principles and retain the same behavioural categories. For example, the Operant Supervisory Team Taxonomy and Index (OSTTI) was developed for use in situations where leaders supervise a team of people; the Operant Supervisor-Subordinate Taxonomy and Index (OSSTI) is used to examine leader–follower interactions, and the OSSTI-S can be used to study how behaviours occur over time (Komaki 1998).

According to Komaki and Citera (1990), the central features of the operant model are performance monitoring and performance consequences. Effective supervisors go beyond simply providing instructions to gather relevant information about subordinates' performance and provide feedback about their performance. Specifically, effective leaders spend more time using work sampling monitoring techniques (e.g. they directly observe employees' on-the-job behaviours, or inspect employees' work products), and provide

Table 4.1 Definitions and examples from the Operant Supervisory Taxonomy and Index (OSTI)

Category	Definition	Example
Performance consequences	Communicates knowledge of performance.	'You're making good progress.'
Performance monitors	Gathers information about performance.	'Are you close to finishing that report?'
Performance antecedents	Instructs, reminds, or conveys expectations about performance.	'Can you have this done by tomorrow?'
Own performance	Supervisors refer to the way they themselves are performing.	'I forgot to give you that information!'
Work-related behaviours	Discussions about work that do not concern performance.	'What day is the meeting?'
Non-work-related behaviours	Supervisor interacts with subordinates, but the conversation is not about work.	'Did you have a good weekend?'
Solitary	Supervisor is not interacting with subordinates.	Reading daily briefings alone in office.

Source: Komaki 1998

equal amounts of positive (e.g. 'Well done!'), negative (e.g. 'No, you've forgotten to include this') and neutral (expressing neither approval nor disapproval (e.g. 'That's a different way to do it') consequences (see Komaki 1998 for review). Research also suggests that the timing of a leader's behaviour impacts employee performance and satisfaction. Effective leaders are more likely to express Antecedent-, Monitoring- and Consequence-related behaviours, or just Antecedent- and Monitoring-related behaviours, in rapid succession. The order in which these three behaviours occur has also been shown to influence leader effectiveness, with those who provide additional antecedents after they monitor being perceived as more effective by subordinates (see Komaki 1998 for review).

The only published study to examine the operant model of effective supervision in a police context was conducted by Brewer *et al.* (1994), who examined the OSTI behaviours and supervisory effectiveness of 20 patrol sergeants from a major Australian police force. To measure sergeants' efficiency, each sergeant's supervisor rated his/her team across 12 performance dimensions (e.g. speed and accuracy with which tasks are completed). Supervisory behaviour was measured using the OSTI (Komaki 1986). Specifically, an observer shadowed every sergeant for 20 sessions, each lasting half an hour. Each session was divided into 30 one-minute sampling intervals which, in turn, were broken into a 10-second observation period, a 40-second period for recording observed supervisory behaviours, and a 10-second period to establish the context of the next observation period.

In general, sergeants spent most of their time engaging in solitary behaviours (58.2 per cent) and discussing work-related behaviour (21.5 per cent). Monitors and consequences were given only 6.6 per cent and 3.4 per cent of the time, respectively. Comparisons with other studies (Komaki 1986; Komaki *et al.* 1989; and Komaki, Zlotnick and Jensen 1986) revealed that police sergeants spent about half as much time as insurance, newspaper, bank and theatre managers when it came to providing antecedents and consequences, but about 53 per cent more time monitoring subordinates' performance. As predicted, sergeants with highly ranked teams spent more time monitoring subordinates' performance and providing (neutral) consequences. Further, the more time supervisors spent performing solitary activities, the less time they spent providing antecedents, monitoring, engaging in work-related discussions, and talking about their own performance. Nevertheless, time spent performing solitary activities did not correlate with team performance. Interestingly, however, better team performance was associated with sergeants who spent more time at their desks doing paperwork and less time in their patrol car, perhaps because sergeants at their desks had more opportunities to solicit information from their officers and to provide consequences (Brewer *et al.* 1994).

As Brewer (1995) notes, although it is important to use monitoring behaviours and to clarify tasks by providing antecedents after monitoring, supervisors should not rely too heavily on these techniques. Indeed, it has been shown that leaders who continually specify how subordinates should perform a task, or who are constantly watching over their subordinates' shoulders, are not viewed positively (e.g. Podsakoff, Neihoff, MacKenzie and Williams

1993). In general, evidence suggests that effective leaders spend no more than 5–10 per cent of their time monitoring (e.g. Brewer *et al.* 1994), although different circumstances may require different levels of supervisory attention. For instance, a police recruit may need more monitoring than an experienced officer (Brewer 1995).

In contrast with previous behavioural theories and observational studies, the operant model of effective supervision is more rigorous in its definition of leaders' behaviours, sampling procedures, and reliability evaluations (Brewer *et al.* 1994). Another advantage of this approach is that it examines leader effectiveness in a real-world setting. Komaki (1998), however, argues that the model is upheld only when: subordinates possess the necessary skills and abilities to perform their jobs and are satisfied with their circumstances (e.g. salary, location, peers); supervisors are knowledgeable about their subordinates and the working environment and have good interpersonal skills; sufficient resources are available to perform tasks; the supervisor has already decided how to execute the task at hand; and when the desired outcome is to maintain subordinate performance rather than to initiate or direct it.

Leadership during critical incidents

Despite the fact that many of the situations faced by police leaders are complex, stressful and urgent, few studies have examined police leadership in such challenging circumstances. As Crego and Alison (2004) note, information about leadership during critical incidents comes primarily from inquiry teams who have scrutinised the breakdown of a police investigation; hence the focus has been on failure rather than success. This highlighted a need to examine critical incident leadership from a less reactive and negative approach. Crego and Alison (2004) conducted an electronic focus group session with 28 senior investigating officers from across the UK who had investigated serious, high-profile cases. (The details of these methods are outlined in Chapter 3.) Delegates indicated that issues relating to external parties' (e.g. the media's) views of a case were the most difficult to deal with and had the most impact on an inquiry. Such concerns may reflect the fact that officers lacked control over these elements, as well as the fact that the perceptions of external parties can leave an enduring legacy on the senior officer, the investigative team and the police force (Crego and Alison 2004). Elements rated as high impact, but slightly less difficult were more individual-oriented factors, such as record keeping and the personal characteristics of the senior investigating officer (e.g. be accountable, be prepared to make tough decisions). Elements beyond the immediate inquiry (e.g. political and cultural aspects of the police service) were rated as having relatively less impact on an investigation, but were considered particularly difficult to manage. Finally, elements that involved creating an effective team atmosphere and assigning clear roles and responsibilities to members of the team were perceived to be easier to manage and to have relatively less impact than the aforementioned elements.

In more recent 10kV sessions, Crego and Alison (2005) identified two generic attributes that senior investigating officers perceived to characterise effective leadership and the expedient resolution of cases: interpersonal skills (e.g. the ability to harness team members' specialties and commitment, the effective use of impression management techniques); and decision-making skills (e.g. open-mindedness, the ability to generate adaptable hypotheses, and the ability to prioritise information and decisions). Crego and Alison (2005) describe a model of critical incident management that recognises that decision-making and interpersonal skills are central across diverse encounters and levels of the incident (see also Chapter 7 for further discussion of this model). These features are summarised in Figure 4.1.

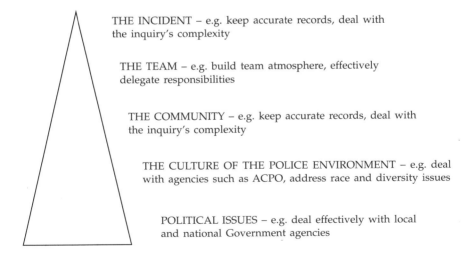

Figure 4.1 Crego and Alison's (2005) management pyramid in critical incidents

Although the studies by Crego and Alison (2004, 2005) represent important first steps in the study of critical incident leadership, more in-depth and detailed research in this area is needed. As noted previously, one lucrative technique for accomplishing such ends may be to use training simulations to observe the behaviours of critical incident managers.

Such research could be informed by organisational and military psychology that examines how groups and teams react to complex, stressful situations (e.g. involving high stakes, heavy workloads, ill-defined problems, and time constraints; McCann, Baranski, Thompson and Pigeau 2000; Oliver and Roos 2003) and how leaders can improve a team's functioning (e.g. Salas, Burke and Stagl 2004a; Salas, Burke, Wilson-Donnelly and Fowlkes 2004b). Although still relatively in its infancy (Salas *et al.* 2004b), this research suggests that leadership has a considerable impact on a team's dynamic processes (e.g. Zaccaro *et al.* 2001), particularly as task and environment complexity increases (Jacobs and Jaques 1987).

Some evidence suggests that teams in adverse situations are more effective when they share mental models about a given task, including models about the equipment, procedures, strategies and constraints involved in the task, the roles, responsibilities, and interdependence of team members, as well as models about team-mates' knowledge, skills and abilities (e.g. Cannon-Bowers, Salas and Converse 1993). These shared mental models are believed to enable individuals to anticipate the type of information/assistance that other team members might require, increase team co-ordination/cohesion, and diminish the need for communication. Additional research indicates that teams performing in situations that require rapid adaptation are more proficient when they have effective meta-cognitive and self-correction processes (i.e. when they are able to effectively review events, and can correct their cognitions, attitudes and behaviours without outside intervention; Blickensderfer, Cannon-Bowers and Salas 1998). Leaders who help promote such processes (e.g. through training (Cannon-Bowers *et al.* 1993)); or by engineering situations in which team members can interact (Oliver and Roos 2003) may therefore increase the efficiency of their teams.

Furthermore, it has been shown that, when the members of a team surrender to stress, information is not properly shared, alternative solutions are not adequately explored, and decision-making accuracy declines as a result (e.g. Argote, Turner and Fichman 1989; Gladstein and Reilly 1985). Although there is a dearth of information about leaders' ability to influence group emotion (Zaccaro *et al.* 2001), research indicates that team members are less likely to react unfavourably towards stressors if leaders provide clear goals, specify team members' roles, and identify performance strategies (Sugiman and Misumi 1988).

Conclusion

In part, the present chapter was prompted by recent concerns about the state and future of police leadership in the UK (e.g. Crego and Alison 2005; Home Office 2001; PSSO 2002). It is important to note, however, that such issues are not specific only to police forces within the UK. In a recent study of the Royal Canadian Mounted Police (RCMP) (Police Futures Group 2001), for example, police chiefs, police governing bodies, police associations, and police middle managers indicated that insufficient learning opportunities exist to prepare RCMP officers properly for supervisory roles. Specifically, each group identified notable deficiencies in the force's leadership training and communication programmes. In response to such findings, the RCMP Human Resources department has begun to develop leadership training programmes in an attempt to guide the next generation of supervisors (Doherty 2004). Improving police leadership is also an area of concern among American (Hansen 1991), Indian (Report for the Patel National Police Academy 2004) and Australasian police forces (Densten 1999; Etter and Palmer 1995). In addition, the International Association of Chiefs of Police (IACP), which represents police leaders from 89 different countries around the world, has recognised the need to produce guidelines that will enhance the success of present and future police supervisors. Towards these ends, the IACP has called for an increased focus on leadership competencies, preparation, functioning and survival, and has established its own Centre for Police Leadership (Polisar 2002). Indeed, the IACP has recommended that, 'Leadership issues should drive [the] profession's [introspective] examination for the next decade or two' (Moody 1999: i).

However, despite the global and ever-increasing importance of police leadership, the present review indicates that little up-to-date research on the topic exists. This is particularly problematic because it means that police forces will have insufficient empirical evidence to consult when attempting to design programmes and policies to enhance the abilities of their leaders. Although several methodological paradigms, such as the trait, skills, behaviour/style, situational, transformational and power-influence approaches, have been used to study police leadership in the past, the information gleaned from this research often lacks shared theoretical elements and does not adequately describe the range of issues in police leadership. At best, such research provides only a partial explanation about the factors involved in effective police leadership and how these interact (Brewer 1995).

References

Alison, L. (2007) Personality factors and resistance to viewing policy as doctrine. Senior Investigative Programme. Leadership Academy, Metropolitan Police Service, 5 March, London.

Argote, L., Turner, M.E. and Fichman, M. (1989) 'To centralize or not to centralize: the effects of uncertainty and threat on group structure and performance', *Organizational Behaviour and Human Decision Processes*, 42: 58–74.

Ash, P., Slora, K.B. and Britton, C.F. (1990) 'Police agency officer selection practices', *Journal of Police Science and Administration*, 17: 258–69.

Bass, B.M. (1985) *Leadership and performance beyond expectations*. New York: The Free Press.

Bass, B.M. (1988) 'The inspirational process of leadership', *Journal of Management Development*, 7: 21–31.

Bass, B.M. (1990) *Bass and Stogdill's handbook of leadership: theory, research and managerial applications* (3rd edn). New York: The Free Press.

Bennis, W.G. and Nanus, B. (1985) *Leaders: the strategies for taking charge*. New York: Harper and Row.

Berson, Y., Shamir, B., Avolio, B.J. and Popper, M. (2001) 'The relationship between vision, strength, leadership style and context', *Leadership Quarterly*, 12(1): 53–73.

Blake, R.R. and Mouton, J.S. (1964) *The managerial grid*. Houston, TX: Gulf.

Blake, R.R. and Mouton, J.S. (1985) *The managerial grid III*. Houston, TX: Gulf.

Blickensderfer, E., Cannon-Bowers, J.A., and Salas, E. (1998) 'Cross-training and team performance', in J.A. Cannon-Bowers and E. Salas (eds), *Making decisions under stress: implications for individual and team training* (pp. 299–311). Washington, DC: American Psychological Association.

Brewer, N. (1995) 'Leadership and supervision', in N. Brewer and C. Wilson (eds), *Psychology and policing* (pp. 291–316). Hillsdale, NJ: Lawrence Erlbaum Associates.

Brewer, N., Wilson, C. and Beck, K. (1994) 'Supervisory behaviour and team performance amongst police patrol sergeants', *Journal of Occupational and Organisational Psychology*, 67: 69–78.

Bruns, G.H. and Shuman, I.G. (1988) 'Police managers' perception of organisational leadership styles', *Public Personnel Management*, 17(2): 145–57.

Bryman, A. (1992) *Charisma and leadership in organisations*. London: Sage.

Bryman, A. (2004) 'Qualitative research on leadership: a critical but appreciative review', *The Leadership Quarterly*, 15: 729–69.

Bolden, R. (2004) *What is leadership?* Exeter: Leadership South West. Retrieved 15 May, 2005, from: http://www.leadershipsouthwest.com

Burns, J.M. (1978) *Leadership*. Oxford: Harper and Row.

Cabinet Office (2001) *Strengthening leadership in the public sector*. London: Cabinet Office.

Cannon-Bowers, J.A., Salas, E., and Converse, S.A. (1993) 'Shared mental models in expert team decision making', in N.J. Castellan (ed.), *Individual and group decision making: current issues* (pp. 221–46). Hillsdale, NJ: Lawrence Erlbaum.

Chemers, M. (2000) Leadership research and theory: a functional integration. *Group Dynamics: Theory, Research, and Practice*, 4(1): 27–43.

Conger, J.A., Kanungo, R.N. and Menon, S.T. (2000) 'Charismatic leadership and follower effects', *Journal of Organizational Behaviour*, 21(7): 747–67.

Crego, J. (2002) 'Training decision-making by team-based simulation', in R. Flin and K. Arbuthnot (eds), *Incident command: tales from the hot seat* (pp. 258–69). Aldershot: Ashgate.

Crego, J. and Alison, L. (2004) 'Control and legacy as functions of perceived criticality in major incidents', *Journal of Investigative Psychology and Offender Profiling*, 1: 207–25.

Crego, J. and Alison, L. (2005) *Celebrating success, learning from experience*. Briefing report for the North Yorkshire Police.

Deluga, R.J. and Souza, J. (1991) 'The effects of transformational and transactional leadership styles on the influencing behaviour of subordinate police officers', *Journal of Occupational Psychology*, 64: 49–55.

Densten, I.L. (1999) 'Senior Australian law enforcement leadership under examination', *Policing: An International Journal of Police Strategies and Management*, 22(1): 45–57.

Densten, I.L. (2003) 'Senior police leadership: does rank matter?' *Policing: An International Journal of Police Strategies and Management*, 26(3): 400–18.

Deszca, G. (1988) 'The communication of ideology in police forces', *Canadian Police College Journal*, 12(4): 240–68.

Dobby, J., Anscombe, J. and Tuffin, R. (2004) 'Police leadership: expectations and impact', Home Office Report 20/04. Retrieved 18 April, 2005, from http://www.mcb.org.uk/mcbdirect/library/uploads/rdsolr2004.pdf

Doherty, D. (2004) 'Building the next generation of leaders in the Royal Canadian Mounted Police', *The Canadian Review of Policing Research*. Retrieved 18 April 2005, from http://crpr.icaap.org/issues/issue1.html

Eagly, A.H. and Johnson, B.T. (1990) 'Gender and leadership style: a meta-analysis', *Psychological Bulletin*, 108: 233–56.

Emans, B.J.M., Munduate, L., Klaver, E. and Van de Vliert, E. (2003) 'Constructive consequences of leaders' forcing influence styles', *Applied Psychology: An International Review*, 52(1): 36–54.

Engel, R.S. (2001) 'Supervisory styles of patrol sergeants and lieutenants', *Journal of Criminal Justice*, 29: 341–55.

Etter, B. and Palmer, M. (1995) *Police leadership in Australasia*. Sydney: The Federation Press.

Fernandez, C.F. and Vecchio, R.P. (1989) 'Situational leadership theory revisited: a test of an across-jobs perspective', *Leadership Quarterly*, 8(1): 67–84.

Flemming, E.G. (1935) 'A factor analysis of the personality of high school teachers', *Journal of Applied Psychology*, 19: 596–605.

Girodo, M. (1998) 'Machiavellian, bureaucratic, and transformational leadership styles in police managers: preliminary findings of interpersonal ethics', *Perceptual and Motor Skills*, 8: 419–27.

Gladstein, D. and Reilly, N. (1985) 'Group decision making under threat: the tycoon game', *Academy of Management Journal*, 8: 613–27.

Glogow, E. (1979) 'The successful leader in law enforcement: what works', *LAE Journal of American Criminal Justice*, 42: 71–77.

Goldsmith, A. (2001) 'The pursuit of police integrity: leadership and governance dimensions', *Current Issues in Criminal Justice*, 13(2): 186–202.

Gosling, J. and Murphy, A. (2004) *Leading continuity*. Working Paper: Centre for Leadership Studies, University of Exeter. Retrieved 1 March, 2005, from http://www.leadershipsouthwest.com

Gowan, M.A., and Gatewood, R.D. (1995) 'Personnel selection', in N. Brewer and C. Wilson (eds), *Psychology and policing* (pp. 177–204). Hillsdale, NJ: Lawrence Erlbaum Associates.

Hackman, J.R. and Walton, R.E. (1986) 'Leading groups in organisations', in P.S. Goodman and Associates (eds), *Designing effective work groups* (pp. 72–119). San Francisco, CA: Jossey-Bass.

Hansen, P. (1991) 'Developing police leaders.' Retrieved 1 March 2005, from http://fux0r.phathookups.com/textfiles/law/2developp04.law

Hemphill, J.K. and Coons, A.E. (1957) 'Development of the leader behavior description questionnaire', in R.M. Stogdill and A.E. Coons (eds), *Leader behavior: its description and measurement, monograph no. 88*. Columbus, OH: The Ohio State University, Bureau of Business Research.

Hersey, P., and Blanchard, K. (1988). *Management of organisational behaviour* (5th edn). Englewood Cliffs, NJ: Prentice Hall.

Hollander, E.P. (1978) *Leadership dynamics: a practical guide to effective relationships*. New York: Free Press/Macmillan.

Hollander, E.P. (1993) 'Legitimacy, power and influence: a perspective on relational features of leadership', in M.M. Chemers and R. Ayman (eds), *Leadership theory and research: perspectives and directions* (pp. 29–47). San Diego, CA: Academic Press Inc.

Hooijberg, R. and Choi, J. (2001) 'The impact of organisational characteristics on leadership effectiveness models: an examination of leadership in a private and a public sector organisation', *Administration and Society*, 33(4): 403–31.

Home Office (2001) *Policing a new century: a blueprint for reform.* Retrieved 5 April 2005, from http://www.policereform.gov.uk/docs/policingsurvey.pdf

House, R.J. (1971) 'A path-goal theory of leadership', *Administrative Science Quarterly*, 1: 321–38.

House, R.J. and Aditya, R.N. (1997) 'The social scientific study of leadership: quo vadis?, *Journal of Management*, 23(3), 409–73.

Jacobs, T.O. and Jaques, E. (1987) 'Leadership in complex systems', in J.A. Zeidner (ed.), *Human productivity enhancement: vol. 2, organisations, personnel and decision making* (pp. 7–65). New York: Praeger.

Jermier, J.M. and Berkes, L.J. (1979) 'Leader behaviour in a police command bureaucracy: a closer look at the quasi-military model', *Administrative Science Quarterly*, 24: 1–23.

Judge, T.A., Picolo, R.F. and Illies, R. (2004) 'The forgotten ones? The validity of consideration and initiating structure in leadership research', *Journal of Applied Psychology*, 89(1): 36–51.

Katz, R.L. (1955) 'Skills of an effective administrator', *Harvard Business Review*, 33(1): 33–43.

Kipnis, D. and Schmidt, S. (1983) 'An influence perspective on bargaining within organisations', in H.M. Bazerman and R.J. Lewicky (eds), *Negotiation in organisations* (pp. 303–19). London: Sage.

Komaki, J.L. (1986) 'Toward effective supervision', *Journal of Applied Psychology*, 7: 270–9.

Komaki, J.L. (1998) *Leadership from an operant perspective.* London: Routledge.

Komaki, J.L. and Citera, M. (1990) 'Beyond effective supervision: identifying key interactions between superior and subordinate', *Leadership Quarterly*, 1: 91–105.

Komaki, J.L., Coombs, T. and Schepman, S. (1991) 'Motivational implications of reinforcement theory', in R.M. Steers and L.W. Porter (eds), *Motivation and Work Behaviour* (5th edn). New York: McGraw-Hill.

Komaki, J.L., Desselles, M.I. and Bowman, E.D. (1989) 'Definitely not a breeze: extending an operant model of effective supervision to teams', *Journal of Applied Psychology*, 74(3): 522–9.

Komaki, J.L., Hyttinen, M. and Immonen, S. (1991) 'Cross-cultural research in work and leader behaviour', in K.R. Thompson (Chair), *Managing across cultures from a behavioural perspective: theory and research.* Symposium conducted at the Meeting of the Academy Management, Atlanta, GA.

Komacki, J.L., Zlotnick, S. and Jensen, M. (1986). 'Development of an operant-based taxonomy and observational index of supervisory behaviour', *Journal of Applied Psychology*, 7: 260–9.

Krimmel, J.T. and Lindenmuth, P. (2001) 'Police chief performance and leadership styles', *Police Quarterly*, 4(4): 469–83.

Kuykendall, J.T. (1985) 'Police managerial styles: a grid analysis', *American Journal of Police*, 4: 38–70.

Kuykendall, J. and Usinger, P. (1982) 'The leadership styles of police managers', *Journal of Criminal Justice*, 10: 311–21.

Lindgren, H.C. (1973) 'Leadership and college grades', *Journal of Social Psychology*, 90(1): 165–6.

Lok, P. and Crawford, J. (2004) 'The effect of organisational culture and leadership style on job satisfaction and organisational commitment: a cross-national comparison', *Journal of Management Development*, 23(4): 321–38.

McCallin, A. (2003) 'Interdisciplinary team leadership: a revisionist approach for an old problem?', *Journal of Nursing Management*, 11: 364–70.

McCann, C., Baranski, J.V., Thompson, M.M. and Pigeau, R.A. (2000) 'On the utility of experiential cross-training for team decision-making under time stress', *Ergonomics*, 43(8): 1095–110.

Mills, C.J., and Bohannon, W.E. (1980) 'Personality characteristics of effective state police officers', *Journal of Applied Psychology*, 65(6): 680–4.

Moody, B.D. (1999) 'Police leadership in the 21st century: achieving and sustaining executive success.' International Association of Chiefs of Police. Retrieved April 3 2005, from http://www.theiacp.org/documents/index.cfm?fuseaction=documentanddocument_id=142

Muir, W.K. (1977) *Police: street corner politicians*. Chicago, IL: University of Chicago Press.

Mumford, M.D., Zaccaro, S.J., Harding, F.D., Jacobs, T. and Fleishman, E.A. (2000) 'Leadership skills for a changing world: solving complex social problems', *Leadership Quarterly*, 11(1): 11–35.

Murphy, S.A. and Drodge, E.N. (2004) 'The four Ls of police leadership: a case study heuristic', *International Journal of Police Science and Management*, 6(1): 1–15.

Murray, T. (2004) 'Policing management and organisation', *The Canadian Review of Policing Research*. Retrieved May 21 2006, from http://crpr.icaap.org/issues/issue1.html

Northouse, P.G. (2004) *Leadership: theory and practice* (3rd edn). London: Sage.

Oliver, D. and Roos, J. (2003) 'Dealing with the unexpected: critical incidents in the LEGO mindstorms team', *Human Relations*, 56(9): 1057–82.

Osborn, R.N., Hunt, J.G. and Jauch, L.R. (2002) 'Toward a contextual theory of leadership', *Leadership Quarterly*, 13: 797–837.

Pearce, C.L. and Sims, H.P. (2002) 'Vertical versus shared leadership as predictors of the effectiveness of change management teams: an examination of aversive, directive, transactional, transformational, and empowering leader behaviours', *Group Dynamics: Theory, Research, and Practice*, 6(2): 172–97.

Petrillo, M.A. and Delbagno, D.R. (2001) *The new age of police supervision and management: a behavioural concept.* Flushing, NY: Looseleaf Law Publications Inc.

Podsakoff, P.M., Neihoff, B.P., MacKenzie, S.B. and Williams, M.L. (1993) 'Do substitutes for leadership really substitute for leadership? An empirical examination of Kerr and Jermier's situational leadership model', *Organizational Behaviour and Human Decision Processes,* 54: 1–44.

Police Skills and Standards Organisation (2002) *Police skills foresight report.* Sheffield, UK: PSSO. Retrieved on 4 April 2005, from http://www.psso.co.uk/publications/ Final%20Report%202002.pdf

Polisar, J.M. (2002) President's message: the IACP Centre for Police Leadership. Retrieved on 4 April 2005, from http://www.theiacp.org/documents/index.cfm?document_id=566andfuseaction=documentandsubtype_id=

Price, B.R. (1974) 'A Study of leadership strength of female police executives', *Journal of Police Science and Administration,* 2: 219–26.

Putti, J.M. and Tong, A.C. (1992) 'Effects of leader behaviour on subordinate satisfaction in a civil service Asian context', *Public Personnel Management,* 21(1): 53–63.

Reams, R., Kuykendall, J. and Burns, D. (1975) 'Police management systems: what is an appropriate model?', *Journal of Police Science and Administration,* 3: 475–81.

Reichman, W., Finkelman, J.M. and Friend, M. (1977) 'The supervisory style of police chiefs', *Canadian Police Chief,* 65: 12–16.

Report for the Patel National Police Academy (2004).

Roberg, R., Kuykendall, J. and Novak, K. (2002) *Police management* (3rd edn). Los Angeles, CA: Roxbury Publishing Company.

Salas, E., Burke, C.S. and Stagl, K.C. (2004a) 'Developing teams and team leaders: strategies and principles', in D.V. Day, S.J. Zaccaro and S.M. Halpin (eds), *Leader development for transforming organisations: growing leaders for tomorrow* (pp. 293–323). Mahwah, NJ: Lawrence Erlbaum Associates.

Salas, E., Burke, C.S., Wilson-Donnelly, K.A. and Fowlkes, J.E. (2004b) 'Promoting effective leadership within multicultural teams: an event-based approach', in D.V. Day, S.J. Zaccaro and S.M. Halpin (eds), *Leader development for transforming organisations: growing leaders for tomorrow* (pp. 293–323). Mahwah, NJ: Lawrence Erlbaum Associates.

Scandura, T.A. and Williams, E.A. (2004) 'Mentoring and transformational leadership: the role of supervisory career mentoring', *Journal of Vocational Behaviour,* 65(3): 448–68.

Silverthorn, C. and Wang, T.H. (2001) 'Situational leadership style as a predictor of success and productivity among Taiwanese business organisations', *Journal of Psychology,* 135(4): 399–412.

Singer, M.S. and Singer, A.E. (1990) 'Situational constraints on transformational versus transactional leadership behaviour, subordinates' leadership preference and satisfaction', *The Journal of Social Psychology,* 130(3): 385–96.

Skinner, B.F. (1974) *About behaviourism*. New York: Vintage.

Southerland, M.D. and Reuss-Ianni, E. (1992) 'Leadership and management', in G.W. Cordner and D.C. Hale (eds), *What works in policing? Operations and administration examined* (pp. 157–177). Cincinnati, OH: Anderson Publishing.

Stevens, D.J. (2001) 'Community policing and managerial techniques: total quality management techniques', *Police Journal*, 74(26): 26–41. Retrieved 5 April 2005, from http://www.vathek.com/pj/contents01-1.shtml

Stogdill, R.M. (1974) *Handbook of leadership: a survey of the literature*. New York: Free Press.

Sugiman, T. and Misumi, J. (1988) 'Development of a new evacuation method for emergencies: control of collective behaviour by emergent small groups', *Journal of Applied Psychology*, 73: 3–10.

Swanson, C.R. and Territo, L. (1982) 'Police leadership and interpersonal communication styles', in J.R. Greene (ed.), *Managing police work: issues and analysis* (pp. 123–139). Beverly Hills, CA: Sage.

Vecchio, R.P. (1987) 'Situational leadership theory: An examination of a prescriptive theory', *Journal of Applied Psychology*, 72(3): 444–51.

Wigfield, D. (1996, April) 'Competent leadership in the police', *The Police Journal*, 99–108.

Wigfield, D., Burton, C., Aitchison, D. and Knill, L. (1998, April) 'Developing leaders in the police service', *The Police Journal*, 99–108.

Witte, J.H., Travis, L.F. and Langworthy, R.H. (1990) 'Participatory management in law enforcement', *American Journal of Police*, 9(4): 1–23.

Wycoff, M.A. and Skogan, W.G. (1994) 'The effect of a community policing management style on officers' attitudes', *Crime and Delinquency*, 40: 371–83.

Yukl, G. (1989) 'Managerial leadership: a review of theory and research', *Journal of Management*, 18(2): 251–89.

Yukl, G.L. (1994) *Leadership in organisations* (3rd edn). Englewood Cliffs, NJ: Prentice Hall.

Yukl, G. (1999) 'An evaluation of conceptual weaknesses in transformational and charismatic leadership theories', *Leadership Quarterly*, 10(2): 285–305.

Zaccaro, S.J., Rittman, A.L. and Marks, M.A. (2001) 'Team leadership', *The Leadership Quarterly*, 12: 451–83.

Zaleznik, A. (1977) 'Managers and leaders: are they different?', *Harvard Business Review*, 55(3), 67–8.

Chapter 5

Command, control and support in critical incidents

Kate Whitfield, Laurence Alison and Jonathan Crego

In recent years, most of the information that describes critical incidents has focused on police performance breakdowns (Crego and Alison 2004), and subsequently public reviews (Macpherson 1999; Laming 2003). It is a poignant truth that the efforts of successful inquiries are seldom publicly acknowledged (Flin 1996). This chapter focuses on several different critical incidents including: a siege, a child abduction, a high-profile murder, a natural disaster, a public order incident, and the detonation of a terrorist bomb in another country where the assistance of the British police services was required. Although many rich themes emerge from the debriefings, we focus directly on the underlying tension between directive command and supportive leadership, and the often difficult negotiation of attaining a successful balance between the two.

Directive and supportive leadership

As noted in Chapter 4, two common themes run throughout the majority of leadership studies. Firstly, *task-oriented* leadership refers to the provision of clear direction (Hemphill and Coons 1957; Judge, Piccolo and Ilies 2004; Lok and Crawford 2004). Such individuals tend to be *autocratic* (Eagly and Johnson 1990) and focus on *initiating structure* (Fleishman 1953). This parallels what situational approaches identify as *directive* behaviour (House 1971; Hersey and Blanchard 1977), and transformational approaches refer to as *transactional* actions

(Burns 1978; Bass 1985). All of these studies describe actions directed at accomplishing the team's goals. These may include, for example, the clear definition of roles, efficient planning and organisation, ensuring directions are understood, and managing complexity.

Secondly, an effective leader offers support to colleagues and team members, with behaviour/style approaches describing such individuals as *socio-emotional-oriented* (Hemphill and Coons 1957; Judge, Piccolo and Ilies 2004; Lok and Crawford 2004), *democratic* (Eagly and Johnson 1990), and regularly displaying *consideration* for others (Fleishman 1953). Situational and transformational approaches classify this behaviour as *supportive* (House 1971; Hersey and Blanchard 1977) and *transformational* (Burns 1978; Bass 1985) respectively. Supportive leadership thus refers to the interpersonal and participative actions of the leader, for example, building rapport, maintaining team relationships, and providing support.

These two facets of leadership are considered to be independent of one another, with leaders providing both direction and support at any one time. As we highlight in Chapter 10, context, specifically organisational context, has a major impact on the ability (and willingness) of leaders to express these behavioural styles. Repeatedly in our examinations of the 10kV debriefs, we found that the media, communities, external agencies, government, investigating team members, and prevailing police organisational culture have a powerful impact on the type of behaviour required of the leader, and his or her response to expressing support or providing direction. In order to be effective, leaders must adapt accordingly (Stevens 2001). As Krimmel and Lindenmuth (2001: 472) note, 'the ability to pigeon-hole police leadership styles offers little utility without considering the social structure in which police function.' For example, during the early stages of a child abduction inquiry, officers leading the inquiry must appreciate complexity, provide rapid responses to prioritising the flood of information, and clearly delegate roles and responsibilities. In the later stages, the senior investigating officer (SIO) must recognise and respond to the potential stressors experienced by staff (such as long working hours and emotional impact).

As a result, police leadership during critical incident management is a continual balancing act between directing and supporting. The remainder of this chapter indicates the sub-components of directive and supportive leader behaviour, with illustrative samples and quotes from the debriefings.

Dimensions of directive leadership

Based on the police officers' reflections during the 10kV debriefings,[1] there are three sub-components of directive behaviour: planning, organising and communicating.

1 Planning

According to Boddy (2005: 14), 'Planning deals with the overall direction of the work to be done.' Successful planning results in clear direction, increased motivation and economic efficiency in the utilisation of resources. Conversely, poor planning leads to confusion, frustration and stress (Boddy 2005). During a critical incident, it is therefore essential that team members *'know what need[s] to be done in what order'*.

Planning and prioritisation was raised in four of the debriefings. In some instances, it was simply a matter of improving the planning of briefings. For example, in one of the debriefings it was stated that there was often *'no agenda at meetings'* and that *'meetings [needed to be] more structured. At times it was a chat whilst having a sandwich.'* In contrast, in another debriefing there were *'business-like meeting structures'* which in essence *'pulled together a structure that meant after a short period of time [they] had good accountability and support.'*

Three of the debriefings, however, suggested long-term planning was especially relevant, as *'the organisation was ill-prepared to manage inquir[ies] of such size and complexity'*. In other cases, the issue was not enough prior planning: *'Emergency procedures had not adequately planned for an incident of this impact.'* In addition, there were *'frustrations in that people were rushing around without any coherence, therefore decisions were not being made in a logical and effective manner, resulting in wasted effort and delays.'*

Other debriefings also revealed individuals feeling unprepared for a critical incident of significant magnitude, both in terms of individuals' skills and the available equipment: *'There was clearly a gap in knowledge of the use of firearms in public order situations'*; leaders *'should have had a better plan for firearms incidents at the start of the operation. The plan [they] came up with later was good, but the public order officers hadn't been trained on it.'* In addition, there were instances of *'officers being deployed to hostile areas not properly "clothed", and having to dress in the middle of a riot situation,' "* as well as *'vehicles [being] unable to carry numbers of staff and equipment necessary'.* Despite this, however, the team *'demonstrated [their] professionalism by drawing together plans that were delivered well, and were proven in the deployment to contain a group armed with a firearm'.*

A consistent emerging theme then is lack of readiness to deal with situations that, by their very nature, may be unique. Simulations assist individuals in preparing for the unexpected and for events of significant magnitude. They encourage delegates to generate 'worst-case scenarios' of what could *possibly* happen during the simulated inquiry. As we will discuss later, this 'worst-case scenario' generation, though seeming bleak in its commitment always to thinking the worst *will* happen, does enable SIOs to develop plans for rapid deployment, and to structure and clarify roles. And, as we noted, operational change is often only recommended after failure. A clear objective then is to allow failure to emerge in the 'simulated world', so as to assist leaders in effective use of directive behaviour and to develop better strategic plans.

Finally, in stressful situations, where time is of the essence and decisions must be made, it is essential that information and tasks be prioritised (Flin and Arbuthnot 2002). In one debriefing an individual commented that the incident *'lacked clearly defined lines of inquiry at early stage'.* This was possibly the result of the *'vast amount of information on every possible aspect of the investigation coming in',* which was often *'held in differing places and modes',* and in some instances, *'there was valuable information incoming that was not available for some days.'* As one officer stated, *'We were not able to capture, process, prioritise the information, and could not act upon, or even identify, the important information.'* Such issues highlight the importance of planning during a critical incident.

2 Organising

During a rapidly unfolding incident, organisation is vital for the effective use of resources and in moving abstract plans closer to realisation. Successful allocation of time and effort may be achieved through efficiently co-ordinating tasks and assigning individual roles (Sarna 2002; Boddy 2005).

Some of the debriefings indicated team members feeling discouraged as a result of lack of efficient co-ordination. One officer stated that the *'poor distribution of workload and deployment of staff ... caused unnecessary frustrations'*. Elements of disorganisation were also felt: *'Everybody was under enormous pressure due to the press hype, lack of resources at an early stage and volume of information. This created an investigation team that was extremely difficult to manage. It also created confusion. The initial days were therefore without focus, the inquiry lacked direction. Decisions were made hastily, without consideration and considering the basics.'*

However, there was effective organisation where the investigation *'co-ordinate[ed] on days well over two hundred staff, support[ed] both the requirements of silver command and the investigation teams'*. In addition, *'resources were made available for the investigation when required and a structure was put in place to provide co-ordination between the investigation, the response to the media appeal and local reassurance.'* The team realised from the outset that there was a *'need to know which staff were on duty and when'*, and ensured that *'by having systems and resources in place, [they] were able to respond in a systematic and professional manner'*.

As well as co-ordinating tasks, organising also involves assigning people to specific roles. An individual's role refers to the behaviours expected of him or her when occupying a particular position (Shaw 1981). During a critical incident, it is important that roles are clearly defined and allocated according to expertise and ability. It is then important that team members get in role and stay in role, rather than deviate and take on others' responsibilities (Sarna 2002).

In some debriefings, difficulties were encountered concerning individual roles. This included (i) lack of definition: *'roles were not properly defined'* (ii) individual and team confusion: *'there was a degree of confusion as to who was performing what role'*; (iii) lack of clarity of responsibility: *'staff seemed unaware of their roles'*; (iv) lack of inter-role appreciation: *'lack of understanding of people's roles'*; and (v) inter-role confusion: *'sometimes the team leader's role became muddled – in that they actually became more like another negotiator, passing even more post notes. They could then not all be processed and things got lost'*. Adopting the roles of others can hinder the operation as a whole; for example, during one incident, *'the command structure was at times vulnerable from officers acting outside of their respective roles'*. As such, many recommendations for change focused around *'ensur[ing] that each [member of the investigating team] is aware of the others' roles, responsibilities and capabilities'*.

However, even when roles are clearly defined and understood, sometimes individuals do not have the necessary expertise or experience for the role they are assigned. This was apparent during one inquiry where *'as the day progressed staff were identified and sent to the scene, but they were chosen on availability and not by their skill, which hampered the task.'* Another debriefing also indicated that *'staff without the required skills were doing specific tasks, [suggesting] very steep learning curves.'* In addition, it was clear that simply because an individual has a specific rank, does not necessarily mean they are suitable for a particular task. This was made plain in the assertion of one officer: *'We need to ask hard questions about not just what roles we need to fill in critical aspects of the operation, but also who is best equipped to do this role ... not all people are good at all roles just because they have the rank.'* We noted earlier the need for preparedness and creativity in generating 'worst-case scenarios' during simulations. An additional component to assist in increasing the effectiveness of directive leader behaviour is to draw upon previous, tacit experience.

The level of organisation during a critical incident inquiry is largely influenced by consistency and continuity of leadership. It is difficult to deliver a co-ordinated response if leaders frequently change or, alternatively, managers constantly alter their messages to the team. Delegates thus noted that there are *'great benefits from using the same staff as much as possible, particularly those engaged in gold/silver roles. It allows for continuity of style and decision-making ... [however, it is] not always possible,'* as *'changing of gold is often necessary due to periods of rest'*.

The existence of *'too many chiefs who all had their own ideas'* and *'gold was a committee rather than an identified commander, [thus] resulting in mixed messages to the workers'*, as well as a *'confused and disjointed command structure'*, resulted in *'briefings [being] stopped midway and the direction changed or process altered. There was no accountability for actions, which meant issues were not addressed. The picture was never assessed on a basic level and as a result issues were missed'*. Because *'continuity and consistency of command will always be an issue in incidents that run over several days'*, serious attention must be devoted to harnessing previous experience. Of course, the debriefings themselves present an opportunity for retaining some aspects of these experiences, as the participating delegates have learned the hard way by being immersed in extremely challenging real events.

3 Communicating

Boddy (2005: 522) asserts that 'Communication happens when people share information to reach a common understanding.' This depends largely on effective two-way transmission of messages, and ensuring that meaning is shared by both parties. Clear and transparent communication networks are essential to the effective functioning of the investigating team. When situations unfold quickly and decisions need to be taken rapidly, communication networks should be strong, and information unambiguous (Davis 2002).

Thus, lack of continual reflective review to key parties can prove problematic: *'There was no general briefing from lead commanders responsible for the operation. This would have helped pull the whole team together. Different departments with staff new to the role do not always understand what others are doing. The system is reliant on internal/external partners knowing what others are doing so that together the key tasks can be achieved'.* Indeed, during the abduction investigation individuals also *'felt very "thrown in the deep end" at the beginning of the inquiry with little guidance and no previous experience on how to handle it'.* Finally, delegates indicated that *'the briefing [they] did for officers on the night ... didn't change as the disorder grew. Officers were deployed with limited intelligence.'*

It is important, however, to get the balance right regarding the frequency of debriefings. For example, although the individuals working on one investigation *'recognised the need for clear, unambiguous communications'* and received *'comprehensive briefings from gold and silver'*, they also indicated that they were in fact *'crippled with briefings – too many too often'.* Indeed, *'the number and length of briefings and other meetings did take key players away from directing the investigation.'*

When an operation is spread over a large area, or individuals are working from different locations, it is vital that networks are retained. There were issues concerning poor contact across some of the incidents. Firstly, it was indicated that *'the main problem was attending the briefings at HQ and then somehow trying to get information out to teams at various locations ... people in those teams did feel as though they were out of the information loop, but it was physically impossible to be everywhere.'* Secondly, *'communication was intermittent at best, having to resort to the use of mobile phones and officers being used as 'runners' on the ground. If this problem had occurred later in the day when there was real disorder many officers could have been exposed to lethal force without support from colleagues.'* Finally, as one incident unfolded, individuals experienced *'isolation issues such as mobiles being turned off ... [this was] balanced with an intelligence operation to a specific and real threat'.* There was, however, *'good contact and support prior to attendance at the scene via telephone'*, such that officers were prepared for the scene and knew what was expected of them.

Dimensions of supportive leadership

Further reflections from officers during the debriefings indicated four broad dimensions of supportive leadership: accessible, inspirational, empathic and appreciative.

1 Accessible leaders

Because of the magnitude of some of these incidents, the media, community and other external players place extreme demands on the SIOs' time, thereby diverting them from the investigation itself. For example, in one inquiry it was recognised that *'the number and length of briefings and other meetings did take key players away from directing the investigation'*. During another incident it was also indicated that *'when bronzes were requesting decisions from silver there were considerable delays, leading to frustration'*. Frustration and job dissatisfaction can emerge in response to situations where leaders are absent from the team.

Sometimes access to leaders, albeit brief, can be direct. For instance, an officer working on one investigation indicated that he *'was given direct access to the SIO when required to ensure that [he] was working with the most accurate and up-to-date information'*. Other times, staff recognise the pressures facing higher-ranking officers, but nevertheless demand some effort from them to signal 'support to the troops'. It was suggested that *'there might have been a benefit for staff at briefings, and subsequently refreshment areas, to see someone of rank higher than usually a Chief Inspector'*.

Visible leaders who are directly involved with the team (through monitoring behaviour) contribute to increased productivity and a more effective workforce (Komaki 1998). For example, one officer stated, *'I was fortunate to have a supervisor who was prepared to listen to and believe in my judgements but, at the same time, guide those judgements in the direction where they could be of most benefit to the overall aim of the task.'* In practice, such continuing monitoring support is neither practical, nor desirable, since several of the inquiries were well over 500 people strong. This returns us to the importance of planning, organisation and, specifically, role clarity, with more effective leadership emerging as a product of manageable systems and hierarchies requiring monitoring. Thus, if the 'top leader' is immersed in dealing with the media, support needs to be directed at deputising other leadership roles. Even visible presence at a more generic level, with words of support that are meaningful for the whole team, can make a considerable difference to morale.

When leaders are inaccessible to team members, and there are no efforts even to try to consider these issues, individual team members will be less aware of the progression of the operation and 'event flow'. During one incident it was felt that *'as a result of the number of meetings the co-ordinator had to attend … on some occasions he did not have a "feel" for what was happening and was making suggestions that were not always appropriate.'* Thus leaders should not compromise the leadership role by spreading themselves too thin.

2 Inspirational leaders

As we have indicated, much of the component of accessibility can centre around perception. Effective leaders, while not necessarily accountable in person, must maintain high morale in their team. This idea of morale boosting in the face of adversity was a consistent theme across *all* the debriefings, and was often expressed as achievements and success, *in spite of* considerable hurdles. Indeed, *'Staff rallied round and worked together … to ensure that things were provided in very difficult and demanding circumstances'* This was reiterated in another debriefing: *'The sense of collective effort was clearly an important factor in keeping staff motivated and focused.'*

Indeed, sharing responsibility and wanting to achieve for 'the greater good' may have emerged *because* of the recognition of adverse conditions. The debriefings suggest that there was a *'sense of staff at all levels coming together with a shared goal and a determination to achieve it'* where *'people wanted to go "the extra mile"'* and *'didn't complain or whinge at the long hours, but got on with the tasks at hand, and achieved remarkable results in a number of different fields'* Another officer stated, *'Morale appeared to remain high despite the length of incident, hours worked and time of year.'*

This shared situational context creates an environment in which officers develop a group identity based on their common fate and experience. Such an explanation can be understood through social identity theory (Tajfel 1978; Turner 1987). Haslam (2001) has used this approach to consider a variety of issues such as motivation and performance, communication and group decision-making, leadership and authority, and change and management. An individual's social identity is a dynamic construct that can change and develop over time. It is influenced by and in turn *reshapes* context. So, a critical incident provides a context that informs social identity. This will subsequently inform a range of possible responses to the incident. The response they choose then creates a new context through which the investigation will proceed. The investigation will continue to be influenced by both the social identity of the investigating officers and the context in which these occur. Choosing an alternative response could create other possible contexts and other possible identities and, ultimately, other directions in which the investigation could proceed.

3 Empathic leaders

Leaders who display consideration and empathy for staff and their welfare promote a stronger and psychologically healthier team. In terms of the critical incidents examined, two common issues arose, namely, number of hours worked and provision of food.

Commonly, and because of the extreme demands, concerns were sometimes expressed regarding long hours, fatigue and the need to ensure a transparent and systematic mechanism to circumvent burn-out: '[Leaders] *could have been more robust re maximum hours worked and sending people home*', with this delegate recognising that '*a tired team will potentially make mistakes*'. This point was also highlighted: '*I understand that the advisors were doing 24-hour shifts. An inquiry following any incident that occurred at the end of an advisor's shift may concentrate on that person's ability to make a decision at that time − whether it was right or wrong.*'

Working long hours can negatively impact on physical and psychological health. For example, it was observed that '*officers worked long hours in extreme heat and unpleasant conditions. All of [them] were ill at some stage, and under a great deal of stress.*' Similarly, an officer made the following observation: '*I watched people around me excel at everything they did in a way that we all thought impossible. On the down side, I saw people working beyond their physical and mental limits and this concerned me.*' Indeed, '*staff were exposed to stress at such levels that their health began to suffer in as little as the first week*'.

In addition to monitoring the amount of hours team members work, concern should be given to basic needs: warmth, food and refreshments. As one officer observed, '*An army marches on its stomach.*

Officers deployed for prolonged periods of time should have provision for regular and suitable feeding.' Although in some incidents *'welfare support … was excellent – no shortage of food and drink'*, in others *'many officers were retained on duty with few if any opportunities to take refreshments or to obtain food'*.

In many debriefs, comments reflected on these most basic of issues. Where inquiries 'got it right' this appeared to have a major impact on morale. For example, in one critical incident, it was greatly appreciated that they were *'supp[lied] upwards of 4,000 meals a week and apart from one or two minor glitches all staff [were] fed and watered as needed 24/7.'* Where the inquiry 'got it wrong' considerable time was spent reflecting on the perceived organisational neglect.

4 Appreciative leaders

Leaders who show consideration and respect for their staff, who are supportive and provide feedback, and make individuals feel important and valued, encourage cohesion and good working relationships (Roberg, Kuykendall and Novak 2002). This was particularly evident in the comment *'soon after the arrest a senior officer personally thanked staff and recognised their professionalism and hard work. With much still to do, that small effort by him went a long way to keep motivated a very tired workforce.'* However, other organisational features can usurp morale and prove highly damaging. For example, *'faced not only the wrath and emotion from the [victim's family] who needed to blame someone, but also constant criticism from within [the] organisation … after three days they were shattered, more from the internal criticism than external.'*

Conclusion

Brewer (1995) suggests that although clear antecedent instructions (such as providing directions and guidance) are necessary in order to co-ordinate an inquiry efficiently, this directive framework alone is insufficient in maintaining the momentum and stamina to sustain a team in these uniquely challenging environments. Individuals remain productive and positive when their expertise is acknowledged; and, rather than being subject to bureaucratic procedures, they need to be guided, supported and monitored by leaders that are participative, adaptive and empathic. A clear example of this is illustrated in comments such as: *'I would like to thank [my supervisors] for the support they gave during the course of [the operation]. They asked questions, listened to answers* [participative, empathic], *and were not afraid to make decisions based on available information* [directive, task-oriented]. *The command structure was very much a two-way street, with a healthy respect for both sides* [participative]. *I had the confidence to do my job with the necessary support in place for those occasions where I needed further guidance or strategic direction* [directive].'

Leading effectively thus requires sensitivity and interpersonal skills, directive task-oriented skills, and the resilience, hardiness and flexibility to know when to use which. We have some evidence from the debriefings that prior planning and familiarity of procedures, grounded in a knowledge of likely challenges, makes this easier for leaders – particularly in the early stages. In contrast, an inadequate supporting framework (no mechanism for assessing hours worked, improper equipment, inadequate resources, poor catering) can compromise the very early stages at which leaders must direct staff, reduce role ambiguity, prioritise tasks and create a framework for communication. As the inquiry gathers momentum, leaders must know when to shift to the interpersonal sensitivities – monitoring, supporting, participating, appearing available, and being willing to engage, empathise, and focus on an approach that has at its forefront a focus on humanity.

Note

1 Delegates' comments in 10kV debriefs are italicised throughout.

References

Bass, B.M. (1985) *Leadership and performance beyond expectations*. New York: Free Press.

Boddy, D. (2005) *Management: an introduction*. Harlow: Prentice-Hall.

Brewer, N. (1995) 'Leadership and supervision', in N. Brewer and C. Wilson (eds), *Psychology and policing* (pp. 291–316). Hillsdale: Lawrence Erlbaum.

Burns, J.M. (1978) *Leadership*. Oxford: Harper and Row.

Crego, J. and Alison, L. (2004) 'Control and legacy as functions of perceived criticality in major incidents', *Journal of Investigative Psychology and Profiling*, 1, 207–225.

Davis, D. (2002) 'Fire commander' in R. Flin and K. Arbuthnot (eds), *Incident command: tales from the hot seat* (pp. 88–104). Aldershot: Ashgate.

Eagly, A.H. and Johnson, B.T. (1990) 'Gender and leadership style: a meta-analysis', *Psychological Bulletin*, 108, 233–256.

Fleishman, E.A. (1953) 'The description of supervisory behaviour', *Journal of Applied Psychology*, 37, 1–6.

Flin, R. (1996) *Sitting in the hot seat: leaders and teams for critical incident management*. Chichester: John Wiley and Sons.

Flin, R. and Arbuthnot, K. (2002) *Incident command: tales from the hot seat*. Aldershot: Ashgate.

Haslam, S.A. (2001) *Psychology in organizations: the social identity approach*. London: Sage.

Hemphill, J.K. and Coons, A.E. (1957) 'Development of the leader behaviour description questionnaire', in R.M. Stogdill and A.E. Coons (eds), *Leader behaviour: its description and measurement*. Columbus: Ohio State University.

Hersey, P. and Blanchard, K.H. (1977) *Management of organisational behaviour: utilising human resources* (3rd edn). New Jersey: Prentice Hall.

House, R.J. (1971) 'A path-goal theory of leadership', *Administrative Science Quarterly*, 16, 321–338.

Judge, T.A., Piccolo, R.F. and Ilies, R. (2004) 'The forgotten ones? The validity of consideration and initiating structure in leadership research', *Journal of Applied Psychology*, 89, 36–51.

Komaki, J.L. (1998) *Leadership from an operant perspective*. London: Routledge.

Krimmel, J.T., and Lindenmuth, P. (2001) 'Police chief performance and leadership styles', *Police Quarterly*, 4, 469–483.

Laming Report (2003) The Victoria Climbié inquiry. Available [Online]: http://www.victoria-climbie-inquiry.org.uk/finreport/finreport.htm [Accessed February 2007].

Lok, P. and Crawford, J. (2004) 'The effect of organisational culture and leadership style on job satisfaction and organisational commitment: a cross-national comparison', *Journal of Management Development*, 23, 321–338.

Macpherson, W. (1999) The Stephen Lawrence inquiry. Available [Online]: http://www.archive.official-documents.co.uk/document/cm42/4262/4262.htm [Accessed August 2005].

Roberg, R., Kuykendall, J. and Novak, K. (2002) *Police management* (3rd edn). California: Roxbury.

Sarna, P.C. (2002) 'Managing the spike: the command perspective in critical incidents', in R. Flin and K. Arbuthnot (eds), *Incident command: tales from the hot seat* (pp. 32–51). Aldershot: Ashgate.

Shaw, M.E. (1981) *Group dynamics: the psychology of small group behaviour* (3rd edn). London: McGraw-Hill.

Stevens, D.J. (2001) 'Community policing and managerial techniques: total quality management techniques', *Police Journal*, 74, 26–41.

Tajfel, H. (1978) 'Interpersonal behaviour and intergroup behaviour', in H. Tajfel (ed.), *Differentiation between social groups: studies in the social psychology of intergroup relations* (pp. 27–60). London: Academic Press.

Turner, J.C., Hogg, M.A., Oakes, P.J., Reicher, S.D. and Wetherell, M.S. (1987) *Rediscovering the social group: a self-categorization theory*. Oxford: Blackwell.

Chapter 6

Leading, co-operation and context in Hydra syndicates

Laurence Alison, Jonathan Crego, Kate Whitfield, Andrea Caddick and Laura Cataudo

In Chapter 4, we reviewed leadership literature and different theoretical models, though with research spanning more than seven decades, there has been continual debate and disagreement over an adequate definition of leadership (Yukl 1989). In fact, after an extensive examination of over 3,000 studies on leadership, Stogdill (1974: 259) concluded that 'there are as many definitions of leadership as there are persons who have attempted to define [it]!' So, with such difficulties, it is worth first reminding ourselves of some general points. Recall that effective leadership plays a critical role in cultivating and maintaining productive team performance, positive task attitudes, and commitment to organisational goals and values (Brewer 1995). Indeed, it has been suggested that successful leaders are able to inspire and motivate their team by generating respect from, and displaying consideration for, fellow team members (Hollander 1993). Additionally, the dimensions of leadership are socially constructed, and are thus embedded in a particular time and place (Osborn, Hunt and Jauch 2002).

In this chapter, we move from the general to the specific – looking at police officers in action in a study that explores the dynamic relationship between choices of leadership style, team co-operation and context in two Hydra syndicate groups. In particular, we focus on two distinct leadership styles at the heart of much leadership research: directive and participative. Directive leaders are seen to 'perceive less value in member input and are less inclined to examine a variety of solution alternatives' (Larson, Foster-Fishman and Franz 1998: 485).

In contrast, participative leaders support shared decision-making, value team members' contributions, consider decision alternatives and create an atmosphere that encourages team participation (Larson *et al.* 1998). Within these distinctions, the further categorisation of production-centred versus employee-centred leadership emerges (Morris and Seeman 1950). This measure highlights the task-oriented components of directive leadership against the relationship-oriented aspects of participative leadership (Hersey and Blanchard 1977). Accordingly, these dimensions clearly reflect two critical functions of leadership, specifically 'team performance', which refers to the leadership functions of task, and 'team development', which focuses on the functions of relational maintenance (Northouse 2004).

With organisations becoming increasingly dependent on team-based structures, research since the 1960s has been concerned with identifying what is necessary for teams to be effective (Northouse 2004). As a result, there is accumulating evidence in support of a shift from the traditional directive approach of leading teams, in favour of a participative alternative (i.e. Kahai, Sosik and Avolio 1997). By adopting an egalitarian approach and promoting shared decision-making, participative leaders stimulate a sense of unity and identification within the group. Indeed, leaders who share problem-solving responsibilities foster more information-sharing, which is associated in some instances with increased team effectiveness (Larson *et al.* 1998). Similarly, Kahai *et al.* (1997) found team members with participative leaders generated more solutions to problems. Of particular interest is the work reported by Tesluk and Mathieu (1999) which found that where leaders encourage team self-management, the team members engage in more problem-management strategies, such as problem diagnosis, solution generation and implementation. These behaviours were subsequently identified as significant determinants of work crew effectiveness.

This method of fostering team members' self-efficacy is indicative of transformational leadership (Bass 1960), where an individual engages with others and creates a connection that raises the level of motivation and morale in both the leader and follower. The aim of such leadership is, therefore, one of mutual stimulation that both encourages team members to reach their potential and converts followers into leaders (Bass and Avolio 1994). With a goal towards independence, the follower of a transformational leader is encouraged to take part in all aspects of group tasks, which reflects a central component of participative leadership.

In a study assessing the job satisfaction of 158 police officers (Jermier and Berkes 1979), greater contentment was found where leaders, firstly, allowed officers to participate in the decision-making process and, secondly, encouraged them to get involved with a variety of tasks. Some studies have since emerged indicating a positive response to participative leadership within police departments. Most notably, Wycoff and Skogan's (1994) research indicates that employees are more satisfied with their work, the organisation and their supervisors where participative approaches are adopted. Furthermore, with increased autonomy, they report greater enjoyment of police work and consider their job to be important.

In this chapter, we are concerned with an applied example of leadership in action and in order to gain a comprehensive understanding of the applicability of leadership styles, it is important to recognise the context in which certain approaches are more effective. Indeed, Fiedler (1967) argues that effective leadership is dependent on the interaction between leadership style and situational factors. His contingency model describes three categories of situational control (high, moderate and low), which are based on three features of a situation. Firstly, 'leader–member relations' assesses the degree of trust and support that followers give the leader. Secondly, 'task–structure' evaluates the clarity of goals and procedures for accomplishing the task and, finally, 'position–power' captures the leader's level of formal authority in terms of his/her ability to issue rewards and punishment. As a result of this model, Brewer (1995) proposes that participative approaches are most effective in a 'moderate control' setting, with intermediate leader–member relations, task–structure and position–power. With specific reference to the policing context, where tasks are often complex and ambiguous, Fiedler's (1967) model suggests an open, considerate and participative style of leadership would prove most effective, as it addresses low morale and creates an environment conducive to successful problem-solving and decision-making (Kellerman 1984).

Effective teamwork is a fundamental component in the management of critical incidents, and since it involves individuals co-ordinating their decisions and activities through sharing information and resources (Brannik, Salas and Prince 1997), the need for efficient co-operation is evident. Indeed, co-operation itself can be viewed as a multifaceted construct as it entails teams autonomously pursuing individual goals, while simultaneously directing their actions towards a common outcome (Hall 1987).

As Hydra exercises simulate group/team activities, the technology provided us with a valuable opportunity to observe intra-group dynamics and assess the level of co-operation between group members, including choice of leadership style. In the following sections, we explore the relationship between choice of leadership style, team co-operation and context in two Hydra syndicates. The study focused on evaluating the officers' behaviour, group activity and interaction within a critical incident environment over time at numerous levels.

The Hydra exercise: scenario and syndicates

The chosen Hydra exercise was a simulated kidnap and rape investigation that ran in real time over three days, although for this study, we confined observations to the first day's activity. Syndicate 1 consisted of two male and two female police officers aged between 27 and 42 years, with their length of service ranging between five and 13 years. Syndicate 2 was made up of five male officers, aged between 29 and 41, with their length of service ranging from two to eight years. The officers have been renamed in order to ensure their anonymity. The first syndicate team was observed to adopt a highly facilitative and participative approach to managing the investigation, while the second syndicate group experienced more conflict and fluctuated between directive and participative leadership.

Data analysis: interpretative phenomenological analysis

Interpretative phenomenological analysis (IPA) was used as the method of analysis, as it focuses on capturing and understanding individuals' behaviour during a particular event, while simultaneously taking into consideration the researchers' interpretations. Care was taken to retain the essence and contextual meaning of the intra-group dynamics, by basing the analysis on communication and behaviour displayed during group interaction. IPA thus offered us a more effective and inclusive means of analysing naturalistic data than the more traditional psychological methods (Smith 1996).

The data analysis was divided into two stages:

1 Constructing a coding dictionary
Through a process of immersion and familiarisation with the

observed syndicates and relevant literature, key themes outlining group co-operation and leader behaviour were identified. To manage the lack of structure of the data, we adopted a common management model as a basis for the construction of a coding dictionary (see the Appendix on page 120), with the aim of accurately assessing group co-operation and leadership in the syndicate groups.

The dictionary was divided into four broad categories relating to management, namely, leading, planning/organising, communicating, and non-participation. *Leading* here refers to the generation of effort and commitment towards meeting group objectives (Boddy 2005). It assesses whether an individual leader emerges, and if so, whether they display a participative or directive style of leadership. *Planning/ organising* describes the overall direction of the work to be done (Boddy 2005). It involves the recording and reviewing of information, which is then prioritised and used to develop targets or objectives, as well as to decide where efforts and resources should be concentrated, and consequently to identify effective structures or roles for this to be effectively carried out. *Communicating* indicates how 'people share information to reach a common understanding' (Boddy 2005: 522). This ranges from sharing and accepting team members' ideas, as well as the extent to which team members ignore, interrupt and challenge each other. *Non-participation* refers to the level of interaction in the syndicate group, that is, how committed each officer is to the task at hand, and whether they follow the directions of others or prefer to work independently.

In each of these four categories were associated themes and corresponding codes. In order to test reliability, two independent researchers used the coding dictionary to analyse identical footage of a syndicate. The inter-rater reliability was established at a percentage of 89 per cent agreement.

2 Observational coding and calculating frequencies

We divided the time that the officers spent in the syndicates into half-hour segments, coding each individual's behaviour separately during each time period. This provided us with an in-depth perspective, so that our comparisons were clearer and we were able to better discriminate between team members' behaviours as the exercise progressed. In the following section, we report the frequencies for each category and theme that formed part of the coding dictionary. We will then discuss the findings and implications of the study in the remainder of the chapter.

Frequencies of coded behaviours

The results based on observations of Syndicate 1 will be presented first, followed by those of Syndicate 2.

Syndicate 1 results

Table 6.1 (below) reflects the frequencies of the participants' behaviours according to the categories and themes in the coding dictionary.

As can be observed in the table, there is some variation in participants' involvement. Figure 6.1 illustrates the overall contribution of each team member during the 5.25 hours of the first day of the simulation. Interestingly, their level of contribution was dictated somewhat by rank and length of service.

Table 6.1   Frequencies of participants' behaviours in Syndicate 1

	Mark	Amy	Sue	Luke
Leading				
Instructing	12	11	5	0
Ensuring understanding	7	8	6	6
Decision-oriented	39	18	6	5
Total	58	37	17	11
Planning/organising				
Cross-checking	1	1	5	14
Prioritising	20	9	4	2
Recording	0	3	0	0
Reviewing	13	9	9	9
Self-appointing roles	2	2	2	4
Autocratic decisions	8	5	5	0
Total	44	29	25	29
Communicating				
Challenging	11	10	4	2
Accepting	16	23	15	19
Total	27	33	19	21
Non-participation				
Working on own	22	31	18	23
Lack of focus	2	8	9	3
Total	24	39	27	26
Follower behaviour	8	5	20	20

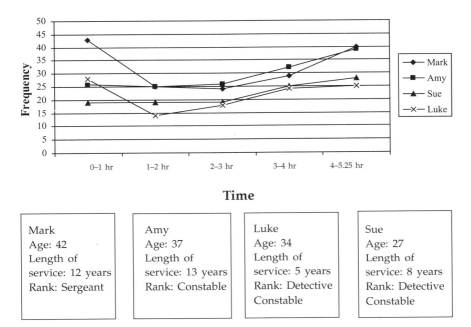

Mark	Amy	Luke	Sue
Age: 42	Age: 37	Age: 34	Age: 27
Length of service: 12 years	Length of service: 13 years	Length of service: 5 years	Length of service: 8 years
Rank: Sergeant	Rank: Constable	Rank: Detective Constable	Rank: Detective Constable

Figure 6.1 Participant contribution in Syndicate 1

With the most years' service, both Mark and Amy consistently showed the greatest amount of involvement in the task throughout the day, while Luke (who only had five years of service) contributed the least. The effect of individual experience is also highlighted when assessing the contribution of each team member within the specific categories of the management model, as presented in Figure 6.2.

Luke showed the least amount of leading behaviours, and he was the team member with the fewest years of service. Needless to say, the number of years in the job is not the only factor to be considered. For example, Mark had one year's experience fewer than Amy, yet he stood out as the overall leader. It is possible that it is his higher rank that has influenced this dynamic.

Syndicate 1 was observed as a highly co-operative group, with leaders adopting participative approaches to guide the team through the simulated investigation. In order to examine the relationship between leadership and team co-operation in this supportive environment, we shall address the frequency scores of each category sequentially.

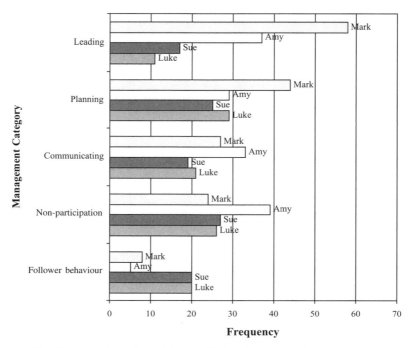

Figure 6.2 Frequencies of participants' behaviours based on the management categories

Syndicate 1: Leading
We have already mentioned that Mark emerged as the definitive leader, exhibiting almost half (47 per cent) of the team's overall leading score. The vast majority of his style of leadership was participative, as defined by the variables 'ensuring understanding' and 'decision-oriented', totalling 79 per cent of participative leadership. Amy also scored highly in this category, contributing to 30 per cent of the overall leading within the group. Similar to Mark's, much of Amy's leading style was participative (70 per cent).

With both leaders adopting a participative approach, it appeared to encourage support from the team, as determined by reference to the 'communicating' category. Both Sue and Luke showed an overwhelming majority of accepting behaviours (85 per cent) in comparison to the challenging interactions they displayed (15 per cent). Furthermore, the variables 'isolated by group' and 'ignored' had to be omitted from the analysis due to lack of frequency. This highlights the consistent support and group collaboration in this syndicate while they made plans throughout the day. In fact, no plans were executed without the approval of all team members, a procedure initially promoted by Mark within the first few minutes of the day when he suggested, *'When any new evidence comes in, we consider it as a group and make decisions as a group.'* Indeed, this proposal was adhered to by all team members, as each routinely sought validation for their plans prior to action, questioning, *'Do you agree?'* or *'What do you think?'*

Syndicate 1: Planning/organising

Mark appeared to be the most involved in the planning and organisation of the simulated investigation (indicated by a frequency of 44). In particular, Mark did the most prioritising of tasks and information, which – when we evaluated it incrementally throughout the day – appeared to mirror the frequency of participative leadership displayed. This pattern is also evident regarding Amy's leadership behaviour and the amount of prioritising she did.

Additionally, the allocation of time and effort can be evaluated through the 'reviewing information' variable, as on many occasions the group re-examined details of the case in order to arrange future actions. This was illustrated by one of the team member's comments, *'... That's why I'm saying [we need] to review what we've done, because there might be stuff that's still a concern that's a bigger priority.'*

Syndicate 1: Communicating

Amy communicated the most of all the team members (33 per cent), which was marginally more than Mark (27 per cent). The frequency scores in Table 6.1 also indicate these two leaders exhibited the most 'challenging' interactions in the syndicate group. These challenges, however, were typically broached amicably with statements such as, *'Can I just make the point though ... I might be wrong or right, but ...'* and *'I'm not trying to be awkward here, it's just ...'* As a result, both Mark and Amy were receptive to negotiation, which is reflected in their high frequency of 'accepting' behaviour (16 and 23 respectively), and comments such as, *'If everyone else disagrees [with the challenging argument], then fair enough.'*

Syndicate 1: Non-participation

The frequencies in Table 6.1 indicate that the two group leaders (Mark and Amy) exhibited the least follower behaviour (8 and 5 respectively). Importantly though, it should be noted that the follower behaviour Mark displayed surfaced only as a result of adopting the role of typist, during which time team members would occasionally dictate what to type in the communicator and decision logs. Similarly, the frequency with which individuals worked on their own appeared to be influenced by the role they adopted. This was particularly true for Amy who undertook the task of preparing notes for the briefing. She was observed working alone throughout the day, and thus emerged as the team member most frequently engaged in lone working (33 per cent).

Amy, along with Sue, also appeared at times to lack focus regarding the task. Although these lapses in concentration were not lengthy (typically lasting only a few minutes), they did instigate most of the task-irrelevant conversations (for example, regarding food and weight) and behaviours (such as trying on one another's glasses).

It is interesting to note that Mark, the established team leader, exhibited the least follower-type behaviour. It is possible that this was due to his assuming the role of leader. Additionally, much of his activity was involved in organising aspects of the task. It appears that once he clarified plans to the syndicate group, the team members were then able to work alone to further the progress of their investigation.

Although 'working on own' was one of the highest-frequency behaviours (94), there was nevertheless an extremely co-operative atmosphere in the syndicate room, with the other highest overall frequencies being 'participative leading' (95) and 'accepting the ideas of others' (73). In a team where participative leadership is prevalent, accepting the ideas of others and working alone *are* key behaviours. Indeed, it is suggested that once Mark highlighted that they '*make decisions as a group*', it resulted in each team member feeling empowered to accomplish successfully the tasks at hand. Consequently, this perhaps encouraged them to be more receptive to the ideas of others, as they did not feel the need forcefully to assert their position in the group.

Syndicate 2 results

Table 6.2 reflects the frequencies of the participants' behaviours according to the categories and themes in the coding dictionary.

Syndicate 2: Overview of participants' individual behaviour
Based on the information in Table 6.2, a snapshot of each participant can be given:

Table 6.2 Frequencies of participants' behaviours in Syndicate 2

	Andrew	Kevin	David	Alan	Carl
Leading					
Physical	7	2	29	4	7
Instructing	39	59	10	8	23
Ensuring understanding	33	27	4	3	20
Decision-oriented	45	43	16	10	16
Total	**124**	**131**	**59**	**25**	**66**
Unreciprocated leading	8	1	9	0	1
Planning/organising					
Cross-checking	15	37	8	6	21
Prioritising	19	17	2	4	7
Recording	24	4	0	15	8
Reviewing	50	39	7	21	29
Identifying/assigning roles	5	3	2	2	3
Self-appointing roles	6	4	17	11	10
Autocratic decisions	19	16	3	1	4
Total	**138**	**120**	**39**	**60**	**82**
Communicating					
Challenging	14	32	18	10	6
Accepting	14	30	7	10	7
Does not listen	7	11	11	2	4
Ignored	10	7	8	15	5
Total	**45**	**80**	**44**	**37**	**22**
Non-participation	52	13	35	7	29
Isolated by group	5	1	0	1	1
Lack of focus	10	7	6	18	14
Total	**67**	**21**	**41**	**26**	**44**
Follower behaviour	34	29	54	29	34

Andrew was the most consistently active team member. He combined a directive and participative leadership style to organise and plan group activity, particularly through reviewing and recording information: '*Shall we do some flip charts on what we know and don't know?*' His early attempts to organise the group were ignored, but rather than be deterred, he carried out many tasks independently. The group response changed as more information became available, and Andrew's relevant expertise in the area became apparent. Indeed, this resulted in team members accepting him as leader, and referring to him as '*Sarge*' and '*Boss*'.

Kevin was also a very active team member, who stayed highly focused on the given task. He too adopted a combined directive and participative leadership approach in order to move the investigation forward. When new information was received, he became more directive in a positive way, so as to organise and guide group members. He regularly cross-checked materials, and reminded the team of tasks to be done and the correct way to do them, for example, *'You've put a decision but you haven't put a reason.'* Kevin was highly communicative where he openly challenged other group members but in a transparent and co-operative manner, such that a group consensus was always reached.

David took a very directive approach to the exercise, predominantly through physical actions (74 per cent), by consistently sitting at the head of the table and using the keyboard as a means of control. Here, decision input was often dictated by him, or alternatively he tended to fast-track decisions independently without group review, which appeared to irritate other group members. This was possibly due to his forceful, challenging approach, with words such as *'Hang on, don't do that.'* He frequently made attempts at unreciprocated leading, was ignored by his team, and often ignored other syndicate members. He seldom participated in the planning and organising of tasks, and rarely moved from his position.

Alan was the least active group member, who was perceived to have low confidence, highlighted by his significantly low leading score. As the day progressed, he developed a more active role and often attempted to lead the planning and organising of group tasks. Here he communicated his ideas and intentions but was often ignored by the group, or backed down halfway through his sentences, for example, *'We could ...'* When this behaviour was observed, it resulted in his becoming less focused and withdrawing from group activity.

Carl was observed to be the quietest member of the group, who sat back and let other team members direct him and the investigation: *'Anything I can be doing?'* However, he was not afraid to share his ideas or voice his concern, which particularly became evident with his more directive approach as the investigation developed and decisions were being made. He actively reviewed new information for the group, and joined in with, rather than initiated, group tasks.

Syndicate 2: Observed overall behaviour of group
The following graph (Figure 6.3) depicts the cumulative frequencies of the entire team for the observed management categories.

Leading behaviour increased steadily throughout the day, particularly when new information arrived, as there was then a need for group structure and organisation. Due to his experience and expertise, Andrew increasingly emerged as the team's leader.

The planning behaviour of the group also increased significantly as the day progressed, peaking during the second hour when information was being recorded and reviewed, and then at times when new information was introduced. During the third and fourth hours, planning and non-participation behaviour were high due to

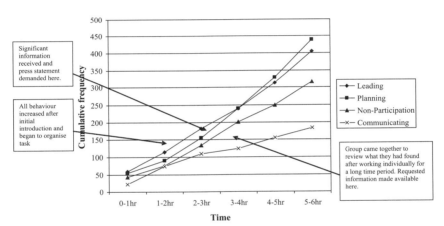

Figure 6.3 Cumulative frequencies of observed management categories

individuals working on independent tasks of cross-checking and recording information. The lack of team interaction at this time generated a low frequency of communicative behaviour.

From the fourth hour onwards, there was an increase in leading, planning and communication as Alan brought the group together to review and share information: *'Do we need to sit down and have a chat together? Because we are all doing different stuff, aren't we?'* Here it became clear that working independently for long periods, with little communication, negatively impacted team co-operation. Additionally, a great deal of time then had to be spent discussing, challenging, reviewing and going back over work that the team as a whole did not agree on. For example, Alan stated, *'We've got over 30 communications there. We could halve that probably'*, as David had been typing decisions in the decision log without consulting the group. This resulted in group conflict, leading to an increase in directive behaviour so as to resolve it.

Syndicate 2 was observed as a group in conflict, as some individuals were *too* directive in approach when attempting to lead, which was consequently not appreciated by their colleagues. In other instances, there was little communication between team members, resulting in there being no shared mental model or awareness as to what was being done to further the investigation. As a result, leaders adopted both directive and participative approaches, depending on what the situation required. In order to look at the relationship between leadership and team co-operation in this difficult environment, the frequency scores of each category will be addressed sequentially.

Syndicate 2: Leading

We observed obvious directive and participative leading in Syndicate 2. However, as can be seen in the graph below (Figure 6.4), some participants were more directive in approach than others.

Indeed, David physically employed a directive approach from the very beginning by sitting at the head of the table. He was, however, ignored by the group, and so took control of the keyboard for the remainder of the day, thus giving himself some power over decision-making.

Andrew displayed fairly consistent directive behaviour, whereas Kevin dramatically increased this form of behaviour as the day progressed. This was done in a positive way as they both used directive leadership to provide structure and guidance for the group. From the fourth hour onwards, both Andrew and Kevin's directive behaviour increased in order to deal with conflicting opinions and information brought about by lack of co-operation and communication in the third to the fourth hour. Here, Kevin became more directive in a challenging and instructing way: *'We need to sit down and look at what we're putting on'*, whereas Andrew was directive so as to organise and maintain a co-operative working environment: *'Right, stop it, stop now!'* Both individuals had a positive impact on the team.

Carl and, in particular, Alan consistently displayed low frequencies of directive leadership, as they generally co-operated and allowed the more experienced individuals to lead the group.

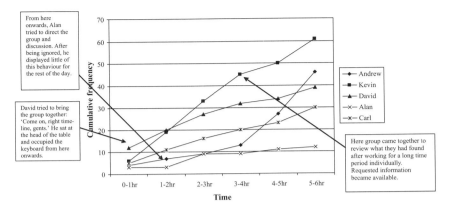

Figure 6.4 Cumulative frequencies of participants' directive behaviour

In terms of participative leadership in the syndicate group, the graph below (Figure 6.5) indicates that Andrew and Kevin displayed the highest frequencies of participative leading from the beginning of the simulation, with it accounting for 63 per cent and 53 per cent of their respective leading behaviour. As the team attempted to maintain a co-operative environment, leadership styles varied to suit the task at hand. This was observed with all team members, apart from David, who was constantly directive in approach, causing him to be ignored by his colleagues.

Figure 6.5 illustrates how Kevin and particularly Andrew's participative leadership increased throughout the day. This is possibly because of the group coming together for discussion. At such times the team was quite co-operative in nature, and although both leaders were directive when organising tasks, they always sought the opinions and approval of their colleagues. Andrew provided a clear example of this behaviour when competing views were debated: *'OK, let's do a vote. Who wants someone to go there and speak to him? Or do a drive by [to observe the house] first?'* As a result of interjections such as this, co-operative decisions were made.

Syndicate 2: Planning/organising

There was consistent planning and organising throughout the day, albeit in different ways at different times. During the middle of the day, individuals were actively cross-checking and recording information, while towards the end of the day they became more involved in reviewing and prioritising it.

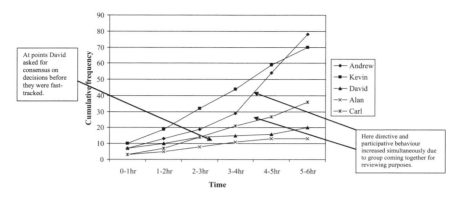

Figure 6.5 Cumulative frequencies of participants' participative behaviour

The frequency of planning behaviour increased whenever new information was introduced, because group members wanted to assess it as efficiently as possible. As can be seen in Table 6.2, high frequencies of planning behaviour appear to be associated with high frequencies of leading behaviour, with Andrew and Kevin achieving the highest scores. It is important to note, however, that planning behaviour is not directly related to a specific leadership approach, as Andrew and Kevin both used a combination of directive and participative styles. Additionally, when the group was working well together, these two leaders tended to identify and carry out particular roles themselves, rather than delegate to someone else. For example, Kevin said, *'We need more than one copy of this. I'll go and find a photocopier.'*

Syndicate 2: Non-participation

The graph below (Figure 6.6) illustrates that there was no strong association between high frequencies of directive behaviour and frequencies of the more negative behaviour in the group, such as not listening and ignoring each other.

Indeed, these negative aspects occurred in low frequency and, when they did, they involved specific individuals rather than the group as a whole; for example, David was ignored by the group due to his abrupt approach.

Follower behaviour appears to increase in conjunction with increasing directive leadership. As previously mentioned, this directive behaviour was a result of the two leaders providing guidance upon the introduction of new information. We observed that this behaviour was not forceful, but rather arose to provide assistance to others. Consequently, group members adopted the role of followers and allowed Andrew and Kevin to direct.

Interpreting the results

We assessed co-operation according to the following categories: leading, planning/organising, communicating, and non-participation. Despite the differences in each syndicate, we found a close relationship in both syndicates between leadership style (directive or participative), context and team co-operation.

Syndicate 1: leading

Eagly and Johnson (1990) report that females are more likely to adopt democratic or participative styles of leadership than their male counterparts, who tend to opt for more autocratic or directive approaches, but that is not what we found in this study. The syndicate, as a whole, favoured a more participative approach and there was relatively little directive leadership behaviour. As the leaders in the group, Mark and Amy both showed a participative approach.

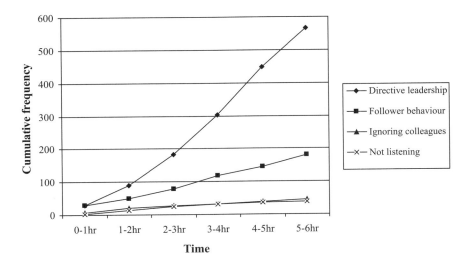

Figure 6.6 Cumulative frequencies of directive leadership and non-participation themes

Monitoring provides recognition and positive reinforcement for good performance, as well as detecting performance breakdowns or errors and providing corrective feedback. However, when we assessed the variable 'ensuring understanding' (part of our participative leading category) we found that there were comparatively few monitoring behaviours in favour of 'decision-oriented' actions. In only 27 instances did leaders check the progress of their team members, asking, for example, *'Are you all right with that?"* Performance monitoring is considered a critical supervisory behaviour (Komaki 1998) though it was largely absent here.

Despite this depleted level of monitoring, the group did not appear to be at any disadvantage, as no one seemed confused regarding team goals or isolated from lack of involvement. In fact, behavioural evidence from a number of occupational settings indicates that effective leaders spend no more than 5 to 10 per cent of their time monitoring, and the level of necessary monitoring can be dictated by the characteristics of the subordinates and the context (Brewer, Wilson and Beck 1994).

The overwhelming majority of participative leading behaviours were recorded under the 'decision-oriented' theme, which captured the leader's concern for achieving group agreement regarding decisions. Throughout the day, all team members were particularly attentive to the ideas of others, often checking: *'... so are we agreed on that?'* Indeed, this contributed to the positive atmosphere in the syndicate room. The creation of such a collaborative climate in a group is described by Larson *et al.* (1998) as resulting from team members being transparent, flexible, having shared mental models and remaining focused on the task.

Syndicate 1: planning/organising

The dominant behaviours we saw in this category were 'prioritising' and 'reviewing' information, both of which we recorded most frequently for the two leaders of the group and in particular, Mark; these specific behaviours are characteristic of tasks expected to be undertaken by leaders (Brewer 1995). Research suggests, however, that in certain situations a more directive approach may be required. For example, Reams, Kuykendall and Burns (1975) found that police officers did not believe participative leadership was either possible or desirable in policing. Rather, in times of crisis, directive leadership was considered crucial to ensure clarity, control and optimal performance from subordinates.

Syndicate 1: communicating

Evaluation of this category indicated that very little 'challenging' behaviour occurred in the syndicate. However, it was observed that Amy did this the most, although it was usually to raise concerns; she usually justified the behaviour by referring to the 'autocratic decisions' she had been subjected to in the workplace, for example: *'You're right, she [the victim] is the priority, but ... whenever I get [assigned] a rape, all I get [from supervisors] is, is there a scene?'* This method of expressing differences of opinion is representative of good communication skills, and appears to be afforded by the participative leadership style adopted. In highlighting her concerns and providing valid reasons for her position, her challenge was not perceived as a criticism, and so promoted and maintained open communication within the group.

All team members, including the two leaders, frequently accepted the ideas of others. This is a characteristic of participative leadership, where the views of subordinates are valued and encouraged. The fact that the leaders in the group displayed 'accepting' behaviour suggests that equality for all team members was practised. Team members are likely to react positively towards participative leaders because this egalitarian means of addressing issues satisfies higher-order needs (Miller and Monge 1986). As a result, this could only have a positive impact on group co-operation, as we observed in this syndicate team.

Syndicate 1: non-participation

The results indicate that 'follower behaviour' and 'working on own' were the most frequent themes to emerge from this category. As this group worked closely as a team, the 'follower behaviour' most typically emerged when they were typing in the decision log, and other team members dictated how to word this. Indeed, this was solely the case for Mark's observed 'follower behaviour'. It is important to note, however, that prior to this they had already agreed collectively as to what actions to take. Additionally – and unsurprisingly enough – it was those team members exhibiting the least leading behaviour who displayed the most 'follower behaviour', typically seeking validation from leaders before carrying out an action, for example, *'is that all right?'* or *'... do I fast-track that?'*

Despite high frequencies for 'follower behaviour', team members were nevertheless often observed working on their own. In an expanded version of the transformational leadership model, Bass (1960) highlights the leader's ability to motivate the group to reach their potential. According to this theory, leaders who communicate high expectations to followers inspire them to be committed to a shared vision, which simultaneously enhances team spirit. Indeed, leaders were observed offering motivational reassurance to Luke, the least vocal member of the group, reassuring him with words such as, '... that's a good idea.'

Interestingly, Mark showed the most non-participation in the group, which could indicate that having co-ordinated the direction of the task, he stepped back to allow others to make their contribution. Additionally, it is important to note that when deciding how to manage the situation, Mark openly sought advice from Amy and Sue, as they had more experience dealing with rape victims, for example, '... so, do you think we've considered the victim enough?'

When considering the input of all team members, there was very little 'lack of focus', as everyone remained involved, which had a positive effect on the overall team co-operation.

Syndicate 2: leading

As the exercise began, there was a lack of co-operation between group members, along with no clear roles or structure. Thus, as found in previous research, group members competed for recognition and control (Heller 1992; Tyler 2002). The observed competitive behaviour was associated with the emergence of a high frequency of directive behaviour, with individuals constantly talking over each other. Indeed, this could possibly be attributed to the fact that the syndicate consisted of five highly motivated men working together. As a means of gaining control, David was physically directive by sitting at the head of the table when trying to bring the group together. However, due to his abrupt and often autocratic approach (for example, 'First of all, you go and get coffee ...'), his pursuit of leadership was often unreciprocated. As a result, and in a further attempt to control decision-making, he adopted the head seat and took on the role of typist. This finding contradicts previous research which states that the person who occupies the head seat tends to emerge as leader (Shaw 1981). Leadership is rather a reciprocal process, which requires acceptance (Tyler 2002).

During the early stages of the task, we did not observe an individual leader but, as the exercise progressed and new information was introduced, someone was required to co-ordinate and direct group activity. Andrew emerged as leader, possibly as a result of his perceived experience, autocratic decisions, and active involvement in group discussion. Although the group identified Andrew as leader (even at times referring to him as 'Boss'), Kevin and Carl often took control when they had relevant knowledge of the task at hand. This supports previous findings that leadership varies depending on expertise required (Shackleton 1995). Indeed, when the group co-operated efficiently, a participative approach was adopted, with Andrew and Kevin consistently ensuring team members understood what they were doing (for example, 'How are you getting on?'). The fact that the two individuals with the highest frequencies of 'ensuring understanding' behaviour were also the two with the highest scores for 'leading' behaviour supports previous research that the most effective and accepted leaders motivate and regularly monitor their team (Komaki 1998).

Syndicate 2: planning/organising

Andrew displayed the highest frequency of planning behaviour, particularly through actively reviewing and recording information. The frequency of 'reviewing information' had an observed impact on leadership style as, after the group came together in the fourth hour to discuss what they had been individually planning, Andrew and Kevin became significantly more directive in order to deal with opposing views when new information was introduced. This was done in a positive way so as to provide structure and to resolve conflict within the group. Here, David's autocratic approach and lack of reviewing information prior to inputting decisions caused irritation. This was noted when Alan stated, 'There's far too much communication [with the control room] here,' to which all the other team members agreed. The increase in directive leading is also associated with an increase in participative leading. This was so as to mediate and come to some sort of shared agreement, for example, 'Let's go through one by one what we have got,' with Andrew reviewing a list of priorities for the group.

From this it is clear that, owing to the combination of competitive and co-operative behaviours, Andrew and Kevin combined a participative and directive approach to suit the team's behaviour and task at hand.

Syndicate 2: communicating

In line with previous research (Mulvey and Ribbens 1999), the lack of co-operation and communication during the third and fourth hours had a negative impact on the group. By adding avoidable time to the investigation, it caused conflict and the need for a lengthy review of information so as to achieve group consensus. As a result, Andrew and Mark's directive leading increased in the sixth hour to bring the group together and resolve disagreements. It is thus important to note that sometimes conflict has a positive impact on the group as it promotes the sharing of ideas and expertise to make more informed decisions (Tjosvold and Tjosvold 1995). Additionally, despite these two leaders taking a directive approach, they both listened and accepted the ideas of others. This stood in sharp contrast to David, who also adopted a directive approach but interrupted and constantly challenged and disagreed with his colleagues, resulting in their ignoring him.

Syndicate 2: non-participation

Group participation was higher when a participative leading approach was employed, with group members seeking validation ('follower behaviour') from each other: *'Do you want me to read it out?'* However, non-participation was high when individuals were working alone or recording information themselves to review later on with the group. Andrew frequently did this through highlighting and carrying out roles himself, rather than delegating them to others.

Additionally, when Andrew and Kevin were particularly dominant in the group, Alan tended to lose focus, as a consequence of being frequently ignored. Andrew was also isolated on a few occasions, as a result of his overwhelming the group with constant reviews and plans.

Conclusion

Both directive and participative leadership was displayed in the simulated team exercise. It goes without saying that it is necessary to lead teams well during the management of a critical incident. However, the decision of which style to adopt in a particular context is crucial to facilitating successful team co-operation. It is clear from observations of the two syndicates that effective leaders should be able to adjust their behaviour according to what the circumstances demand; circumstances evolved and changed as the hours unfolded in this simulated incident. They constitute a similarly organic phenomenon in real-life incidents.

In Syndicate 1, where there was excellent rapport and working relationships, very little direction was required, as team members shared mental models about the given task and got on with the job together. In such a supportive and collaborative environment, team members were empowered through a participative leadership approach. In contrast, Syndicate 2 was a competitive group with many opposing views. They worked independently for long periods of time and did not encourage 'quiet voices' to be heard. Leadership, therefore, had to fluctuate between directive (so as to regain structure and order) and participative (so as to facilitate group discussion) styles.

We would argue, of course – as one of the central themes of this book – for the importance of the broader context, and Krimmel and Lindenmuth (2001) emphasised that 'the ability to pigeon-hole police leadership styles offers little utility without considering the social structure in which police function' (p. 472). It is thus essential that leaders adopt an approach that suits the team and the task at hand as the situation unfolds, such that performance is enhanced, morale elevated, team members empowered, and the investigation concluded successfully.

References

Bass, B.M. (1960) *Leadership, psychology and organisational behaviour*. London: Harper and Row.

Bass, B.M. and Avolio, B.J. (1994) *Improving organisational effectiveness through transformational leadership*. London: Sage.

Boddy, D. (2005) *Management: an introduction*. Englewood Cliffs: Prentice-Hall.

Brannik, M.T., Salas, E. and Prince, C. (1997) *Team performance assessment and measurement: theory, methods and applications*. New Jersey: Lawrence Erlbaum.

Brewer, N. (1995) 'Leadership and supervision', in N. Brewer, and C. Wilson (eds), *Psychology and policing* (pp. 291–316). Hillsdale: Lawrence Erlbaum.

Brewer, N., Wilson, C. and Beck, K. (1994) 'Supervisory behaviour and team performance amongst police patrol sergeants', *Journal of Occupational and Organisational Psychology*, 67, 69–78.

Crego, J. and Harris, C. (2002) 'Training decision-making by team-based simulation', in R. Flin. and K. Arbuthnot (eds.), *Incident Command: Tales from the Hot Seat* (pp. 258–69). Aldershot: Ashgate.

Eagly, A.H., and Johnson, B.T. (1990) 'Gender and leadership style: A meta-analysis', *Psychological Bulletin,* 108: 233–56.

Fiedler, F.E. (1967) *A theory of leadership effectiveness.* New York: McGraw-Hill.

Hall, R.H. (1987) *Organisations: structures, processes and outcomes.* Englewood Cliffs: Prentice-Hall.

Heller, F. (1992) *Decision-making and leadership.* Cambridge: Cambridge University Press.

Hersey, P. and Blanchard, K.H. (1977) *Management of organisational behaviour: utilising human resources* (3rd edn). New Jersey: Prentice Hall.

Hollander, E.P. (1993) 'Legitimacy, power and influence: a perspective on relational features of leadership', in M.M. Chemers and R. Ayman (eds), *Leadership theory and research: perspectives and directions* (pp. 29–46). New York: Academic Press.

Jermier, J.M. and Berkes, L.J. (1979) 'Leader behaviour in a police command bureaucracy: a closer look at the quasi-military model', *Administrative Science Quarterly,* 24: 1–23.

Kahai, S.S., Sosik, J.J. and Avolio, B.J. (1997) 'Effects of leadership style and problem structure on work group processes and outcomes in an electronic meeting environment', *Personnel Psychology,* 50: 121–46.

Kellerman, B. (1984) *Leadership: multidisciplinary perspectives.* Englewood Cliffs: Prentice-Hall.

Komaki, J.L. (1998) *Leadership from an operant perspective.* London: Routledge.

Krimmel, J.T. and Lindenmuth, P. (2001) 'Police chief performance and leadership styles', *Police Quarterly,* 4: 469–83.

Larson, J.R., Foster-Fishman, P.G. and Franz, T.M. (1998) 'Leadership style and the discussion of shared and unshared information in decision-making groups', *Personality and Social Psychology Bulletin,* 24: 482–95.

Miller, K.I. and Monge, P.R. (1986) 'Participatory satisfaction and productivity: A meta-analysis review', *Academy of Management Journal,* 29: 727–53.

Morris, R.T. and Seeman, M. (1950) 'The problem of leadership: An interdisciplinary approach', *Journal of Sociology,* 56: 149–55.

Mulvey, P.W. and Ribbens, B.A. (1999) 'The effects of intergroup competition and assigned group goals on group efficacy and group effectiveness', *Small Group Research,* 30: 651–67.

Northouse, P.G. (2004) *Leadership: theory and practice.* London: Sage.

Osborn, R.N., Hunt, J.G. and Jauch, L.R. (2002) 'Towards a contextual theory of leadership', *Leadership Quarterly,* 13: 797–37.

Reams, R., Kuykendall, J. and Burns, D. (1975) 'Police management systems: what is an appropriate model?', *Journal of Police Science and Administration,* 3: 475–81.

Shackleton, V. (1995) *Business leadership.* London: Routledge.

Shaw, M.E. (1981) *Group dynamics: the psychology of small group behaviour* (3rd edn). London: McGraw-Hill.

Smith, J.A. (1996) 'Beyond the divide between cognition and discourse: using interpretive phenomenological analysis in health psychology', *Psychology and Health*, 11: 261–71.

Stogdill, R.M. (1974) *Handbook of leadership: a survey of the literature*. New York: Free Press.

Tesluk, P.E. and Mathieu, J.E. (1999) 'Overcoming roadblocks to effectiveness: incorporating management of performance barriers', *Journal of Applied Psychology*, 84: 200–17.

Tjosvold, D. and Tjosvold, M.M. (1995) *Psychology for leaders: using motivation, conflict and power to manage more effectively*. Chichester: John Wiley and Sons.

Tyler, T.R. (2002) 'Leadership and cooperation in groups', *American Behavioural Scientist*, 45: 769–82.

Wycoff, M.A. and Skogan, W.G. (1994) 'The effect of a community policing management style on officers' attitudes', *Crime and Delinquency*, 40: 371–83.

Yukl, G. (1989) 'Managerial leadership: a review of theory and research', *Journal of Management*, 15: 251–89.

Appendix

Coding Dictionary of Team Co-operation

Code

LEADING

Directive leading

A directive leader asserts authority by issuing commands and providing direction.

1 Physical

Asserting authority or dominance through physical actions, e.g. standing up and speaking to the group, sitting at the head of the table, using keyboard to gain control of decision-making (NOTE: this does not refer to delegates who are told what to type – see 17).

2 Instructing

Telling team members what to do, e.g. 'You go put up the time-line', dictating what to type (NOTE: this does not refer to interrupting – see 15). Using rhetorical questions, i.e., statements phrased as questions.

Participative leading

A participative leader treats team members as equals and promotes shared decision-making.

3 Ensuring understanding

Monitoring/checking what others are doing, e.g. 'Are you all right, you just getting on with it?' Helping others to understand new information and how to use equipment.

4 Decision-oriented

Asking others what they think/want to do, e.g. 'What do you want?' 'If it suits everyone, shall we do X?' Checking other people agree with the decision, e.g. 'Is that OK?'

5	Unreciprocated leading	Code this behaviour when anyone thwarts the above.

PLANNING/ORGANISING

Information

6	Cross-checking	Compares one piece of evidence with another to check that it is consistent, e.g. replaying videos, comparing different sources of information (e.g. comparing map with video).
7	Prioritising	Actively ordering tasks and information, e.g. 'The order in which we are going to do this ...', 'You can send this information, and then we can think about X.' Highlighting priorities, e.g. 'We should do X and Y as a priority'.
8	Recording	Recording information on flip charts, e.g. 'What do we think we know? What do we know for sure?' Maintaining time-lines.
9	Reviewing	Sharing information aloud with the team, e.g. after receiving information, reading it aloud to the team. Summarises what the group knows so far, e.g. 'So, shall we just review what we've done up to now?' Provides reminders, e.g. 'Don't forget ...'

Roles

10	Identifying/ assigning	Identifying specific roles, e.g. 'So we've really got specific roles: someone updating the policy log, someone who's doing the communication ...' Assigning each other roles.

11	Self-appointing	When an individual takes on a role without specifically being asked to do it, e.g. taking on the role as typist or writing a press release without being asked to do this.
12	**Autocratic decisions**	Bases decision on previous experience and policy. Has valid grounds for a decision.

COMMUNICATING

13	Challenging	Considering alternatives. Questioning suggestions, e.g. 'We should put X in the press release' – 'Why?' Debating ideas. Proposing a different suggestions to the majority's decision, e.g. 'I know we make our decision first, and I'm not trying to be awkward here, it's just that ...' Dismissing ideas, e.g. 'I don't think we should do X, rather Y ...'
14	Accepting	Accepting the ideas of others, e.g. 'I agree, let's do X.'
15	Does not listen	Does not consider the views of others, ignores alternative suggestions. Walking away while someone is talking to him/her. Interrupting, i.e. talking over each other (overriding). Speaking loudly while others are talking. Individual makes a suggestion and is ignored.

NON-PARTICIPATION

17	Working on own	Working in isolation by choice, e.g. familiarising self with information/policy, so working on own/writing personal notes.
18	Isolated by group	Working on own as a result of the group isolating the person, e.g. when an individual's suggestion is ignored, he/she then does the task on their own. Due to competition, working on own.

| 19 | Lack of focus | Not staying focused on the task, e.g. wandering around the room aimlessly. Distracting other team members from task. Engaging in irrelevant behaviour and conversation. Making telephone calls. Doing unrelated tasks, e.g. making coffee. |
| 20 | Follower behaviour | Seeking validation from other group members before doing a task, e.g. before entering information in the decision log, checking with other group members that it is correct. Deference towards the leader ('... do you think that's all right?'). Asking others what he/she can do. Takes on role of unquestioning typist. |

Chapter 7

Towards a taxonomy of police decision-making in murder inquiries

Sam Mullins, Laurence Alison and Jonathan Crego

This chapter outlines a model of Senior Investigating Officer (SIO) decision-making in murder inquiries. Specifically, we focus on: (i) *'Decision environment'* (including intra-organisational features such as accountability, hierarchy and external pressures such as publicity, type, stage and area of investigation); (ii) the individual *'Decision-maker'* (including the ultimate accountability of the SIO) and whether he or she has a participatory or autocratic role; and (iii) *'Decision bases'* (the material foundations of particular decisions – from hunches to evidence).

Our model is based on the attendant psychological and sociological literature, as well as examples from the debriefs we have examined and a variety of archival resources (notably public reviews). We consider the psychological impact of time pressure, uncertainty, responsibility, reversibility and control, and evaluate how these may be more or less relevant at various stages of an inquiry. In drawing upon these various levels of complexity that influence decisions, we argue that both naturalistic and traditional decision-making approaches are informative within the context of critical incidents and suggest that a synthesis of these historically 'at odds' paradigms is likely to prove most fruitful in furthering our understanding of the role of the SIO in murder investigations.

A model of decision-making in murder inquiries

While practitioner interest in police decision-making is increasing (it is

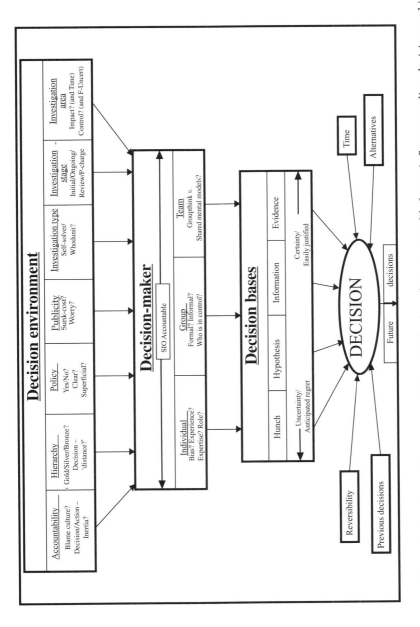

Figure 7.1 Proposal for the preliminary model, with the key factors most likely to influence police decision-making within murder investigations.[2]

one concern of the NPIA, formerly NCPE,[1] 2005), there has been little explicit psychological study of this domain. A clear first step involves identification and description of the domain of interest. With that in mind, we seek to outline the various levels at which organisational, individual and environmental factors impact upon decisions within murder inquiries.

This chapter begins with a brief overview of a preliminary model and the myriad of approaches that we have drawn on and then goes on to explore further this unashamedly eclectic range of issues in greater depth. Echoing the call in Chapter 3, we emphasise the utility of synthesising previously 'at odds' decision-making paradigms, noting how both traditional and naturalistic perspectives can make an important contribution. Along the way, we give several examples, by reference to public reviews (specifically, the 1999 Macpherson report on the Lawrence inquiry) of where things can go wrong, as well as attempting to identify the factors that conspired to generate those very significant errors.

Decision environment

The decision environment is made up of factors pertaining to overall organisational context as well as factors specific to the context of a murder investigation. Often these factors are interrelated, for example, hierarchy, policy and publicity all relate to accountability.

1 *Accountability*. This encourages justification, either promoting (on a positive note) more considered decision-making (e.g. Janis and Mann 1977) or (on a negative note) fostering a blame culture, thereby contributing to inertia (see Chapter 10).

2 *Hierarchy*. The UK police service has formalised a command structure, split into three levels: gold (strategic planning); silver (tactical means of achieving strategy); and bronze (operational implementation of tactics) (Lancashire Constabulary 2004). Broadly, this structure may also correspond to 'time to decide' and, therefore, reflects opportunities to consider all the relevant information, with the strategic level more likely to reflect on considerable amounts of information with possible alternatives and the operational level operating in a more time-sensitive environment.

3 *Policy versus decision*. Policy and legal requirements guide decisions. This distinction relates to how policies are carried out and is useful for distinguishing between considered and superficial decisions (the latter relating to decision avoidance).

4 *Publicity.* Societal scrutiny and political pressures relating to accountability. Potentially contributes to decision avoidance via anticipatory negative thoughts/emotions (Anderson 2003) or inertia via desire to avoid responsibility (See Chapter 10). May also be linked to sunk-cost effects (Arkes and Blumer 1985).

5 *Type of investigation.* Self-solver versus Whodunit (Innes 2003). The former may involve more policy-driven decisions, less uncertainty (see Lipshitz and Strauss 1997) and less need to revise existing strategies. The latter involves greater uncertainty, especially incomplete information and undifferentiated alternatives and may require assumption-based reasoning/hypothesis/story-building and multiple revisions of strategy (thus, confirmation bias would present more of a problem).

6 *Stage of investigation.* Initial stages generally involve more time pressure; thus, early decisions may require the ability to apply experience, attend to important situational cues and act rapidly. Reviews present the best opportunity to spot mistakes or alternative courses of action (weighing alternatives), since they involve 'stepping back' from ongoing events. Post-charge may involve a resurgence of workload and time pressure as well as the need to carry out meticulous reviews of material (a psychological paradox in terms of the situational demands).

7 *Area of investigation.* Different tasks may involve decision-making strategies. Any taxonomy of decision-making must be intimately entwined with a taxonomy of investigative tasks. Possible themes include 'Impact' on investigation and level of perceived 'Control' (Crego and Alison 2004). Impact may relate especially to time and other pressures, while Control may relate to experienced uncertainty regarding future outcomes.

Decision-makers

The decision-maker must act within the decision environment and is influenced directly by it, both as an individual and as part of a group or team. However, the SIO is still most likely to retain overall accountability for decisions made.

1 *SIO.* Retains overall accountability and is the key decision-maker, even when decisions involve input from others. The role of SIO can be compared to that of a musical conductor, using generic understanding to guide individuals with different expertise to

achieve a concerted effort. Thus, their own level of expertise and experience will define the extent to which their decisions are considered and exhaustive. Conversely, experience and expertise may allow decision strategies such as situation-matching rules (Lipshitz, Klein, Orasanu and Salas 2001) or story-building (Kaempf, Klein, Thorsden and Wolf 1996), based on particular cues.

2 *Individual versus Group/Team.* Relates to hierarchy but with specific consideration of whether the decision-maker is an individual, group or team. Lone decision-making may be more prone to individual biases such as confirmation bias or the availability heuristic (Tversky and Kahneman 1974), while groups and teams may be subject to (on a negative note) group processes such as groupthink (Janis 1982) but also (on a positive note) to shared mental models (Cannon-Bowers, Salas and Converse 1993) (consideration of relevant information and of viable alternatives). A further consideration is whether members of other organisations are involved, as this relates to inter-organisational politics and such themes as social identity and group membership (see e.g. Hogg, Abrams, Otten and Hinkle 2004).

Bases of decisions

Finally, the particular bases of decisions must be considered in terms of quality and quantity of material, alongside such factors as whether the decision is reversible, how much time is available, what alternative options might be, and how the decision 'fits' the ongoing decision chain; any current decision affects future decisions.

1 *Bases for particular decisions.* Relates to uncertainty, generally (including concepts of Lipshitz and Strauss 1997, and specific 'future-uncertainty'). At least three levels of 'reliability' may exist, linked to differing levels of uncertainty, potential negative thoughts/ emotions regarding accountability, and different likelihoods of decision avoidance or inertia as follows:
   (a) hypotheses based on existing, incomplete material may involve consideration of alternatives and allow lines of logic to be followed.
   (b) Information – depending on the quantity and quality, this affords some direction and certainty for decision-makers.
   (c) Evidence – generally the most solid grounds for decision-making, providing there is opportunity for its use and that it is adequately understood.

An even more tentative basis for decisions, preceding the above, would involve 'hunches' or intuition/tacit knowledge that cannot be expressed.

Although in drafting our model the views are essentially speculative, certain key themes are identified from the academic literature as well as from public reviews and the attendant experience of debriefing and training senior officers who have dealt with high-profile murder inquiries.

We assert that at the most general level there are organisational themes of accountability, hierarchy, policy, and individual/group/team decision-making that provide a background to more context-specific influential factors. These factors include the individual characteristics of the SIO, the type and stage of investigation, the investigative area or task, bases of particular decisions (from intuition to evidence), and the impact of the media and other sources of external scrutiny. Underlying each of these themes are differences in levels of time pressure, uncertainty, responsibility, reversibility, and control.

A pragmatic definition of decision-making

Historically, research and theory on decision-making has been divided into two main camps – Traditional Decision-Making Theory (TDT) and the Naturalistic Decision-Making approach (NDM) (see Chapter 3). Eyre and Alison (2007) have recently argued that TDT and NDM should not be treated as contradictory or mutually exclusive paradigms. Both approaches acknowledge, to varying extents, the limited nature of human rationality, and both seek to explain the process of deciding – in making choices, what is considered under what circumstances and how. Further, Eyre and Alison argue that different types of decision-making at different stages of an inquiry might more helpfully be considered by one or other paradigm, and have argued that what is required is a synthesis of both approaches within the broader framework of various organisational processes.

Organisational context

The complexity and uniqueness of different situations within policing makes devising a taxonomy a daunting task. One central component of organisational context is its formal structure. Sentamu, Blakey and Nove (2002) note that the UK police service's gold, silver, bronze structure can be applied to the command and control of any serious crime or major incident although, in criminal investigations, the divisions are arguably more blurred since the SIO still apparently controls the direction of the investigation and retains accountability for decisions, even if these decisions are supported or advised by others. What emerges is a picture of 'qualified autonomy' held by the SIO and varying levels of input from players with different roles within the hierarchy.

Hierarchy and 'distance' between decisions and actions

The gold, silver, bronze distinction represents the most basic taxonomy by drawing attention to the potential importance of how far temporally and physically removed from the action the decision-maker(s) can be. Sir William Morris, in discussing leadership competencies with the Assistant Commissioner of the Metropolitan Police (Morris, Burden and Weekes 2004: 54) pointed out that, 'There are some people in the organisation who are managers … but they are not operational police officers'. This divergence of role may also result in conflicting agendas (see Chapter 4 for the differences between managers and leaders) and different operational, tactical and strategic requirements. For example, Macpherson, Cook, Sentamu and Stone (1999) describe a state of general confusion among on-site senior officers. More importantly, this raises the idea that different tasks may require different decision-making strategies. Strategic and tactical decisions within investigations often operate on a significantly longer time-scale than operational ones since, at this latter level, there is no 'distance' between decision and action. The implication is a difference in the amount of information considered as a function of time available, and this might be conceptualised as roughly analogous to the difference between traditional and naturalistic decision-making strategies, with the former as more relevant in less time-pressured environments than the latter.

The Military Operations Research Society (MORS) (2003) has distinguished between deliberate and crisis decisions, with the former taking months of planning, and the latter concerning current events and being more flexible and time sensitive. According to this dichotomy, deliberate decisions allow time for information search and analysis with advice and support while crisis decisions must be made quickly, based only on the available information and the decision-makers' expertise and judgement.

Although progress across a murder investigation may be incremental or deliberate (Innes 2003), the time-scales for different investigations and investigative tasks vary considerably and the fact remains that some decisions are likely to be deliberate while others are spontaneous and unplanned. For example, according to the Police and Criminal Evidence Act (PACE) (1984), a suspect can be held for up to 36 hours without charge[3] (with the exception of suspected terrorists). This gives officers time to plan and co-ordinate interview strategies and consider the most effective approach for gathering information. In contrast, if an officer has attended the scene of a gang-related murder and is with a variety of witnesses at the scene, he or she may have to make a rapid decision as to whether to garner information immediately. Johnstone, Driskell and Salas (1997: 615) argue that in naturalistic, time-pressured settings, 'Decision-makers can make effective decisions without carrying out an elaborative and exhaustive analytical procedure.' This so-called 'hyper-vigilant' decision-making involves attending to the barest minimum of required information, while ignoring all other sources not of immediate interest.

Time-scales are likely to vary with seniority, with more junior officers being asked to make snap decisions and managers generally being given more opportunity to make considered decisions. However, 'slower-burn' decisions are also more likely to be accompanied by larger swathes of information as well as more conflicting information. Thus, greater cognitive effort and processing time is brought to bear on more senior managers, alongside the attendant comparative stressful chronicity associated with longer-term processing. Furthermore, SIOs in particular must have a generic interpositional knowledge and awareness of investigations at all levels and they must be able to employ different decision-making strategies according to the situation and task demands. At times, this may involve the ability to recognise certain situational cues that may allow rapid decisions and, at other times, the ability to consider simultaneously large amounts of information and make choices between alternative courses of action.

Accountability

In Chapter 10, we expand on the work of Anderson (2003) and highlight the importance of organisational context in terms of accountability and a blame culture that can permeate the police and emergency services. In particular, multi-agency work and the onus on various organisations to officially record and justify any decisions made can result in increasing negative emotion.

The police service maintains a strict and very onerous policy of accountability, reflected in the keeping of crime reports and decision/policy logs, as a series of legal requirements under the Criminal Procedure and Investigation Act (1996) and the Human Rights Act (1998). Needless to say, there are many quality assurance and moral and legal issues involved in the provision of such documents but the burden of too 'iron-fisted' an accountability system, in which there is considerable scope for twisting information or the obfuscation of genuine intent, can foster a climate of distrust that can prove highly counter-productive. Such a climate can encourage individuals to seek ways round the system, thereby providing an entirely false impression of the justifications behind a decision.

Individuals/groups/teams

Tversky and Kahneman (1974, 1981) have identified a number of heuristics and biases that can affect decision-making. We give these due attention in Chapter 8 but examples include the availability heuristic (reasoning based upon instances that easily spring to mind, essentially ignoring base-rates) and framing effects (whereby the way in which a situation is presented affects how it is processed, a form of anchoring). Such mental 'short cuts' are often characterised as deficiencies in thinking that must be guarded against. Innes (2003: 185) reports that, 'There is, in effect, a degree of [confirmation] bias that gravitates towards interpreting new material in such a way as to support the established theory about the crime.' In a similar vein, in the Stephen Lawrence public inquiry report, Macpherson (1999) noted the dangers of adopting a 'colour blind' approach while investigating the potential influence of racism in murder.

Individual SIO/decision-makers are frequently exposed to considerable pressure, often with incomplete or contradictory information and with limited time/resources. Conversely, each SIO brings with him or her a wealth of experience and expertise that guides their decision-making. The importance of experience has been highlighted under the heading of situation/action-matching decision rules (Lipshitz *et al.* 2001) and as part of Klein's (1993) Recognition Primed Decision-Making (RPD) model. Both describe processes in which situations are identified by means of pattern matching and choosing new courses of action, by comparing limited ranges of possible alternatives, and by opting for preferred actions based on what has worked in similar situations in the past. They argue that experienced decision-makers often 'get it right first time' by considering only a limited range of options (Klein, Calderwood and Macgregor 1989).

However, Klein (1998) notes how RPD strategies are less likely to be employed when decisions must be (i) justified, and (ii) when different stakeholders' views must be considered. The emphasis on justification and the need to consider competing parties' needs, as well as the observation that, in criminal investigations, each case is characterised by its own unique complexities, means that the task of describing the range of decision-making categories in murder investigations is frustrated by considerable complexity. This limits and potentially precludes situation-matching rules as a fully integrated meta-theoretical model of criminal investigative decision-making.

However, Kaempf et al.'s (1996) story-building models are extremely useful in helping to understand how narratives inform the ways in which officers interpret information. The process is described as mentally simulating a story to explain how particular events might have been caused, to be used when information is insufficient or contradictory. Such processes are described by the National Centre for Policing Excellence (NCPE) (2005) and The Association of Chief Police Officers' (ACPO) Crime Committee (1998) under *assumption-based reasoning* where they draw upon Lipshitz and Strauss's (1997) RAWFS (Reduction, Assumption-based reasoning, Weighing pros and cons, Forestalling, and Suppression) heuristic model of coping with uncertainty. Such accounts bear comparison to Innes's (2003: 166) description of a 'process of narrative construction' – a theme developed during his observations of 'live' murder investigations.

What is central, however, to all these approaches is the notion that detectives generate meaning from incomplete, ambiguous and contradictory information. Further, these scripts/schemas/narratives are developed not in isolation but rather are informed by contributions from colleagues, from parties external to the service, and by the organisational infrastructure and climate of the police force.

Alongside all the vagaries of individual decision-making, then, there are group processes such as polarisation (Moscovici and Zavalloni 1969) groupthink (Janis 1971, 1982) and self-categorisation theory (SCT) (Turner, Hogg, Oakes, Reicher and Wetherell 1987) that can all impact decision-making. Importantly, Sentamu et al. note that "It is ... very rare for an SIO to be detached from the investigation team with which they normally work' (2002: para. 3.2.3).

A relevant contribution from the NDM perspective is the concept of shared mental models where shared understanding of the situation enhances communication and planning (Cannon-Bowers et al. 1993).

Table 7.1 Hypothetical relationships between individual/group/team decision-making and bias, expertise and accountability

	Bias	Expertise	Accountability
Individual	Without significant input from others, individuals may be most prone to biased decision-making.	Allows recognition of situational cues and salient issues. Here, it is limited to individual experience.	Regardless of who has input into a decision, it may always be an officially responsible individual who is ultimately accountable. In murder investigations, this seems most likely to be the SIO. How this affects formal and informal group/team dynamics and the responsible individual's perceptions of accountability are topics for future research.
Groups	Multiple perspectives may guard against bias, although a single meeting may involve a narrow focus on certain issues and allow the decision-making process to be dictated by official relationships (rank).	Groups can encompass a range of experience and expertise; however, as with bias, if processes are dictated by rank, this range of expertise may not come into play. Conflicting agendas are also a possibility.	
Teams	Multiple perspectives along with free-flowing communication potentially allows expression of diverse viewpoints, avoiding individual bias and resulting in shared mental models in terms of key issues and goals. Conversely, cohesion may result in groupthink.	If communication is unrestricted, the variety of expertise can be expressed. There is no guarantee different 'experts' will agree.	

Fully formed consistent teams might be expected to have better integrated shared mental models compared to relatively transiently formed groups based on the principle that the former will spend more time together, develop more regular assessment procedures and allow for more free-flowing communication up and down the hierarchical chain. Such groups may also benefit from opportunities to 'try out' each other's roles – the concept of *interpositional knowledge* – a factor that has been linked to enhanced team performance (Cannon-Bowers *et al.* 1993).

These factors may also have an impact on personnel selection in terms of assembling teams based on psychological attributes of individual team members. For example, how does a team with similar attitudes and personalities, as revealed by psychometric testing, perform compared to a team of individuals with disparate attitudes? Table 7.1 summarises key issues.

Decision or policy?

The final organisational level factor is the impact of formal organisationally driven policy. While the terms 'policy log' and 'decision log' are used interchangeably, certain procedures cannot really be classified as decisions, insofar as they are 'if-then' rules that drive actions. For example, cordoning off a crime scene or appointing a Family Liaison Officer (FLO) is standard practice given specific circumstances. Wright and Alison (under review) have suggested that decisions with less documented justification 'may be bureaucracy-driven judgements that are standard across all cases and therefore require little thought'. However, the precise means by which these actions are initiated does require some thought. For example, what are the parameters for the crime scene? Which specific person should be appointed as FLO? Innes (2003: 209) describes an SIO's quite particular directions for fingerprinting certain areas of a crime scene and not others so that 'past experience and a particular form of investigative logic [were used to inform policy and avoid] swamping the investigation' with extraneous evidence in the form of fingerprints to be analysed.

It is incumbent on researchers to try to pick apart decision from policy and recognise, where policy is in play, the breadth of the parameters involved. Further, attention needs to be drawn to instances where individuals eschew the responsibility of enacting a course of action by relying wholly on the 'party-line'. This decision omission by reference to organisational policy can be critically damaging and stultify creativity and flair in decision making.

The context of murder investigations

Given an overview of generic organisational factors including structure, culture, individual versus multiple decision-makers, and policy, it is useful to consider investigations as 'entities' in themselves in order to provide focus within a wider context. This raises the importance of identifying the various types and stages of murder investigation.

In cases of murder, the initial response is often by uniformed officers. First aid may be applied if the victim is still alive at this point as, for example, in the cases of Stephen Lawrence and Damilola Taylor (See Macpherson 1999 and Sentamu *et al.* 2002, respectively). Efforts are made to secure the crime scene and to retain a comprehensive crime scene log. Senior officers are notified and other necessary departments will attend, such as the Serious Crime Group. An SIO will be appointed, who will act as key decision-maker, with overall responsibility for every aspect of the investigation (ACPO Crime Committee 1998). Various officers are appointed to different roles and a major incident room (MIR) will be set up according to Major Incident Room Standard Administration Procedures (MIRSAP). The computerised system known as the Home Office Large Major Enquiry System (HOLMES 2) will be utilised for organising the 'information burst' (Innes 2003).

Aside from the variety of formal processes such as forensic analyses, house-to-house inquiries, searches for weapons, utilising various intelligence databases, carrying out surveillance, interviews and so forth, murder investigations invariably involve liaisons with family of victim(s) and any witnesses, as well as with a range of different community groups, local organisations and the media. Thus, there is a range of different areas an SIO must be aware of and a number of different tasks he/she must manage, perform and delegate.

Different types of murder investigation

Innes (2003) has classified murders into a relatively simple dichotomy: *Self-solvers* and *Whodunits*, with various hybrids in between. He argues that 'The quantity and quality of knowledge available to detectives at an early stage of an enquiry is crucial in terms of how quickly they will be able to begin to progress the investigation' (p. 198). A key distinction is whether or not suspect(s) are identified early on. Innes describes Self-solvers as involving an initial large number of actions that gradually decline while Whodunits are more frequently demarcated as having an initial surge of actions followed by peaks and troughs of activity.

Thus, where suspects are immediately apparent, there is a narrower focus and less information (or at least, less conflicting information) to consider. Situational models are likely to be more constrained, since more is known and there are fewer parameters to consider. In contrast, where suspects are not apparent, progress is made in smaller, incremental and erratic steps, and initial information may be sparse, contradictory or ambiguous – all factors that are likely to increase the number and complexity of situational models and open up increased margin for error. Indeed, some preliminary studies are beginning to hint at the relationship between ambiguity, complexity of situational models and proneness to confirmation bias (Doran and Alison 2005). This may also frustrate the potential for fully and clearly justifying all decisions, since the potential for arguing optimality of any single decision is only possible with the benefit of hindsight.

Investigative cues and superficial decisions

Innes (2003) also refers to the location of the crime scene as particularly important in forming the adoption of particular strategies, for example, the preservation of physical evidence, dictating search parameters, likelihood of witnesses, and generating hypotheses about the offender's movements. However, in the case of Stephen Lawrence, the offence took place outdoors in a heavily populated urban area at a time when many people were still awake and active (around 10:30 p.m.), there was an eyewitness/co-victim present and information from different sources implicated the same suspects. In many respects, then, this murder had many hallmarks of being a Self-solver, but due to problems that arose in failing to act decisively in the initial stages, and the adoption of a *laissez-faire* approach (Macpherson 1999), these cues were not imperialised in the way that they might have been.

Of course, the Lawrence inquiry is a painful reminder that the early identification of the right cues to assist in interpreting decisions and the resultant lines of inquiry is critical in successful resolution of any case. If such cues are incorrectly interpreted and decision-makers fail to take advantage of the early opportunities, crushing inertia may impede subsequent progress. Macpherson argued that the lack of purchase officers made in the early stages led to a point at which the inquiry had gone beyond the threshold for arrest. Having failed to recognise this (experiencing uncertainty in terms of inadequate understanding), the inquiry team and, ultimately, the SIO appeared to have adopted a strategy of decision deferment, or as Macpherson more robustly indicated, the team were engaged in a process of 'burying their heads in the sand, and simply waiting in the somewhat forlorn hope that [a more reliable] eyewitness would turn up' (1999: para. 15.20). The decision to arrest appeared not to have been considered an option and the resultant action (surveillance) was 'deployed in an "ad hoc" fashion, with no apparent direction towards the achievement of specific objectives, or the collation of evidence to assist in the prosecution of an offence' (Mr Philip Pitham, Head of Training at the Regional Crime Squad National Training Centre 1997, cited in Macpherson 1999, para. 18.17). The superficial *ad hoc* decision-making reported in the Lawrence inquiry shares similar antecedents to processes that underlie decision inertia or avoidance and might be described as deferment under the guise of action. The exact circumstances that lend themselves to this 'scratch the surface' decision-making requires a dedicated research agenda but one might reasonably speculate that the perceived need to be seen to be doing something – indeed, anything – may partly be explained by too many onerous and redundant procedural practices that stifle reflective thinking.

Stages of investigation

Investigations, regardless of type, are dynamic entities and vary in pace and intensity dependent on the stage at which they are examined. A recurring theme throughout accounts and documents relating to murder investigations and identified in the previous section is the fact that the initial stages are particularly important. Macpherson (1999: para. 15.9) notes that the first few days are inevitably 'hectic and extremely busy', with 'vital' decisions opening time-limited options. Examples of 'golden hour' opportunities include pursuing and apprehending suspect(s) before they escape, or gathering physical evidence before it can decay or be corrupted. Many tasks are conducted in parallel under considerable time pressure and uncertainty. These conditions frustrate considered decision-making strategies and initial stages might therefore be best described under the recognition-primed, hyper-vigilant or crisis decision-making models. Nevertheless, the SIO must justify all these rapid decisions and commit them to paper. It is not unreasonable to assume, given such circumstances, that there may be a tendency to justify decisions on a post-hoc basis. An area pertinent to the sort of heuristics that emerge in such an environment is the phenomenon of hindsight bias (the process of updating justifications based on known outcomes) (Hoffrage, Hertwig and Gigerenzer 2000) and pilot studies on post-hoc decisions in firearms incidents (Villejoubert, O'Keeffe and Alison 2006) suggest that such biases are strongly dependent on preconceived narratives shaped by ambiguous information. For example, the perceived threat and subsequent justification for a lethal force decision appears to be influenced by what can only be known after the event.

Thus, different stages will necessitate the incorporation of different decision-making paradigms, with the influence of time pressure and uncertainty (and, therefore, NDM models) emerging as relevant in the early stages, and search and inference processes (and, therefore, TDT models) in the latter stages. Furthermore, investigation does not end with charging a suspect and discussions with The Crown Prosecution Service (CPS) will inevitably involve a whole new swathe of decisions.[4] Sentamu *et al.* draw attention to how large and difficult a task it is to develop robust post-charge investigations, noting that, 'The criminal justice process imposes time limits on the prosecution of offenders and ... there are often incomplete or unresolved lines of enquiry at the time of charge' (2002: para. 4.2.2). Thus, there may be a curious symmetry to murder inquiries in terms of expeditious decisions having to be made at the early and final stages. Preparing the case for prosecution involves meticulous planning under considerable time constraints.

The final stage involves the fact that murder investigations are often subject to review. For example, the investigation of the murder of Damilola Taylor was subject to a standard 28-day Progress Review carried out by the MPS[5] Murder Review Group (MRG) and involved 50 recommendations (Sentamu *et al.* 2002). The process of review involves detailed attention to a mass of information and might be characterised more as *'Have I missed anything?'* rather than *'What should I do next?'*[6]

Bases of decisions

At every stage of an inquiry (particularly regarding formal investigative duties), there are decisions to pursue certain courses of action based on different quantities and qualities of information.[7] Quantity might not easily be defined in this context but must involve some consideration of the sheer number of different sources of information that corroborate as well as contradict one another (e.g. two independent witnesses reporting the same sequence of events, CCTV confirming the same and forensic evidence linking the implicated suspect to the crime). Quality must involve consideration of the reliability and validity of individual sources, with witness information as less reliable and valid compared to many forms of forensic evidence.[8] Recognition of the distinction between information and evidence has been referred to by Macpherson (1999) as critical for the formulation of any case where information, although considered acceptable as a basis for informing actions, including arrest and charge, is less sound than evidence as grounds for decision-making.

Any taxonomic description of decision-making must, therefore, take into account whether a decision is based upon information or evidence, since different types of decision may arise from these foundations; for example, while the decision to arrest can be driven by information, 'Consideration needs to be given to the likelihood of evidence being secured within 96 hours of that arrest and the impact of release without charge if such evidence is not forthcoming. If there is a better chance of securing evidence pre-arrest as opposed to developing it quickly after having arrested on "reasonable suspicion" then this may justify delay' (Macpherson 1999: para. 13.88). In such cases, the SIO must consider the current information and unique features of the case and anticipate which option is most likely to lead to evidence (weighing of pros and cons). In the event that evidence already exists, the decision to arrest is more likely to be effectively pre-made and will not involve dilemma over alternative options. The basis for decisions within an investigative context is likely to form a key part of any investigative decision-making taxonomy. At least three different types of basis have been identified within this paper:

1   Hypotheses used to bridge gaps where information is very sparse may involve high degrees of uncertainty and, therefore, are more likely to form the basis of decisions that do not have severe consequences, or are reversible, such as decisions to carry out searches of particular areas.
2   Information can vary in quality and quantity but, broadly speaking, may provide a direction for decisions. Degree of uncertainty is likely to be related to issues of quality and quantity, as well as consideration of accountability and, hence, anticipatory thoughts and emotions. Nevertheless, information can drive important decisions such as the decision to arrest, which impact future opportunities.
3   Evidence, although again varying in quality and quantity, represents the strongest foundation for making decisions and ultimately informs a case for prosecution.

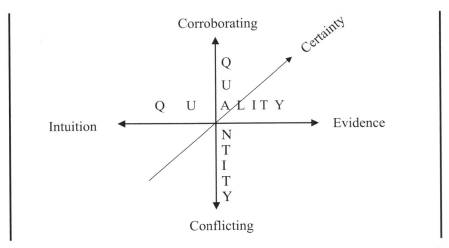

Figure 7.2 Proposed relationship between different bases of decisions and degree of perceived certainty.

Thus, the basis of any decision affects issues of uncertainty, accountability and anticipated regret. Evidence involving little uncertainty might make related decisions obvious, providing that the decision-maker has an adequate understanding of that evidence (and, if not, expert advice might be sought to reduce that uncertainty). Information may involve a wider range of levels of uncertainty and, depending on the context of the decision-environment, decision-making might involve deferment and further information searching, comparing alternatives, or assumption-based reasoning. Decisions based on hypothetical reasoning or 'guesswork' from very limited information are most likely to be plagued by uncertainty and, by definition, involve assumption-based reasoning.

Figure 7.2 illustrates the proposed relationship between degree of certainty and the quality and quantity of material, expressed as continua. Quality ranges from intuition, through information to solid evidence, and quantity ranges from conflicting to corroborating. As certainty increases, decision difficulty decreases.

Decision chains

Whatever the type or stage of investigation, and whatever the basis of decisions, a final concern is that it may be unproductive to view decisions in isolation from each other. While this is implicit in recognising that certain opportunities will be lost if not acted upon, or that certain decisions are irreversible (affecting future opportunities), it is important to be explicit about this cumulative process. Any decision made is likely to take into account previous and concurrent decisions and, to some extent, by considering consequences, the future decisions that will have to be made. Thus, more may be learned about police decision-making processes and how they develop over the course of an investigation by paying particular attention to decision chains. Of relevance within this context are processes such as sunk-cost-effects (where decision-makers show a tendency to commit to earlier decisions that involved investment of time and effort, even when a change of strategy may be more appropriate (Arkes and Blumer 1985)). This could conceivably interact with other common biases, including confirmation bias and status quo bias.

In terms of the former, if considerable effort has been invested in pursuing a particular course of action, there might be a greater tendency to ignore disconfirming information. Sunk-cost effects might also be influenced by the fact that murder investigations are often the subject of considerable publicity. To continue belligerently with a course of action might be attractive to the decision-maker (although entirely inappropriate) because it could be used to justify it. In contrast, the decision-maker may perceive changing strategies as providing fertile ground for crucifixion by the media. Thus the 'decision' not to arrest in the case of Stephen Lawrence appeared to have been hastily reversed only under escalating public and political pressure (Macpherson 1999: ch. 23).

Non-decisions

The picture so far suggests that once a decision has been made, albeit by different processes and depending on the situation, that decision is then acted upon. However, there are many examples where no decision is reached or where there is decision not to act. Anderson (2003) describes a rational–emotional model of decision avoidance, which expands upon the notion that active decisions are not inevitable and introduces the role that emotions play in decision inertia. Although discussed in greater detail in Chapter 10, it is worth noting here that it can take different forms, including choice deferral[9] (refusing to choose, including searching/waiting for better alternatives and avoiding responsibility altogether), status quo bias (a tendency to prefer options that do not effect change), omission bias (a tendency to prefer options which do not require action by the decision-maker) and inaction inertia (the tendency of a person to omit action when he or she has already passed up a similar, more attractive opportunity to act). These are all affected by simple, rational cost-benefit assessments and by anticipated regret (consideration of blame/accountability, factors such as reversibility and anticipated future opportunities) and selection difficulty (when it is unclear which option will most likely meet one's goals).

The Macpherson Report is once again an example – where the decision to arrest was postponed for approximately two weeks. The public inquiry concluded that 'no proper considered decision making took place, and the investigation was allowed to drift in' (Macpherson 1999: para. 13.44).[10] In the Damilola Taylor murder inquiry, there was considerable controversy over the decision to endorse a reward announced by a national newspaper. 'Benefits and difficulties were identified ... [and] ... In the event the existence of the reward was endorsed but some unease also remained about its potential effects' (Sentamu *et al*. 2002: para. 3.10.9). Thus, there was apparent selection difficulty and weighing of costs and benefits as well as some unease or concern over potential regret while the consequences of the (irreversible) decision gradually unfolded. Nevertheless, a decision was made. This also forces us to consider, not only whether the consequences of a decision gradually unfold, but also whether a decision seems to be more correctly identified as an act of volition or a response to the decisions/actions of some other party.

Previous studies of police decision-making

In a series of immersive simulation inquiries, Wright and Alison (under review) explored SIOs, recorded justifications for decisions regarding different areas of a simulated critical incident inquiry. They observed that different domain areas of investigation (i.e. forensic evidence *v*. appointing family liaison officers) are more or less likely to employ either fairly robust or less adequate levels of accountability and legal and evidence-based practice. Recorded decisions also focus on positive action (i.e. what to do rather than what not to do). This relates to previously discussed issues regarding the purpose of justifying decisions and raises questions about when it may be appropriate to record alternative options or why other choices were not considered.

Control and impact

In Crego and Alison's (2004) early debriefing work, 15 key themes

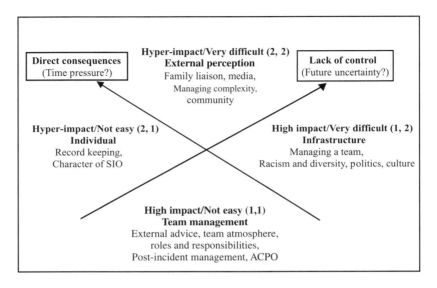

Figure 7.3 The facets of impact (directness of consequences) and ease (degree of control) as they are seen to relate to different areas or themes in investigations. The additions here are consideration of whether impact may be related to time pressure and whether ease/control may be related to uncertainty as to future events (see below). Adapted from Crego and Alison (2004).

emerged that can be considered along two dimensions of difficulty and ease. These were 'managing external perceptions' (rated as Hyper-impact/Very difficult) with elements including family liaison, media, managing complexity and community; 'individual qualities' (Hyper-impact/Not easy) with elements including record keeping and character of SIO; 'infrastructure' (High impact/Very difficult) with elements including managing a team, racism and diversity, politics, and culture; and finally 'team management' (High impact/ Not easy) consisting of external advice, team atmosphere, roles and responsibilities, post-incident management, and ACPO. Crego and Alison (2004) speculate that the defining dimension that leads to perceptions of difficulty and impact relates to the degree of control that an SIO has over the various elements, with less control over external perceptions and more control over internal factors such as team management.

Further, the immediacy of consequences may be linked to degree of time pressure when dealing with such diverse management areas.

Thus, issues such as family, media and the community may be factors that demand an immediate response and, in turn, generate swift reactions to the decisions that are made. In contrast, record keeping relates to issues of accountability and there will be pressure to document and justify decisions while also ensuring that they are carried out. As one experienced practitioner stated, 'In a very busy schedule many decisions and the rationale are not being captured' (Crego and Alison 2004: 218). Perceived time pressure may interact with negative anticipatory thoughts/emotions regarding potential consequences of making the 'wrong' decisions. The net result would be that decision-makers are under pressure to be decisive and act upon decisions, while at the same time experiencing all the antecedents of decision avoidance or inertia.

The level of perceived control over domains of investigations may relate to experienced uncertainty. To control a situation is to be certain of the outcome, while lack of control means the outcome is uncertain. This represents a notion of uncertainty that is distinct from the three types examined by Lipshitz and Strauss (1997). Although one might accept a degree of uncertainty with respect to future events or outcomes, anxiety may be intensified by perceived anticipated lack of control, especially when aware that, ultimately, one's own position might be under threat as the SIO recognises that he or she is accountable. This process of *worrying* (see Wells and Butler 1997) predicts that those areas of investigation perceived as harder to control are subject to more negative thoughts regarding the future (e.g. 'How will the media or the team react to particular decisions?' 'I expect they will hate what I am about to do – what are the consequences for me if it does go wrong?').

An interesting finding from the world of financial analysts is also relevant, where Stotz and von Nitzsch (2005) found support for the hypothesis that the greater the perception of control, the more overconfidence intensifies. Granted, no areas of investigation in Crego and Alison's (2004) study were rated as easy and, thus, overconfidence may not be at the forefront of most investigators' minds but the idea that certain areas might be more prone to optimism would be worth exploring. The Macpherson Report (1999: ch. 16, para. 27.10) is also instructive in this context, with the review noting that inadequate staffing was taken for granted and one officer was performing five different roles.

Uttaro (2002) has also identified control as an important concept in police-decision making with several case studies of American officers working at a federal level. In two of these cases, decisions were made operationally, on scene, in situations requiring split-second decisions that deviated from the detailed planning that had taken place previously. The third case involved remote, tactical/strategic decision-making with slightly more time to decide but still under heavy pressure as lives were at stake. The model Uttaro (2002) proposes surrounds unanticipated events caused by other parties, which decision-maker(s) deal with by using their experience and preparation to assess the context (including consideration of uncertainty and potential consequences) and making decisions aimed at controlling the situation. Key to this process was a level of situational awareness (see Endsley 1995) and construction of a cognitive map of the situation, brought about by planning and scanning for environmental cues. Thus, efforts were made to reduce uncertainty (incomplete information and future uncertainty) *a priori*, such that previous strategic and tactical decisions guided and informed operational, reactive decisions at the extreme end of the time pressure continuum.

One implication would be that less controllable elements might be subject to more careful planning as well as enhanced training. Tentative support for this comes from Wright and Alison's (2006) observations, where they noted that most claims/decisions were made regarding the media/community (e.g. to set up meetings to discuss media strategy) rather than general investigative strategies. One might argue that there is something of the 'tail wagging the dog' approach in focusing so intensely on the perceptions of external parties (and especially the media), particularly if it is to the detriment of the investigation itself. The key, perhaps, though, is balance – individuals need the courage to concentrate on and enact the best possible decisions while also considering the longer term impact of the perception that those decisions, while 'right for the time', were subject to deliberate distortion that have now led to a longer term, damaging effect on (for example) the community.

Summary and conclusion

This chapter has attempted to lay the foundations for establishing a taxonomy of themes that influence police decision-making, specifically within murder investigations. A range of theoretical and research-based issues has been considered, with outlines of the relevant organisational context and investigative processes involved. What is most apparent is the considerable complexity of dissecting the many elements that operate at different levels and that may interact inter and intra level. We have hinted at how different forces may influence decision-makers in predictable ways, some towards decisive action, and others towards deferment, inaction or surface-level decision-making, and some preliminary research has begun to tease apart these various influences.

Notes

1 National Centre for Policing Excellence.
2 'P-charge' under 'Investigation Stage' refers to post-charge. 'F-Uncert' under 'Investigation Area' refers to future uncertainty.
3 An inspector may grant up to 24 hours' detention. This may be extended to 36 hours with permission from an officer of superintendent rank or above; police must apply to the courts for permission to detain for longer periods (Police and Criminal Evidence Act Code of Practice C, Section 42 (1)).
4 See Macpherson (1999), chapter 39.
5 Metropolitan Police Service.
6 See Nicol, Innes, Gee and Feist (2004) for more on murder reviews.
7 The NCPE (2005) discusses similar issues and the police have a grading system for assessing reliability of information known as the 5x5x5 system (see Bichard *et al.* 2004).
8 For an overview of eyewitness issues, see Ainsworth (1998) and for forensic science issues, see Kiely (2000).
9 Compare this to Lipshitz and Strauss's (1997) concept of forestalling. Also, confirmation bias can be conceptualised as a form of status quo bias.
10 It is possible that certain cues of the situation contributed to this decision avoidance, a point discussed above.

References

Ainsworth, P. (1998) *Psychology, law and eyewitness testimony*. Chichester: John Wiley & Sons.

Anderson, C. (2003) 'The psychology of doing nothing: forms of decision avoidance result from reason and emotion', *Psychological Bulletin*, 129: 139–67.

Arkes, H. and Blumer, C. (1985) 'The psychology of sunk cost', *Organizational Behavior and Human Decision Processes*, 35: 124–40.

Association of Chief Police Officers (ACPO) Crime Committee (1998) *Murder investigation manual*. ACPO.

Bichard, M., Nicholson, J., Brudenell, K., Manjdadria, J., Eadie, J., Gallafent, K., Smith, N. and Taylor, B. (2004) *The Bichard inquiry*. Retrieved 20 April 2006, from http://www.bichardinquiry.org.uk

Cannon-Bowers, J., Salas, E. and Converse, S. (1993) 'Shared mental models in expert team decision making', in N. Castellan (ed.), *Individual and group decision making: current issues* (pp. 221–46). Hillsdale, NJ: Erlbaum.

Crego, J. and Alison, L. (2004) 'Control and legacy as functions of perceived criticality in major incidents', *Journal of Investigative Psychology and Offender Profiling*, 1: 207–25.

Criminal Procedure and Investigations Act (1996) Retrieved 10 April 2006, from http://www.opsi.gov.uk/acts/acts1996/1996025.htm

Doran, B. and Alison, A. (2005, December) 'Stressors and stress moderators in critical incident management'. Paper presented at 8th International Investigative Psychology Conference, London, UK.

Endsley, M. (1995) 'Toward a theory of situation awareness in dynamic systems', *Human Factors*, 37: 32–64.

Eyre, M. and Alison, L. (2007) 'To decide or not to decide: decision making and decision avoidance in critical incidents', in D. Carson (ed.), *Applying psychology to criminal justice*. Chichester: Wiley.

Hoffrage, U., Hertwig, R. and Gigerenzer, G. (2000) 'Hindsight bias: a by-product of knowledge or updating?', *Journal of Experimental Psychology, Learning, Memory and Cognition*, 26: 566–81.

Hogg, M., Abrams, D., Otten, S. and Hinkle, S. (2004) 'The social identity perspective: intergroup relations, self conception and small groups', *Small-Group-Research*, 35: 246–76.

Human Rights Act (1998) Retrieved 12 March 2006, from http://www.opsi.gov.uk/acts/acts1998/19980042.htm

Innes, M. (2003) *Investigating murder*. Oxford: Oxford University Press.

Janis, I. (1971) *Stress and frustration*. New York: Harcourt Brace.

Janis, I. and Mann, L. (1977) *Decision making: a psychological analysis of conflict, choice and commitment*. New York: Free Press.

Janis, I. (1982) *Groupthink: psychological studies of policy decisions and fiascoes* (2nd edn). Boston, MA: Houghton-Mifflin.

Johnstone, J., Driskell, J. and Salas, E. (1997) 'Vigilant and hyper-vigilant decision making', *Journal of Applied Psychology*, 82: 614–22.

Kaempf, G., Klein, G., Thorsden, M. and Wolf, S. (1996) 'Decision making in complex naval command-and-control environments', *Human Factors*, 38: 206–19.

Kiely, T. (2000) *Forensic evidence: science and the criminal law*. Florida: CRC Press.

Klein, G., Calderwood, R. and Macgregor, D. (1989) 'Critical decision method for eliciting knowledge', *IEEE Transactions On Systems, Man And Cybernetics*, 19: 462–72.

Klein, G. (1993) 'A recognition-primed decision (RPD) model of rapid decision making', in G. Klein, J. Orasanu, R. Calderwood and C. Zsambok (eds), *Decision making in action: models and methods*. Norwood, CT: MIT Press.

Klein, G. (1998) *Sources of power: how people make decisions*. Cambridge, MA: MIT Press.

Lancashire Constabulary (2004) 'Gold, silver, bronze command and control policy', retrieved 8 February 2006, from http://www.lancashire.police.uk/ Gold Silver Bronze Policy.doc

Lipshitz, R. and Strauss, O. (1997) 'Coping with uncertainty: a naturalistic decision-making analysis', *Organizational Behavior and Human Decision Processes*, 69: 149–63.

Lipshitz, R., Klein, G., Orasanu, J. and Salas, E. (2001) 'Focus article: taking stock of naturalistic decision making', *Journal of Behavioural Decision Making*, 14: 331–52.

Macpherson, W. Advised by Cook, T., Sentamu, J. and Stone, R. (1999) *The Stephen Lawrence inquiry. Presented to Parliament by the Secretary of State for the Home Department by Command of Her Majesty*. Retrieved 14 February 2006, from http://www.archive.official-documents.co.uk/document/ cm42/4262/4262.htm

Morris, W., Burden, A. and Weekes, A. (2004) *The Morris inquiry*. Metropolitan Police Authority. Transcript of Public Session with Assistant Commissioner B. Hogan-Howe, Tuesday 15th June, p.29 (if printed). Retrieved 12 February 2006, from http://www.morrisinquiry.gov.uk/transcripts/2004-06-15-1-hogan-howe

Military Operations Research Society (2003) *Terms of reference: MORS workshop on decision aids/support to joint operations planning*. Dougherty Conference Centre, Offutt AFB, NE. Retrieved 20 April 2006, from http://www.mors. org/meetings/decision_aids/DecisionAids-tor.htm

Moscovici, S., and Zavalloni, M. (1969) 'The group as a polarizer of attitudes', *Journal of Personality and Social Psychology*, 12: 125–35.

National Centre for Policing Excellence (2005) Practice advice on core investigative doctrine produced on behalf of the Association of Chief Police Officers, ACPO Centrex.

Nicol, C., Innes, M., Gee, D. and Feist, A. (2002) 'Reviewing murder investigations: an analysis of progress reviews from six police forces', Home Office Online Report 25/04. Retrieved 20 April 2006, from http:// www.homeoffice.gov.uk/rds/pdfs04/rdsolr2504.pdf

Police and Criminal Evidence Act (1984) The Stationery Office. Retrieved 20 April 2006 from http://police.homeoffice.gov.uk/operational-policing/ powers-pace-codes/ pace-codes.html

Sentamu, J., Blakey, D. and Nove, P. (2002) *The Damilola Taylor murder investigation review report*. Presented to Sir John Stevens QPM DL Commissioner of Police of The Metropolis at his invitation. Retrieved 20 April 2006, from www.met.police.uk/damilola/damilola.pdf

Stotz, O. and von-Nitzsch, R. (2005) 'The perception of control and the level of over-confidence: evidence from analyst earnings estimates and price targets', *Journal of Behavioural Finance*, 6: 121–28.

Turner, J.C., Hogg, M.A., Oakes, P.J., Reicher, S.D. and Wetherell, M.S. (1987) *Re-discovering the social group: a self-categorisation theory*. Oxford: Blackwell.

Tversky, A. and Kahaneman, D. (1974) 'Judgements under uncertainty: heuristics and biases', *Science*, 185: 1124–31.

Tversky, A. and Kahaneman, D. (1981) 'The framing of decisions and the psychology of choice', *Science*, 211: 453–58.

Uttaro, M. (2002) 'Naturalistic decision-making in law enforcement practice – exploring the process', unpublished dissertation (Virginia Polytechnic Institute and State University). Retrieved 20 April 2006, from http://scholar.lib.vt.edu/theses/available/etd-04102002-114630/

Villejoubert, G., O'Keeffe, C. and Alison, L. (2006, September) 'Hindsight bias and shooting incidents', paper presented at 23rd Annual Cognitive Section Conference, Lancaster, UK.

Wells, A. and Butler, G. (1997) 'Generalized anxiety disorder', in D. Clark and C. Fairburn (eds), *Science and practice of cognitive behaviour therapy* (pp. 155–78). Oxford: Oxford University Press.

Wright, A. and Alison, L. (under review) 'The structure, content, and justification of police officers' decisions during a simulated critical incident enquiry.'

Chapter 8

Heuristics and biases in decision-making

Louise Almond, Laurence Alison, Marie Eyre, Jonathan Crego and Alasdair Goodwill

The importance of context is a central theme of this book, and various situational and contextual features can affect decision-making but we need to draw a distinction. Even though some influences on decision-making may be attributable to the situation, it is not necessarily the case that those influences are exclusive to a specific type of situation or decision environment; in other words, some situational factors may influence decisions whether someone is acting in extremis, for example, in a critical incident environment, or merely making one of the many mundane decisions we each of us make every day of our lives. So, in this chapter, we turn our attention to some of the factors that have an impact on decision-making across a range of situations. With a focus on heuristics and biases, we shall review some of the generic features and also offer some practical examples of how those factors might impact on critical incidents and police investigative work more generally.

It is worth noting that we are in the land of probabilities not certainties here. It would be simplistic and, indeed, wrong to imply that all people in all situations will be affected, for example, by the biases below – they might affect someone's decisions, they might not. It depends on many things and the topic is far too big to do justice to it here. We merely offer a tour of empirically well-established influences on decision-making – common to many people and which may emerge in many decision environments.

Heuristics

Heuristics are cognitive 'short cuts' – rules of thumb that we employ to reduce complex problems, observations, interactions, decisions and so on into simple, efficient rules that work well in most circumstances. In the 1970s Kahneman and Tversky did much seminal work in the area. Not only did they borrow the term 'heuristic' (it had originated in the field of artificial intelligence study), they described these judgemental heuristics and their purpose, and set out the conditions in which they were likely to be employed.

Although the area has been much developed since, Tversky and Kahneman (1974) originally described three canonical judgemental heuristics: representativeness, availability, and anchoring/adjustment. They argued that people rely on heuristic principles to simplify judgemental decisions and that heuristics are likely to be deployed under conditions of uncertainty where important information is indeterminate or unavailable. Generally, heuristics can be useful aids to or means of decision-making – not least under time-pressured conditions – but they can, Tversky and Kahneman established, sometimes lead to severe and systematic errors. In the following sections, we shall describe some of the most empirically well-established heuristics and biases that affect decision-making for critical incident managers and lay people alike. First, though, we must cover some research on base rates and probabilities to familiarise ourselves with Kahneman and Tversky's work.

Base rates fallacy

Base rate information refers to reliable, broad-based information that is available to us, such as statistical information; for example, below, our base rate information tells us that the Blue Cab Company has 85 per cent of the city's cabs. Likewise, we have base rate information to help us predict the probability of sunshine in Florida versus Britain or the percentage of men or women in a random sample of people. However, Kahneman and Tversky (1973) reported a series of studies, which showed that when people make judgements, they often ignore or misuse base rate information and they termed this phenomenon the base rate fallacy. The best-known example of this is the 'cabs' problem (Kahneman and Tversky 1973) where participants are told that there are two cab companies in the city: the Blue Cab Company which has 85 per cent of the city cabs, and the Green Cab Company which has 15 per cent. A cab is involved in a hit-and-run accident and a witness later identified the cab as a green one. Under tests the witness was shown to be able to identify the colour of a cab correctly 80 per cent of the time but would confuse it with the other colour 20 per cent of the time. The participants are then asked whether it is more likely that the cab is green or blue. The majority of participants think the correct answer is green when, in fact, it is blue due to the high percentage of cabs in the town being blue. It is interesting to see how the tendency to ignore base rate information has been assimilated into the performance evaluation culture in recent years. There are statistics aplenty to suggest that crime rates have fallen in recent years but the fear of crime has not mirrored this decline (e.g. Collier 2005). However, public (mis) perceptions are not judged invalid; instead, reducing 'fear of crime' has become a measure of police performance to be found reported on any local authority website.

In another study Kahneman and Tversky (1973) presented participants with a series of short personality sketches. Participants were given descriptions of several individuals allegedly taken from a random sample of 100 professionals – engineers and lawyers. Participants were told either that there were 70 engineers and 30 lawyers or that there were 30 engineers and 70 lawyers. The participants were asked to assess the probability that the description belonged to an engineer rather than to a lawyer. The participants have different base rate information and should be guided by it – the probability that any description belongs to an engineer should be higher in the first condition. However, participants did not use the given probabilities to evaluate the likelihood of someone being an engineer; instead, they formed their judgements based on the degree to which the description was representative of a stereotypical lawyer or a stereotypical engineer. When they had no other information, the participants used prior probabilities correctly but this was effectively ignored when a description was introduced. Numerous studies involving similar tasks have shown that, generally, when participants make probability judgements, they will ignore or severely neglect base rate information. With regard to personal descriptions, Kahneman and Tversky (1980) argued that when people make judgements of diagnosicity from these personal descriptions, it is their use of the representativeness heuristic that causes them to ignore the base rate information.

The representativeness heuristic

The representativeness heuristic (Tversky and Kahneman 1974) is a heuristic wherein we assume commonality between things that are similar to a prototype. An individual then assesses the probability of an event by judging the degree to which that event corresponds to an appropriate prototypical model, such as sample and a population or an act to an actor (Payne, Bettman and Luce 1998). Of course, it is extremely helpful to be able to make a fast judgement when we encounter something novel by saying, 'Oh, this is similar to/ a typical case of X,' and proceed with a decision accordingly. The unfortunate downside is that problems can occur when there is no commonality between the two things we are comparing, they are merely superficially similar and/or when the prototype we have as a mental representation is awry. For example, we hear someone say, 'Oh, my granny has smoked 40 a day for decades; she's 95 and has never had a day's illness.' Granny is merely a lucky individual but anyone who uses her to *represent* the population of smokers as a whole – and argue on that basis that smoking isn't so bad really – is likely to allow one healthy granny to override the statistics, that is, they may tend to ignore all the base rate information on the probability that smoking will kill you long before your 95th birthday.

A policing example of assuming commonality was seen in the media's attempt to draw comparisons between the Yorkshire Ripper murders and the murders of five women who worked as prostitutes in Ipswich at the end of 2006. The media portrayed the murders as very similar with the only caveat being that Peter Sutcliffe, the Yorkshire Ripper, also murdered women who were not prostitutes. However, given the likelihood and prevalence (i.e. base rates) of serial murder it is highly unlikely that the cases, although similar, would share any significant commonality. The representativeness heuristic is similar to the idea that correlation does not assume causation; that is, the fact that two things are similar does not necessarily mean that one has any bearing upon the other.

This can lead to what is termed an illusory correlation (Chapman 1967) and can often be misleading when base rates are not considered. For example, a typical starting point in an investigation is to interview the individuals who last saw/spoke to the victim(s). In the case of the Ipswich murders, a man who had recently seen *all* the victims (i.e. high correlation) may be of great interest to the investigators but the typical base rate pattern of men who frequent prostitutes may suggest that they do so with many different prostitutes, thus making a high correlation of recent suspect–victim(s) interaction potentially no more than the 'norm'. In other words, the man may well have seen all the victims but he also happened to visit many other prostitutes in the same time period, who are all still alive.

Kahneman and Tversky (1973) further illustrated the use of the representativeness heuristic in a series of experiments, which showed that people often make predictions by selecting the outcome (e.g. occupation) that is most representative of the input (e.g. description of a person). Moreover, they showed that people's confidence in their prediction depends primarily upon the degree of representativness – that is, the quality of the match between the selected outcome and the input – and people tend to have little or no regard for the factors that limit predictive accuracy. Thus, as with the earlier experiment using lawyers and engineers, if you give people a description of a personality that happens to match the stereotype of librarians, people express great confidence in the prediction that a person is a librarian even if the description is unreliable, incomplete or outdated (Kahneman, Slovic and Tversky 1982).

One of the most striking manifestations of representativeness reasoning is to be found in the so-called conjunction fallacy. Here the predicted outcome is typically a combination of a high probability and a low probability event, where the first is a good and the second is a poor match for the model. The original demonstration of this conjunction fallacy devised by Tversky and Kahneman (1983) is described below:

> Linda is 31 years old, single, outspoken and very bright. She majored in philosophy. As a student, she was deeply concerned with issues of discrimination and social justice, and also participated in anti-nuclear demonstrations.

Participants were asked which of the two alternatives was more probable:

> Linda is a bank teller (T)
> Linda is a bank teller and is active in the feminist movement (T and F)

Now it is a straightforward mathematical fact that the probability of a conjunction of two events can never be greater than the probability of one of its constituents; sounds complicated in the abstract but if we pause to think, this makes sense – it's always going to be more likely that one thing will happen than two things will happen together, so T above is the correct answer. However, 85 per cent of Kahneman and Tversky's participants chose T and F. Tversky and Kahneman argued that this fallacy was induced by the representativeness heuristic as participants based their judgements on the *similarity* between the description of Linda and the two alternatives; since Linda had been described as having qualities that might typically be associated with being a feminist and T and F contained the word feminist, people believe that T and F is more probable.

Indeed, our use of this heuristic is so pervasive in the social processing that we undertake in everyday life that it can initially be a little hard to understand what the problem is with making the leap from the description of Linda's personality to forming judgements about her to deciding that it is more likely that she is a bank teller *and* an active feminist, but the facts about probabilities are bald: one thing is more likely than two things in conjunction – participants were asked about probabilities and the probabilities are not altered whether Linda's personality description contains many, moderate or no similarities to the statements; it is a fallacy to conclude that things in conjunction are more probable than one of its constituents.

Not everybody agrees that the representativeness heuristic is responsible for people's tendency to ignore base rate information when they make judgements. Nisbett, Borgida, Crandall and Reed (1976) offer another explanation; they suggest that base rate information is ignored in favour of individuating information because the former is remote, pallid and abstract while the latter is vivid, salient and concrete. Bar-Hillel (1980) has argued that the notion of relevance is central to why people ignore base rate information. He argued that participants ignore base rate information because they feel that it is irrelevant to the judgement they are making. One determinant of perceived relevance is causality; that is, we *will* take notice of information if it fits in as one of our links in a causal chain of who, what, why. For example, performance on the 'cabs' problem has been found to improve greatly if participants are told that there are equal numbers of blue and green cabs but that 85 per cent of the cabs involved in accidents are blue cabs. This provides participants with a causal connection between blue cabs and accidents, which facilitates utilisation of the base rate – it's now deemed relevant.

Despite differences in opinion on what causes people to ignore base rate information, we can at least agree that we necessarily select what information we will make use of. As social beings, we are always making sense of the world, processing it and inferring meaning from what goes on around us as we make decisions. As we strive to make sense of it, it is perhaps a natural human tendency to endeavour to seek patterns. The trouble is, we will do this even where none actually exists. This is known as the clustering illusion. If a data set is large enough, patterns will inevitably appear. For investigative decision-makers who, par excellence, are faced with having to make sense of incomplete information, it is important to be wary of the clustering illusion. There are, of course, many potential benefits in looking for patterns, especially in serial crime, but problems can occur if it is not acknowledged that patterns are not always meaningful. For example, an investigator may isolate the pattern of victimology and infer meaning from the fact that all victims in a murder investigation were prostitutes. It may or may not be meaningful; danger also lies in attributing the wrong meaning to a pattern, extrapolating from it and speculating, say, that the offender has a particular sexual motive – especially if lines of inquiry shift as a result. There may be no need for an explanation any more complicated than this one: people who work as prostitutes are more easily accessible; hence, they are available as – and, therefore, more vulnerable to becoming – victims. Even simpler, the pattern is meaningless.

Availability

Unlike representativeness, which involves comparing events to a particular model, availability as defined by Kahneman and Tversky (1973) involves evaluating events according to the ease by which they can be imagined or retrieved from memory. People tend to assume that if a number of instances can be readily recalled, then that instance occurs frequently and it is predicted with a high probability to happen again in the future; on the other hand, instances that are harder to recall are regarded as less frequent and less probable. We find it easier to retrieve the memory of the times the bus sailed past just as we reached the bus stop than we do to remember the times we caught the bus without bother; hence, we are likely to overestimate the probability of buses that arrive 30 seconds too early and even consider such an event typical when it is almost certainly not. Schwartz *et al.* (1991) suggested that it is not the number of instances recalled that is the most important determinant but the ease of recall. Therefore, availability relates primarily to feelings of effort or effortlessness of mental productions (Keren and Tiegen 2004).

Lifelong experience teaches us that, in general, we can recall instances of large frequencies better and faster than instances of less frequency; we know that likely occurrences are easier to imagine than unlikely ones and that the association connection between events is strengthened when the events frequently co-occur. As a result, availability is a useful clue for assessing frequency or probability by the ease with which they are retrieved from memory. Like other heuristics, it is useful in forming judgements with minimal effort but the availability heuristic is also affected by a number of additional factors that can affect retrievability.

If some information is more readily retrievable than other information, it follows that there is a possibility of systematic biases. There are different influencing factors, which are a result of cognitive constraints – for example, in the way human memory is organised (Evans 1989). One such cognitive constraint is familiarity, so a sample whose instances are easily retrieved will appear more numerous than a sample of equal frequency whose instances are less retrievable. This bias is due to the selective storage of the more memorable instances. Tversky and Kahneman (1974) carried out an experiment, which demonstrated that people judge words with K as the initial letter to occur more frequently in the English language than those with K as the third letter. Objectively, the answer is incorrect. The problem, they argue, is not that people do not know more words with K in the third position, but rather retrieval by initial letter is much easier. After all, nobody ever played 'I spy with my little eye, something with "k" in the middle', so the familiarity of retrieval by the first letter allows a greater number of words to come to mind and so they seem more frequent.

Another influencing factor is salience, which refers to distinctive stimuli that disproportionately engage attention; for example, actually seeing an event occur will have a greater impact on the subjective probability of such an event occurring than reading about the same event in, say, a journal article. Biases in availability can also arise from events that have been retrieved accurately from memory, but the events being recalled constitute a biased set of examples. This may be brought about by media coverage, which produces heavily distorted perceptions of risk. Evans (1989) argued that people radically overestimate the likelihood of dying from accidents compared with illnesses, due to the media providing highly selective coverage of violent and spectacular deaths but very little coverage of deaths by routine causes. Timing is also an influencing factor; recent occurrences are more likely to be available than earlier occurrences. For example, it is common for individuals' subjective probability of traffic accidents to rise after seeing a car overturned by the side of the road. Anecdotally, a police officer reported that he had immense sympathy for the complainant in the eighth rape investigation of his career. He was concerned that he might fail to treat the victim with due sensitivity because in every one of the first seven rape investigations he had led, the allegations had turned out to be false. As a result, he couldn't help but doubt the latest woman's account and he stated that he had to make a conscious effort to adjust his thoughts during the eighth case. He knew rationally that he ought to be as sensitive as possible towards the traumatised victim of a serious crime yet his past experience meant that doubts surfaced. It is easy enough to understand how such an experience might intrude into someone's thoughts and be a possible factor in decision-making, which simply wouldn't be present in another officer with a different experience.

Anchoring and adjustment

When people have to make judgements about uncertain quantities, they are often influenced by initial values and the initial values are usually suggested by an external source. These initial values serve as a salient comparison value or 'anchor' from which upwards or downwards adjustments are made. This process of anchoring and adjustment creates estimates that tend to be biased, or assimilated in the direction of the anchor. For example, when asked to estimate the length of the Mississippi River, people will give a higher estimate after they have been asked whether it is longer or shorter than 5,000 miles than when they have considered whether it is longer or shorter than 200 miles (Jacowitz and Kahneman 1995). In other words, you are likely to be anchored by 5,000 or 200, depending on which one was set as the initial value; so, who sets the anchor might be something to bear in mind next time you decide to haggle over the price of an item you wish to buy.

When the anchor is informative and relevant then, despite the inbuilt bias, anchoring and adjustment is clearly an adaptive heuristic. However, when people are uncertain they can be influenced by an irrelevant or completely implausible anchor value. For example, Tversky and Kahneman (1982) asked participants to spin a wheel of fortune to generate a starting number point between 0 and 100. The participants were asked whether the percentage of African countries in the United Nations was higher or lower than the starting number point they had just generated. They were then asked to give an absolute estimate value. These starting number points had a marked effect on estimates even though they were completely arbitrary. For example, the median estimate for participants who spun 10 as a starting point was 25 (African countries in the UN) while participants whose starting point was 65 gave a median estimate of 45. Originally this anchoring and adjustment heuristic was interpreted thus: people start by rejecting the anchor value and then adjust until they reach a satisfactory answer. However, adjustments tend to be insufficient and final estimates were thought to be biased because they require mental effort that people are either unwilling or unable to expend (Tversky and Kahneman 1973). This explanation would predict that the anchoring effect would vary with the amount of effortful thinking that individuals devote to the task. Accordingly, manipulations which should increase a person's willingness to engage in effortful adjustment were introduced; participants were offered incentives for accuracy or warned that the anchor value was generated randomly and would, therefore, not be a useful clue to the absolute estimate. They have not been found to reduce the anchoring effect (Tversky and Kahenman 1982; Wilson, Houston, Etling and Brekke 1996) so the idea that anchoring effects are caused by a failure to make the necessary mental effort did not seem to have much explanatory power.

One study gave some insight into the processes that contribute to anchoring effects and suggests mental effort is not relevant. Epley and Gilovich (2005) argued that the anchoring paradigm as described above initially involves people assessing whether the target value might be equal to an externally provided anchor. Because people evaluate hypotheses by trying to confirm them, this comparative assessment involves – even if only for one moment – activating information that is consistent with the anchor being the target value. When participants are then asked to give an absolute estimate value, the evidence they have just collected during the comparative assessment is disproportionately accessible; hence, it yields an estimate that is skewed in the direction of the initial anchor value (Jacowitz and Kahneman 1995). Further, such knowledge activation processes tend to be largely automatic and are, therefore, unlikely to be affected by additional effortful or deliberate thought.

However, not all anchors are externally provided. Many anchors are generated by individuals themselves to simplify an otherwise complicated assessment by calling to mind a value known to be close to the right answer but one that is in need of only slight adjustment. Tversky and Kahneman (1974) described these as self-generated anchors. Self-generated anchors differ from externally provided anchors because they are known from the beginning to be wrong and, thus, do not need to be considered as possible answers to the target question. For example, one might not know the cost of next year's Ford Focus but you can adjust up from the cost of last year's model to allow for inflation. These self-generated anchors do not activate the same accessibility mechanisms that novel externally provided anchors do; instead they require a process of effortful serial adjustment. Epley and Gilovich's (2005) experiments revealed that, unlike externally provided anchors, self-generated anchors are influenced by incentives for accuracy and by forewarning people of a likely anchoring bias in their judgements.

Lab studies give us valuable insights into influences on decision-making because they can tightly control variables to explore: for example, the detail of how spinning wheels of fortune can generate anchors that influence something as unrelated as UN membership estimates. In the policing domain (and, indeed, other professional and non-professional domains), anchoring may manifest as a tendency to rely too heavily – or 'anchor' – on one piece of information or aspect of a case when making decisions. This is often likely in high-profile investigations where the pressure to identify the culprit often outweighs the potential harm of arresting or focusing on the wrong suspect. Once a decision of investigative focus or arrest has been made, investigators tend to 'anchor' their views on the culprit and may actively reject information that goes against that decision (i.e. exonerating evidence or reasonable doubt evidence).

This occurred quite disastrously during the failed investigation into the murder of Rachel Nickell in 1992. The case attracted intense media interest due to the emotional and emotive details of the case. Sexually assaulted and stabbed 49 times, the young mother's murder had been witnessed by her two-year-old son. The child had reportedly been found clinging on to her body, pleading for mummy to wake up. Amidst the pressure to arrest, police anchored on the description of a socially and sexually unsuccessful 'outsider' provided by an offender profiler. They turned substantial efforts and resources towards an individual who fitted the profile – a 30-year-old virgin named Colin Stagg – to the exclusion of exonerating evidence and other lines of inquiry. Stagg became such a strong anchor that police implemented a 28-week 'honeypot' operation in which an undercover policewoman was used to try to lure Stagg into revealing guilty knowledge. When it eventually came to court, the trial judge dismissed the case with a stern rebuke for the investigation team.

It is worth repeating that although factors are necessarily discussed sequentially here, it should be borne in mind that, in practice, heuristics may overlap or operate in conjunction or through causal links with each other. In particular, heuristics are seen to derive from biases. For example, if investigators 'anchor' on a piece of information or a particular suspect, they may then tend to fail to look for or ignore evidence against that which they have already favoured or anchored to. This is known specifically as a confirmation bias and we shall discuss this and other biases in the next section.

Biases

Biases are used to describe deviations from the norm or as an inclination towards one judgement rather than another. Although biases do not in themselves indicate errors in judgement they are often regarded as systematic, suboptimal judgement. Biases can be the result of cognitive limitations, processing strategies, specific motivations and cognitive styles. They are traditionally regarded as being the by-product of heuristics (Keren and Tiegen 2004).

Belief persistence

Once a belief or opinion has been formed, it can be very resistant to change and this has been described, unsurprisingly enough, as belief persistence. Early work on this issue investigated the extent to which first impressions persevere when new information appears to disconfirm people's initial beliefs. Asch's (1946) study of impression formation suggested that, when adjectives were presented in sequence, the first adjectives in the list had more of an impact on people's impressions than the adjectives that were presented later. Asch gave participants a list of adjectives describing someone's personality, and when adjectives with positive connotations were presented first (e.g. intelligent, industrious) and the words with negative connotations were shown afterwards (e.g. stubborn, critical), the participants rated the person positively; but when the adjectives were presented the other way around, participants had a less positive view of the person described. Hence, subsequently introducing new (negative) evidence after the initial belief had been formed did not change the participants' initial belief about that person.

Later researchers investigated people's responses to the discreditation or invalidation of the 'old' evidence on which they had based their initial beliefs. Logically, the negation of the original evidence should result in the eradication of the belief. However, numerous studies have found that people stick to their beliefs even when the original evidential basis for those beliefs is shown to be flimsy or even downright fictitious. Ross, Lepper and Hubbard (1975) presented participants with a task requiring them to discriminate between genuine and fictitious suicide notes. They then supplied the participants with fabricated feedback on their performance so that they were led to believe that they had done either much better or much worse than average. Following the task, they told participants that the feedback had been fabricated. Despite this total invalidation of their apparent performance at the task, participants who had been given 'success' feedback still believed that they had performed better than the average while participants exposed to fabricated 'failure' feedback continued to believe that they had done much worse. Tversky and Kahneman explained this finding thus: they argued that people generate causal explanations to account for observed events. These causal explanations, scripts or schemas provide an effective way of organising and understanding social phenomena and, just like heuristics, they can be an efficient means of reducing processing time but once a causal explanation has been created, it becomes functionally independent of the original evidence so that if this evidence is discredited, the explanation remains intact to sustain the belief (Tversky and Kahneman 1973).

Davies (1997) examined whether belief persistence after evidential discrediting was related to the source of the explanations. In other words, did it make a difference whether participants generated their own explanations for an event as opposed to being provided with an explanation by the experimenter? He found that belief persistence was significantly greater for explanations that the participants themselves had generated. The elaboration likelihood model of persuasion (Petty and Cacioppo 1986) can be used to explain this finding. This model proposes that individuals who think about issues and evaluate arguments engage in central processing, whereas people who devote little thought to the issues and arguments engage in peripheral processing. Petty and Cacioppo (1986) argued that central processing leads to beliefs that are stronger, more persistent and more resistant to counter-persuasion than beliefs produced by peripheral processing. An important factor in belief persistence is the tendency for people to retrieve or generate evidence that confirms their initial belief (Ross and Anderson 1982).

Let us consider belief persistence in a policing context. Belief persistence effects may arise during the course of an investigation due to investigating officers generating story-like narratives in order to make sense of the information they gather (Ormerod, Barrett and Taylor 2005). This cognitive elaboration is needed to help determine who did what to whom and why; in turn, these causal explanations are required to convince jury members of the validity of the police account (Innes 2002). In this respect, it is a beneficial mechanism, but cognitive elaboration has been shown to result in attitudes that are stronger, more persistent and more resistant to counter-persuasion than attitudes produced by peripheral processing, so belief persistence is a potential danger. In Marshall and Alison's (in press) study of investigative biases and the role of offender profiles, they found belief persistence when participants exerted significant cognitive effort when generating initial hypotheses about a case, as would occur in a real police investigation.

It's possible, then, that individuals in an investigative context may be particularly susceptible to this phenomenon. This is not to say that such individuals are peculiarly stubborn types who are simply resistant to changing their minds but rather that they are subjected to features of their environment that may make some biases more likely; in concrete terms, the unknown (and the attendant need to hypothesise and generate causal explanations) is a central part of an investigative context in a way that is not the customary experience of other professionals. Shopkeepers do not have to hypothesise from day to day what each customer wants to buy; people walk right in and tell them – honestly. Teachers do not have to speculate on nor discover where the scene of today's lesson might be; the classroom is exactly where it was yesterday and there is minimal cognitive effort invested in finding it.

By contrast, major investigations are seldom straightforward and missing or ambiguous information can sometimes make for complex decision-making and often complicated theories. A danger here is that an investigative team can easily be drawn into developing *overly* complex theories and strategies to explain offending, that isn't necessarily warranted, causing errors in decision-making and judgement. The principle of Occam's razor can help to minimise this danger. Based on the idea that one should 'shave off' any unnecessary elaborations, it states that the most valid and reliable methods, theories or strategies are those that make the fewest assumptions and postulate the fewest hypothetical arguments. It perhaps makes more sense to look for complex solutions to complex problems but the best solution is often the simplest.

Let us consider a real-life case. Mabel Leyshon, a 90-year-old lady, died in her home. Her killer removed her heart and laid it on a silver platter; he drained the blood from her legs into a vessel, on the rim of which he left traces of his lip marks. He arranged candlesticks next to her body, placed a red candle on the mantelpiece as if it were an altar and positioned two pokers in the shape of a crucifix at her feet. Add in that the murder took place on a small windswept island off the coast of Wales dotted with ancient Druid ruins and relatively isolated rural communities, the case was bound for notoriety. Narratives of ritualistic sacrifice, vampires and the occult are easy to generate from such lurid and strange details but they are the stuff of movies rather than objective police investigations.

In terms of probabilities, it was extremely unlikely that there was an organised vampiric cult – or anybody else for that matter – travelling purposely to a small island to commit murder. In terms of prioritising suspects, base rate information suggests that murderers tend to live near their crime scene and so it was in this case. The offender had left a shoeprint when he broke into the pensioner's home. That and other forensic evidence were used to trace the 17-year-old from the same village who delivered the papers. Applying Occam's razor here would suggest: prioritise suspects nearby and use the available evidence. There may well be a grim fascination for some in speculating on the motives of such a murderer but for the purposes of solving the crime, more complicated explanations were redundant.

There may be other features of the broader context that overlay individual biases. A key element to consider in major inquiries is that of organisational inertia or momentum. Naturally, the organisation in any profession will have an impact on decision-makers, and the decision environment specific to policing is discussed in detail in Chapter 7 but we can pause for an example here. Organisational momentum, in investigative terms, refers to the ability to change direction in the midst of a major inquiry. Amidst intense media, public and organisational scrutiny, it can be particularly difficult to change direction from an established theory or suspect and admit that the original direction was wrong. However, the inability to recognise organisational momentum/inertia as a factor, favouring stability over responsiveness, say, can have catastrophic results. Therefore, it is essential to strike a balance between investigative stability (e.g. setting goals and hypothesising outcomes) and responsiveness to new information and priorities. A tendency to stick with an established theory or suspect, then, is a factor that may operate at the organisational or individual level so, in the next section, we shall discuss confirmation bias.

Confirmation bias

Confirmation bias is a phenomenon whereby decision-makers have been shown to actively seek out and assign more weight to evidence that confirms their hypothesis, and ignore or underweigh evidence that could disconfirm their hypothesis. This bias can result from belief persistence. Nickerson (1998: 175) noted that, 'If one were to attempt to identify the single problematic aspect of human reasoning that deserves attention above all others, the confirmation bias would have to be among the candidates for consideration.' Confirmation bias can be said to operate by two mechanisms – selective information search and biased interpretation of available information.

Selective information search

Watson (1960) was the first to demonstrate confirmation bias by devising the 2, 4, 6, concept attainment task. In this task, participants are told that the experimenter has a rule of thumb in mind that produces series of three numbers (each series of three is referred to as a 'triple'), an example of which is 2, 4, 6. The participants were told to produce triples of numbers in order to figure out the experimenter's rule of thumb. Every time they produced a triple, the experimenter indicated whether the triple conformed to the rule or not. The subjects were told that once they were sure of the correctness of their hypothesised rule, they should announce it. Participants seemed to test only 'positive' examples; that is, triples that would conform to their rule and thus confirm their hypothesis. What the participants did not do was attempt to falsify their hypotheses by testing triples that they believed did not conform to their rule. Therefore, people tend to seek information that they consider supportive of favoured hypotheses or existing beliefs, described as positive testing strategies. Conversely, they tend not to seek, and perhaps even to avoid, information that would be considered counter-indicative with regard to those hypotheses and beliefs and supportive of alternative possibilities (Koriat, Lichtenstein and Fischhoff 1980).

Studies have found that people interpret available information in ways that support their existing beliefs (Synder and Swann 1978); so why does this biased interpretation occur? For a number of reasons: firstly, if you entertain only a single possible explanation for an event or phenomenon, you preclude the possibility of interpreting data as supportive of any alternative explanation; in other words, you can't evaluate how data fit with other hypotheses if you have only come up with one to begin with. Secondly, this issue of restricted attention to a favoured hypothesis relates to the tendency to give greater weight to information that supports existing hypotheses (rather than giving weight to information that runs counter to them). This does not necessarily mean completely disregarding the counter-indicative information but it does mean that individuals are less receptive to it and therefore either discredit or explain away the information. Third is the clustering illusion we mentioned earlier; that is, people's tendency to see patterns in information that they are looking for regardless of whether the patterns are there or not.

It is pretty well established, then, that people are generally biased towards confirming the hypotheses and beliefs they already hold. Even if you give two different hypotheses and the same set of evidence, people will tailor it to support their own beliefs. An early study by Kelley (1950) showed that students' perceptions of the social qualities of a guest lecturer were influenced by what they were led to expect from a prior description of the individual, showing that people with initially conflicting views can examine the same evidence and each still finds reasons to support their existing opinions. Similarly, where information is ambiguous, it is more likely to be seen as confirming rather than disconfirming prior hypotheses (Ross and Anderson 1982).

The bias also operates in a law enforcement context. Ask and Granhag's (2005) study of confirmation bias in criminal investigations has shown that participants' processing of case material was influenced by the hypothesis that had initially been presented to them (either suspect's motive or alternative culprit); further, as the participants had all been presented with a fixed amount of information, confirmation bias here was not a result of selective information searching but rather that they were interpreting the available information to be consistent with their hypotheses. In their study of investigative bias and offender profiles, Marshall and Alison (in press) found evidence of the confirmation bias for participants who engaged in cognitive elaboration. These participants appeared to be more influenced by a profile that supported their judgements than a profile that was incongruous. Therefore, the influence of a profile in an investigation may depend on the degree to which the profile is consistent or inconsistent with an investigating officer's belief about a case. It is also likely that investigating officers interpret information contained within offender profiles in ways that support their existing beliefs by giving greater weight to information that supports their hypotheses than to information that runs counter to them.

Confirmation bias seriously derailed the police inquiry into the

Yorkshire Ripper murders in the late 1970s and early 1980s when the hoaxer who became known as Wearside Jack sent in a tape to police, claiming to be the Ripper and taunting that they were nowhere near to catching him. Adhering to the hypothesis that the man on the tape was the Ripper, confirmation bias led the investigation team to implicate only men with Wearside accents. In an inquiry where the (pre-computers) incident room floor was literally collapsing under the weight of information in filing cabinets, this direction gathered organisational momentum and, in a clear example of selective information search, information on suspects who didn't have the same accent as the man on the tape was all but ignored. Peter Sutcliffe – with a Yorkshire accent – eventually killed 13 women.

Hindsight bias

Hindsight bias is the inclination to see past events as having been predictable and reasonable to expect even though such information was not known and/or could not have been known *at the time*. Everybody has had the experience of believing that they 'knew all along' the outcome of a football game or a political election. These 'natural' hindsight experiences seem especially likely to occur when the focal event has well-defined alternative outcomes (e.g. win–lose), when the outcome has emotional or moral significance and when the event is subject to imaginative consideration before the outcome is known (Hawkins and Hastie 1990). For example, Labine and Labine (1996) asked participants to examine mental health professionals' treatment of patients. Participants judged that violent behaviour had been more foreseeable in a patient who they knew, in hindsight, had actually become violent. Similarly, Hawkins and Hastie (1999) found that an environmental accident was judged to have been more foreseeable (and hence the company was more liable for the outcome) when the participants knew such an accident had actually occurred.

So, why might hindsight bias occur? Researchers have identified three different mechanisms to help explain why people are prone to hindsight bias: memory impairment, biased reconstruction and motivation. Fischhoff (1975) suggests that being told the outcome information impairs memory by altering the person's knowledge about the question or event, either by altering or deleting memory traces or by rendering them less accessible. According to Fischhoff, outcome information is automatically encoded into a person's existing knowledge structure, and this results in an inevitable permanent modification of their prior representation of the question. Put simply, people cannot undo the knowledge they now have in their memory any more than someone can go back to undo a wrinkle or a grey hair once it has appeared.

Other researchers have specified more precisely in the memory processing stages where hindsight bias originates. These researchers have proposed that it does not originate in the encoding stage; instead, hindsight bias originates in the retrieval stage. Because outcome information is encoded more recently than the original prediction, it is fresher and newer and this makes it more accessible during the retrieval stage. This accounts for why the outcome information plays a more important role in the hindsight judgement (Hell, Gigerenzer, Gauggel, Mall and Muller 1988).

The sharp-eyed reader will have noticed that this contradicts some explanations for belief persistence, which findings are sometimes interpreted as a memory bias towards the oldest rather than the newest information. So in which direction is memory biased? The answer is – it depends. The bias towards information that was encoded first (i.e. the oldest) is known as a primacy effect. Conversely, the preference for the most recently encoded (newest) information is known as a recency effect. Some may wish to claim that academics just want to have their cake and eat it; others may be spurred on to delve further and untangle the many different conditions under which primacy or recency effects might obtain. Perhaps we can take comfort that there is no bias towards preferential encoding/retrieval of information that is presented in the middle; let us at least endorse our view on the complexity of decision-making and the many factors therein.

With respect to hindsight bias, other researchers have highlighted biased reconstruction as a major source (Hoffrage, Hertwig and Gigerenzer 2000). This is how it has been explored: if you tell people the correct outcome of an event and then ask participants what their original estimate was, then, naturally enough, some will be able to remember and some will not, so researchers have been able to exploit this natural variation in good or not so good memories. People who do remember should be able to reproduce their estimate. However, people who have forgotten are forced to reconstruct their estimate and are likely to utilise the outcome information as an anchor (see earlier section on anchoring). Schwartz and Stahlberg (2003) demonstrated how participants use this anchor by giving them feedback about their performance. They found that the direction and the magnitude of the hindsight bias was determined by people's subjective assumptions about how close or distant their original estimate had been from the outcome information. Hindsight biases were also more pronounced when participants were told that their initial estimate had been good than when participants were told that their estimate had been poor.

While cognitive explanations have received a large amount of attention there is a small body of research that has shown that hindsight bias can be governed or moderated by motivational factors. Verplanken and Pieters (1988) proposed a distinction between 'person-related' and 'decision-related' motives. Person-related motives could be defined by individual differences. Campbell and Tesser (1983) showed a correlation between the magnitude of hindsight bias and individual differences in the need to maintain a favourable image of oneself (known as favourable self-preservation). They also found that self-rated ego involvement in the task was also correlated with the magnitude of the hindsight bias. However, Pohl (1999) conducted a review of empirical studies and concluded that there is insufficient reliable evidence to support the association between individual differences and hindsight bias so, in this respect, the jury is still out unless or until more empirical evidence is garnered. Decision-related motives do, though, vary as a function of the task involvement. Mark, Boburka, Eyssell, Cohen and Mellor (2003) examined how hindsight bias can result from a self-protecting process, which occurs when the participants feel responsible for the negative outcome. Using a stock-marked decision game, Mark *et al.* showed that participants perceive negative, self-relevant outcomes as less foreseeable than neutral observers do.

Perhaps it is worth pausing to consider how this might apply in the world beyond the lab. Let's suppose the television-watching public see reports of tragic outcomes of a critical incident on the news. Hindsight bias leads them to judge events as having been foreseeable. Moreover, they are more likely to be prey to hindsight bias than those professional responders who actually managed the incident. The outcomes are negative *and* self-relevant for responders so – in line with Mark *et al.*'s findings above – responders are less likely to judge events as having been foreseeable than a neutral public; the difference between the two groups with regard to perceptions of responsibility may have a detrimental impact on public relationships in the long term. Importantly, this assumes at best that the public is a neutral observer; in reality, they may well be influenced by a 'who's to blame?' framework fostered by the media. We can see, though, how hindsight bias may play a part in perpetuating the conditions of a blame culture.

The hindsight bias, then, has important implications for the fields of psychology and law, and Villejoubert, O'Keefe, Alison and Cole (2006) described how hindsight biases could affect people's judgements of negligence in police shooting incidents. Overall, participants who had hindsight knowledge (participants were told it transpired that there had been no gun) were significantly more inclined to believe that the officer should be blamed for the outcome of his decision than those in the foresight condition (i.e. participants not told that there was no gun). Their key finding was that motivational factors played an important role in judgements. Participants playing the police officer responded in a bias-free way reflecting, they argued, possible self-serving motives.

It is likely we can all bring to mind real cases of shooting and other incidents where police or other professionals have got it 'wrong', though we should, perhaps, reflect that it is inherent in the very word 'news' that it focuses on the novel, the unusual, and it is often due to their rarity that critical incidents make the news; as members of the public, it seems we are all happy to make a judgement and form a view. Due criticism is, of course, necessary and desirable as it is an essential springboard to improvement but one should at least recognise the impact of factors such as hindsight bias before we categorise decisions as errors and condemn individuals unfairly for things they somehow ought to have acted upon, which, in truth, they couldn't possibly have known at the time.

Other influences on decision-making

It makes sense that there exist many ways for humans to conserve cognitive effort besides the relatively few heuristics we have discussed here; thus, there are many other influences on decision-making besides established heuristics and biases to be considered, which are not exclusive to the critical incident environment. As with heuristics, they can be extremely beneficial but also carry similar inherent dangers; that is, any rough and ready 'one size fits all' solution is never going to be perfectly tailored to a situation and can lead to decision errors as a result. In this section, we shall focus on some that – though they are generic findings that may affect decision-making in many situations – have been chosen because they marry fairly well with some aspects of a critical incident environment though they are certainly not exhaustive.

Stereotyping

To avoid attribution errors and mistaken inferences, we are not making a crude statement that stereotyping is attributable to individuals in the emergency services. Rather, there are features – such as time pressure and intense cognitive demands – that typify a critical incident decision-making environment. In turn, this may mean people have a greater tendency to resort to stereotypical processing. In studies of time pressure, as well as finding that primacy effects were significantly more pronounced when time pressure was high as opposed to low, Kruglanski and Freund (1983) also found that time pressure significantly enhanced the tendency towards stereotyped judgements.

Even someone completely unfamiliar with the field of psychology and heuristics and biases research will understand the problems of stereotyping. A stereotype is defined as a standardised conception or image of a specific group of people or objects. Research has shown that stereotypical expectations play a major role in the way that information about a person is processed, what information is preferentially retrieved from memory and the way these expectations affect impressions and judgements. Tajfel (1981) suggested that stereotypes result from the need for coherence, simplicity, and predictability in the face of an inherently complex social environment. Stereotyping can be explained therefore as an inevitable by-product of normal cognitive processes in that people are cognitive misers; that is, they conserve mental resources when they are overwhelmed by socio-environmental complexity (Hamilton 1981) and the environment of a critical incident can be extremely complex. Macrae, Hewstone and Griffiths (1993) showed that, under conditions of cognitive overload, people preferentially recall stereotype-consistent information, process stereotype-consistent information faster than non-stereotypic information and, given the choice, preferentially search for stereotype-matching information (Johnson and Macrae 1994).

The issue is not a matter of straightforward individual differences regarding prejudiced people because Devine (1989) showed that people automatically activate stereotype content in the presence of a member of the stereotyped group irrespective of high or low prejudice. However, subsequent processes do vary as a function of prejudice level. For people low in prejudice, the stereotype content is replaced, via controlled cognitive processes, by more egalitarian personal beliefs about the group. In contrast, highly prejudiced people's personal beliefs simply match the activated stereotype content. Low-prejudiced people therefore intentionally inhibit stereotype content. However, Devine demonstrated that this intentional inhibition was only possible in contexts of sufficient attentional resources so it is a concern that, in some circumstances, people may stereotype others despite an explicit intention to do otherwise (Fiske 1989). Also pertinent to decision-making in the typical critical incident environment is the finding that as well as facilitating access to confirmatory material, stereotypes also inhibit access to disconfirmatory material (Dijksterhuis and van Knippenberg 1996); this may compound the tendency towards confirmation bias which we mentioned earlier as a potential difficulty to be aware of in an investigative context.

Primacy and recency effects

The primacy and recency effects we outlined earlier can also pose problems. Marshall and Alison (2006) found that offender profiles were judged more influential when presented before rather than after the presentation of a suspect. Kruglanski and Freund (1983) argued that these primacy effects can be interpreted as 'epistemic freezing', whereby the decision-maker becomes less aware of plausible alternative hypotheses and/or inconsistent bits of evidence that compete with a given judgement. Individuals may therefore attain closure in the informational sequence and be relatively impervious to later information.

Anderson (1976) theorised that primacy effects may occur because of decreases in attention shown to successive items of information. He found that primacy effects were eliminated in conditions where participants were instructed to attend to all the pieces of information including those presented later in the series. Hence, individuals' motivation to think acts as a moderator of this primacy effect, but such cognitive effort is easy to induce in a lab setting; it may be unrealistic or even platitudinous (albeit desirable) to recommend it in a critical incident setting. Recall our example of unwilling stereotyping; it manifested even among the low-prejudiced when attentional demands were high, so it is not always enough merely to urge people to think or to trust that their motivation will suffice as decision aids. Attentional demands may supersede a person's best intentions and, in a real-life incident, the volume of information alone may exceed cognitive resources.

Communication

Even the ways in which people communicate may have an impact on decision-making. For example, Reagan, Mosteller and Youtz (1989) reported 282 different verbal expressions to express states of uncertainty in English (e.g. probably, likely, possibly). Numerous studies have shown that verbal probabilities are very vague (Tiegen and Brun 1995) and the most robust finding is that variability is very high between individuals when judging the same term; people perceive the meaning of verbal probabilities consistently but differently from each other.

Despite our earlier discussion about people's bias towards ignoring base rate information, it is not altogether neglected when processing probability phrases. For example, contextual information about the perceived base rate probability of an event can affect the interpretation of probability phrases. Compare the two statements: 'It is likely that it will rain in Liverpool, England, next June' and 'It is likely that it will rain in Barcelona, Spain, next June.' In this example, the expression 'likely' will receive a different numerical interpretation due to the base-rate probability of it raining in June in these two cities.

Using a clinical scenario, Weber and Hilton (1990) demonstrated that the effects of context on the numerical interpretation of verbal probabilities could be attributed to the perceived base-rate probability of the predicted events. They also demonstrated that another contextual factor which influences interpretation is the perceived severity of the event. Bonnefon and Villejoubert (2006), again using a medical scenario, demonstrated that the same probability word was interpreted as a higher numerical probability when it referred to a more severe condition (deafness) than when it referred to a less severe but equally prevalent condition (insomnia). If the severity of an event strengthening people's understanding of probability phrases is a transferable finding (i.e. it applies in investigative as well as clinical decision environments), this tendency may have decision-making implications in an investigative context if an SIO were to hypothesise to his or her team by saying, 'I think X is *probably* the man who killed these children.'

Ambiguity and Barnum effects

Earlier, we referred to some of the particular difficulties of an investigative decision-making environment and mentioned how decision-makers have to make sense of ambiguous information to a degree that is not the customary experience of other professionals; recall also that humans may be subject to clustering illusions. Studies have shown that ambiguous information can lead individuals to construct meaning from the ambiguity by a process of 'creative interpretation'.

The Barnum effect – named after the circus entrepreneur who said he always tried to 'have a little something for everyone' – is a term coined by Meehl (1956) and it refers to the tendency to regard vague, high base rate, but non-obvious statements as self-descriptive. This phenomenon has been used to explain why people find horoscopes, fortune telling and graphology convincing (Dickson and Kelly 1985; Fichter and Sunerton 1983). In a classic illustration of Barnum effects, Forer (1946) gave a personality test to his students, completely ignored their answers and gave each student the same evaluation, which included statements such as, 'You have a need for other people to admire you and yet you tend to be critical of yourself.' He asked them to evaluate from 0–5 (5 meaning excellent) how accurate they thought the evaluation was. The class average was 4.26.

Hence, Forer convinced people that he could successfully read their character when the results were, in fact, attributable to the natural human tendency to strive to make sense of ambiguity. Indeed, Beyerstein (2001) argued that because humans are constantly trying to make sense out of the barrage of disconnected information we face daily, and become so good at making reasonable scenarios out of disjointed information, we sometimes make sense of nonsense. He stated that individuals would often fill in the blanks and provide coherence to what we see, read or hear, even though evidence would reveal the data as vague, confusing and inconsistent. When Snyder, Shenkel and Lowery (1977) conducted a review of 25 years of research on the Barnum effect, they reported that all people are susceptible to this phenomenon, especially if they believe the statements are tailored specifically to them.

In a policing example of Barnum effects, Alison, Smith and Morgan (2003) gave participants a 'pen portrait' description of either offender A or B, each of whom was distinctly different. When given the same ambiguous offender profile, the majority of participants rated the profile as at least somewhat accurate, thus showing how people strive to find meaning in the information. Thus, there is a danger that officers may exaggerate the merits of information that fits a particular suspect without appreciating the extent to which that information could also fit a wide range of other individuals.

Conclusion

In this chapter, we have covered influences on decision-making that obtain across a range of situations and which are not necessarily exclusive to the critical incident environment. We discussed base-rate fallacies, conjunction fallacies and illusory correlations; representativeness heuristics, availability heuristics and anchoring and adjustment; hindsight biases, confirmation biases and several other factors that may undermine the erstwhile idea of humans as exclusively rational decision-makers.

Indeed, influences on decision-making constitutes such a vast research area that a book rather than a chapter could be devoted to it without difficulty. As a consequence, we have but scratched the surface but there is a more important consideration. In such a research area, it becomes comparatively easy to find sufficient empirical evidence to support almost any argument or draw the facile conclusion that a fudgy compromise is acceptable – 'Well, it's a bit of both' or 'The answer lies somewhere in the middle'. Before anyone is tempted to do so, consider our earlier example of primacy and recency effects. In information recall, sometimes there will be a bias due to recency effects; sometimes, there will be a bias due to primacy effects. What resolutely does not happen is that 'middle effects' emerge. Indeed, it is important to note that this is manifestly the (almost only) way to get it wrong so it is vital not to settle for the easy answers in complex research areas.

Thus, having begun the chapter by stating that we were going to consider influences that obtain across different contexts (and, perhaps, inviting a disregard for context), we end by urging its importance. Investigating two or three of the most disparate, ostensibly unconnected variables imaginable may throw up relationships between them somewhere, somehow, in some situation. Of course, we do want to know the relationship between specific variables but the approach should not be too narrow or reductionist. Decontextualised research can bring particular problems in complex areas. Instead, we must embrace approaches that help us to discover the relationships between the individuals, the different factors and influences to which they are subjected and, reciprocally, which they shape, while taking sufficient account of the social and organisational environment in which they exist and with which they interact.

References

Alison, L., Smith, M. and Morgan, K. (2003) 'Interpreting the accuracy of offender profiles', *Psychology, Crime and Law,* 9: 185–95.

Anderson, N. (1976) 'Equity judgments as information integration', *Journal of Personality and Social Psychology*, 33: 291–9.

Asch, S. (1946) 'Forming impressions on personality', *Journal of Abnormal and Social Psychology*, 41: 258–90.

Ask, K. and Granhag, P. (2005) 'Motivational sources of confirmation bias in criminal investigations: the need for cognitive closure', *Journal of Investigative Psychology and Offender Profiling*, 2: 43–63.

Bartlett, F.C. (1932) *Remembering: an experimental and social study*. Cambridge: Cambridge University Press.

Bar-Hillel, M. (1980) 'The base rate fallacy in probability judgements', *Acta Psychologica*, 44: 211–33.

Beyerstein, B.L. (2001) 'Fate to skeptical inquirer', in P. Kurtz (ed.), *Skeptical odysseys: personal accounts by the world's leading paranormal inquirers* (pp. 43–62). Amherst, NY: Prometheus Books.

Bonnefon, J. and Villejoubert, G. (2006) 'Tactful or doubtful? expectations of politeness explain the severity bias in the interpretation of probability phrases', *Psychological Science*, 17: 747–51.

Campbell, J. and Tesser, A. (1983) 'Motivational interpretations of hindsight bias: an individual difference analysis', *Journal of Personality and Social Psychology*, 51: 605–20.

Chapman, L.J. (1967) 'Illusory correlation in observational report', *Journal of Verbal Learning and Verbal Behavior*, 5: 151–5.

Collier, P.M. (2005) 'Managing police performance', in J. Hartley and A. Pike, *Managing to improve public services: a report by the advanced institute of management research public service fellows*. London: AIM Research/ESRC.

Davies, M. (1997) 'Belief persistence after evidential discrediting: The impact of generated versus proved explanations on the likelihood of discredited outcomes', *Journal of Experimental Social Psychology*, 33: 561–78.

Devine, P. (1989) 'Stereotypes and prejudice: their automatic and controlled components', *Journal of Personality and Social Psychology*, 56: 5–18.

Dickson, D. and Kelly, I. (1985) 'The "Barnum effect" in personality assessment: a review of the literature', *Psychological Reports*, 57: 367–82.

Dijksterhuis, A. and van Knippenberg, A. (1996) 'The knife that cuts both ways: facilitated and inhibited access to traits as a result of stereotype activation', *Journal of Experimental Social Psychology*, 32: 271–88.

Epley, N. and Gilovich, T. (2005) 'When effortful thinking influences judgemental anchoring: differential effects of forewarning and incentives on self-generated and externally provided anchors', *Journal of Behavioral Decision Making*, 18: 199–212.

Evans, J. (1989) *Bias in human reasoning: causes and consequences*. Hillsdale, NJ: Erlbaum.

Fichter, C. and Sunerton, D. (1983) 'Popular horoscopes and the "Barnum effect"', *Journal of Psychology*, 114: 123–4.

Fischhoff, B. (1975) 'Hindsight foresight: The effect of outcome knowledge on judgement under uncertainty', *Journal of Experimental Psychology: Human Perception and Performance*, 1: 288–99.

Fiske, S. (1989) 'Examining the role of intent: towards understanding its role in stereotyping and prejudice', in J. Uleman and J. Bargh (eds), *Unintended thought*. New York: Guilford.

Forer, B. (1949) 'The fallacy of personal validation: a classroom demonstration of gullibility', *Journal of Abnormal and Social Psychology*, 44: 118–23.

Gilbert, D., Fiske, T. and Lindzey, G. (1998) *Handbook of social psychology*. Boston: McGraw-Hill.

Hamilton, D. (1981) *Cognitive processes in stereotyping and intergroup behaviour*. Hillsdale, NJ: Erlbaum.

Haugvedt, C. and Wegener, D. (1994) 'Message order effects in persuasion: an attitude strength perspective', *Journal of Consumer Research*, 21: 205–18.

Hawkins, S. and Hastie, R. (1990) 'Hindsight: biased judgements of past events after the outcomes are known', *Psychological Bulletin*, 107: 311–27.

Hell, W., Gigerenzer, G., Gauggel, S., Mall, M. and Mueller, M. (1988) 'Hindsight bias: an interaction of automatic and motivational factors?', *Memory and Cognition*, 16: 533–8.

Hoffrage, U., Hertwig, R. and Gigerenzer, G. (2000) 'Hindsight bias: a by-product of knowledge updating?', *Journal of Experimental Psychology, Memory and Cognition*, 26: 566–81.

Innes, M. (2002) 'The process structures of police homicide investigations', *British Journal of Criminology*, 42: 669–88.

Jacowitz, K. and Kahneman, D. (1995) 'Measures of anchoring in estimation tasks', *Personality and Social Psychology Bulletin*, 21: 1161–7.

Johnson, J. and Macrae, C. (1994) 'Changing social stereotypes: the case of the information seeker', *European Journal of Social Psychology*, 24: 237–65.

Johnson, J., Cain, L., Falke, T., Hayman, J. and Perillo, E. (1985) 'The "Barnum effect" revisited: cognitive and motivational factors in the acceptance of personality descriptions', *Journal of Personality and Social Psychology*, 49: 1378–91.

Kahneman, D. and Tversky, A. (1973) 'On the psychology of prediction', *Psychological Review*, 80: 237–51.

Kahneman, D. and Tversky, A. (1980) 'Loss aversion in riskless choice: a reference dependent model', *Journal of Economic Behavior and Organization*, 1: 39–60.

Kahneman, D., Slovic, P. and Tversky, A. (1982) *Judgement under uncertainty: heuristics and biases*. Cambridge: Cambridge University Press.

Kelley, H. (1950) 'The warm-cold variable in first impressions of persons', *Journal of Personality*, 18: 431–9.

Keren, G. and Tiegen, K. (2004) 'Yet another look at the heuristics and biases approach', in D. Koehler and N. Harvey (eds), *Blackwell handbook of judgement and decision making*. Oxford: Blackwell Publishing.

Koriat, A., Lichtenstein, S. and Fischoff, B. (1980) 'Reasons for confidence', *Journal of Experimental Psychology: Human Learning and Memory*, 6: 107–18.

Kruglanski, A. and Freund, T. (1983) 'The freezing and unfreezing of lay-inferences: effects on impressional primacy ethnic stereotyping and numerical anchoring', *Journal of Experimental Social Psychology*, 19: 448–68.

Labine, S. and Labine, G. (1996) 'Determinations of negligence and the hindsight bias', *Law and Human Behavior*, 20: 501–16.

Macrae, C., Hewstone, M., and Griffiths, R. (1993) 'Processing load and memory for stereotype-based information', *European Journal of Social Psychology*, 23: 77–87.

Mark, M., Boburka, R., Eyssell, K., Cohen, L. and Mellor, L. (2003) ' "I couldn't have seen it coming". The impact of negative self-relevant outcomes on retrospections about foreseeability', *Memory*, 11: 443–54.

Marshall, B. and Alison, L. (in press) 'Stereotyping, congruence and presentation order: interpretative biases in utilizing offender profiles', *Psychology, Crime and Law*.

Meehl, P. (1956) 'Wanted – a good cook-book', *American Psychologist*, 11: 262–72.

Nickerson, R. (1998) 'Confirmation bias: a ubiquitous phenomenon in many guises', *Review of General Psychology*, 2: 175–220.

Nisbett, R., Borgida, E., Crandall, R. and Reed, H. (1976) 'Popular induction: information is not necessarily informative', in D. Kahneman., P. Slovic and A. Tversky (eds), *Judgement under uncertainty: heuristics and biases*. Cambridge: Cambridge University Press.

Ormerod, T.C., Barrett, E.C. and Taylor, P.J. (2005) *Investigative sense-making in criminal contexts*. Proceedings of the seventh international NDM conference. J.M.C. Schraagen (ed.) Amsterdam, The Netherlands, June.

Payne, J., Bettman, J. and Luce, M. (1998) 'Behavioral decision research: an overview', in M. Birnbaum (ed.), *Measurement, judgment and decision making*. USA: Academic Press.

Petty, R. and Cacioppo, J. (1986) *Communication and persuasion: central and peripheral routes to attitude change*. New York: Springer-Verlag.

Pohl, R. (1998) 'The effects of feedback source and plausibility of hindsight bias', *European Journal of Cognitive Psychology*, 10: 191–212.

Reagan, R., Mosteller, F. and Youtz, C. (1989) 'Quantitative meanings of verbal probability expressions', *Journal of Applied Psychology*, 74: 433–442.

Ross, L. and Anderson, C. (1982) 'Shortcomings in the attribution process: on the origins and maintenance of erroneous social assessments', in A. Tversky, D. Kahneman. and P. Slovic (eds), *Judgement under uncertainty: heuristics and biases*. Cambridge: Cambridge University Press.

Ross, L., Lepper, M. and Hubbard, M. (1975) 'Perseverance in self-perception and social perception: biased attributional process in the debriefing paradigm', *Journal of Personality and Social Psychology*, 32: 880–92.

Schwartz, S. and Stahlberg, D. (2003) 'Strength of hindsight bias as a consequence of meta-cognitions', *Memory*, 11: 455–72.

Schwartz, N., Strack, F., Hilton, D. and Naderer, G. (1991) 'Base rates, representativeness and the logic of conversation: the contextual relevance of "irrelevant" information', *Social Cognition*, 9: 67–84.

Snyder, C., Shenkel, R. and Lowery, C. (1977) 'Acceptance of personality interpretations: the "Barnum effect" and beyond', *Journal of Consulting Clinical Psychology*, 45: 104–114.

Synder, M. and Swann, W. (1978) 'Hypothesis-testing processes in social interaction', *Journal of Personality and Social Psychology*, 36: 1202–12.

Tajfel, H. (1981) *Human groups and social categories: studies in social psychology.* Cambridge: Cambridge University Press.

Teigen, K. and Brun, W. (1995) 'Yes, but it is uncertain: direction and communicative intention of verbal probabilistic terms', *Acta Psychologica*, 88: 233–58.

Tversky, A. and Kahneman, D. (1974) 'Judgement under uncertainty: heuristics and biases', *Science*, 185, 1124–31.

Tversky, A. and Kahneman, D. (1982) 'Judgements of and by representativeness', in D. Kahneman., P. Slovic and A. Tversky (eds), *Judgement under uncertainty: heuristics and biases*. Cambridge: Cambridge University Press.

Tversky, A. and Kahneman, D. (1983) 'Extensional versus intuitive reasoning: the conjunction fallacy in probability judgement', *Psychological Review*, 91: 293–315.

Verplanken, B. and Pieters, R. (1988) 'Individual differences in reverse hindsight bias: I never thought something like Chernobyl would happen. Did I?', *Journal of Behavioral Decision Making*, 1: 131–47.

Villejoubert, G., O'Keeffe, C., Alison, L. and Cole, J. (2006) 'Hindsight bias and shooting incidents', in D. Canter (ed.), *Psychological aspects of legal processes*. Liverpool: IA-IP Publishing.

Watson, P. (1960) 'On the failure to eliminate hypotheses in a conceptual task', *Quarterly Journal of Experimental Psychology*, 12: 129–40.

Weber, E. and Hilton, D. (1990) 'Contextual effects in the interpretation of probability words: perceived base rate and severity of events', *Journal of Experimental Psychology: Human Perception and Performance*, 16: 781–9.

Wilson, T., Houston, C., Etling, K. and Brekke, N. (1996) 'A new look at anchoring effects: basic anchoring and its antecedents', *Journal of Experimental Psychology: General*, 4: 387–402.

Zadeh, L. (1965) 'Fuzzy sets', *Information and Control*, 8: 338–53.

Chapter 9

The emotional legacy of homicide investigations

*Jonathan Crego, Laurence Alison,
Jennie Roocroft and Marie Eyre*

Introduction

If a lay person were given a definition of a critical incident and asked to give an example, murder inquiries would likely be the first (and probably immediate) answer as such events have an obvious and very emotional impact on a community and the perceived safety of its citizens; yet, thus far, the emotionality of critical incidents in general and homicide investigations in particular, have remained relatively neglected as a research topic. This may be due to methodological issues such as access to officers involved, and time constraints placed upon such individuals – they rarely have time to participate in experimental studies with time and cost implications. Nonetheless, assessment and evaluation of such incidents is vitally important. In this chapter, we consider emotion within a policing context on the premise that an understanding of this issue is crucial to anyone interested in critical incidents. We begin with a brief introduction, then, in relation to the literature, go on to discuss some of the issues in researching emotions. In the second section, we discuss emotions within a policing environment and conclude by outlining the main findings of a case-based 10kV study into the emotional impact of homicide investigations.

Researching emotions

In the past decade, there has been a revised interest in examining the relationship between emotions and decision-making but a majority of this research has been directed by the field of economics and a significant proportion has utilised the more traditional experimental approach. Valuable though it is to understand how people weigh up probabilities to decide which of several options is most profitable, such studies offer limited insight into emotions involved in police decision-making. Furthermore, although the resurgence of interest in the topic is a step in the right direction, research has primarily focused on those emotions that the decision-maker *predicts* they will experience should they make a certain decision (Lucey and Dowling 2005) rather than those that are actually experienced by the decision-maker whether that be: a) at the time of the decision or b) after the decision has been made; for example, being asked how you *might* feel if you choose to purchase Car A instead of Car B does little to replicate the alarm and urgency felt when a police officer must decide immediately whether to make a lethal force decision. Neither can the officer simply leave the experimental lab and go home unscathed by the decision he or she makes in such a situation. The long-term emotional legacy of such policing decisions is very real.

In the literature, different terms are used to describe emotions elicited at different points in the decision-making process. *Predicted* emotions are known as 'anticipated'. Alternatively, they are described as 'real' if they are actually felt (whether it be at the time of making the decision or later on, after the event). As described in Chapter 3, the 10,000 Volts and Hydra technologies provide new techniques for exploring the impact emotions have on decision-making at different points within a given scenario – prior to the decision, at the time of the decision and after the decision has been made. These simulation/prebrief/debrief approaches to research can also facilitate understanding of the emotions elicited within real and simulated critical incidents.

Positive and negative

New methods and technologies may help, then, to advance the study of emotion but first we need to take a step back – what is emotion? What may seem obvious enough to describe is actually a curiously nebulous concept. One of psychology's founding fathers, William James, published an article entitled 'What is Emotion?' back in 1884 but today, researchers have yet to agree on a single or even a few distinct definitions (Hastie 2001). At a very superficial level there is a general assumption that emotions can be classified according to a dichotomous simple division: positive and negative. We may all have the ability to distinguish between emotions that are thought of as positive (e.g. happiness and joy) and those considered negative (e.g. anger and fear). We may even find it relatively easy to identify some individual differences where, for example, one person experiences positive emotion whilst bungee jumping whereas it is a negative experience for someone else, but this gives us little insight into degrees of intensity. Is leaping off a cliff tied to a piece of elastic mildly uplifting or utterly joyous and thrilling? Is it merely worrying or desperately frightening? Hence, a straightforward dichotomy is an obvious oversimplification (see e.g. DeSteno, Petty, Rucker, Wegener and Baverman 2004).

Degrees of emotion

Russell and Feldman-Barrett (1999) considered negative and positive emotion alongside intensity and devised a circumplex model in which the first of two axes is defined according to arousal and the second according to pleasantness–unpleasantness. The primary assumption of a circumplex model is that when a set of variables is arranged around a circle, greater contiguity between certain variables indicates greater correlational strength between them (Romney and Bynner, 1997). In other words, the more features that variables have in common, the closer they are together; those that share none are directly opposite each other (Wiggins 1979). A further assumption is that the more extreme a particular behaviour is, the further it will be away from the mid-point of the circle (Kiesler 1983).

Purpose

The purpose of emotions also needs to be considered, particularly in relation to their social or adaptive function. The different specialist interests, theoretical stances and affiliations of different researchers may influence academic approaches in this respect. A researcher interested in making a contribution to the human communications literature may emphasise the view that emotions convey information (e.g. Toda 1980) whereas some stress the interpersonal role of emotions (e.g. Howard, Tuffin and Stephens 2000); others with a biological focus or cognitive evolutionary approach may maintain that the role of an emotion is to stabilise the internal state of an organism in its environment (e.g. Plutchik 1997).

The study of emotion, then, has moved beyond simplistic dichotomies of positive versus negative; degrees of intensity have been incorporated into circumplex models and the very purpose and functionality of emotions has also been addressed. Of course, the more factors that are acknowledged as relevant, the more complex the study of emotion becomes. Indeed, Russell (1997: 207) proposes that six properties are required for a full understanding of what constitutes an emotion. They are:

(1) An emotion is 'a member of a category, indeed many categories';
(2) 'Membership in each category is a matter of degree';
(3) 'Emotion categories are related to each other as described by a circumplex';
(4) 'Emotions fall along certain continua, such as intensity, degree of pleasure or displeasure (hedonic value), and amount of arousal';
(5) 'Emotion categories are understood in terms of a script, which is a prototypical sequence of causally connected and temporally ordered constituents';
(6) 'Emotion categories are embedded in a fuzzy hierarchy'.

Note that Russell's properties illustrate the difficulty of pinning down emotions definitively and precisely – hence it is acknowledged that category membership and boundaries must be flexible and fuzzy. Not only are the positive versus negative as well as degree of intensity included, they also have regard for horizontal and vertical categorisation as well as causal connections over time.

Such seemingly comprehensive explorations of emotions do not, however, mean the matter is settled. The six properties above may cover the definitions and categorisation of the emotions themselves; thus, we may know which 'box' to put a particular emotion in, we may know how it relates to another emotion and, indeed, how to catalogue its intensity but what about the individuals that actually feel the emotion? Russell (1997) provides a very useful taxonomy but the focus isn't on the organism (e.g. human) that experiences the emotion.

Individual responses

Other theorists have sought to address the responses of the individual. Hastie (2001: 671) states that emotions are 'reactions to motivationally significant stimuli and situations, including three components: a cognitive appraisal, a signature physiological response, and a phenomenal response'. In concrete terms, if you give someone a particular stimulus (favourite football team losing), they will react physiologically (increased heart rate, butterflies), cognitively (being out of the cup is disastrous and induces miserable, depressive thoughts/feelings) and respond phenomenally or behaviourally (run away from the stimulus – leave the ground early and drown sorrows in the pub).

One of the most influential approaches focusing on the response of the individual is appraisal theory. The assumption here is that 'each emotion can be related to specific patterns of evaluations and interpretations of events' (van Dijk and Zeelenberg 2002: 322) such that the individual's cognition and interpretation of an event is key to understanding their emotion. Most theorists argue that there is a causal relationship – in essence, how you view an event will by and large determine what you feel about it. Roseman, Antoniou and Jose (1996) argue that such appraisal relationships should be stated explicitly so that researchers can be sure exactly which emotion is being reported. Accordingly, Roseman *et al.* posit no fewer than nine appraisal dimensions such as 'unexpectedness' (of an event), 'situational state' and 'motivational state'.

Range of emotions

Finally in this section is the simplest but perhaps most central issue. Make a mental list of emotions – how many are there? We have no easy answer and we could likely complete another chapter just discussing criteria for inclusion. Notwithstanding the wide range of emotions, some emotions have been researched more than others. Primarily research has focused on the emotions of regret, disappointment, fear and anger and the effect that they can have on persuasion and decision-making. This focus may be due to the fact that most research is conducted within a laboratory and such emotions can be readily manipulated by the experimenter.

Summary

In summary, emotion is a complex area of study and the section above is just a brief outline of some of the many features that need to be considered. Taxonomy is a fundamental issue; there is no point trying to study emotions in any arena if two researchers are trying to compare apples with pears while a third refuses even to agree that they are fruit. Some are interested in the evolutionary or socially adaptive purpose of emotions in the animal kingdom as a whole while others focus exclusively on humans, but even restricting interests to human emotions alone, the area is vast. How many emotions do humans experience? Are we interested in physiological responses and the neural substrates of emotion? Are we interested in cognitive constructs or behavioural responses to emotion or both? Do we want to look at individual traits or the impact of particular social contexts?

Despite the difficulties entailed in reaching consensus on definitions, it is likely that most of us would agree that emotions play a central role in everyday life, obviously to varying degrees depending on the situation, the individuals and so on. They have a role in cognition and behaviour, are embedded within a social context (Drodge and Murphy 2002) and generate many opportunities for specialist study (see e.g. DeSteno, Petty, Rucker, Wegener and Braverman 2004, on persuasion; Fischhoff, Gonzalez, Lerner and Small 2005, on risk-estimates; Luce, Bettman and Payne 1997, on perceived task difficulty). Indeed, emotion is so ubiquitous that one could probably choose any journal article at random and attach the phrase, 'The role of emotion in ...' to any title without straining credulity.

Nonetheless, we must narrow the field somewhat and turn our attention to decision-making in general and the policing domain and critical incidents in particular. Critical incidents, of course, constitute a very particular specialist area. Decision stakes may be life or death so we may intuitively expect people *in extremis* to experience intense emotions, any of which may impact on responses and decision-making behaviour. For example, in fearful situations perceived risk estimates of a decision may be increased, whereas in anger-inducing situations risk estimates may be decreased. Further, if an individual experiences a negative emotion then this may direct their attention towards the importance of an accurate decision (Luce, Bettman and Payne 1997). However, our intuitions about intense emotions may be wrong; it could be said that police officers have to detach themselves from the situations they face every day and, hence, become socialised against explicitly showing emotions (Drodge and Murphy 2002). Howard, Tuffin and Stephens (2000: 305) found that police officers did not show a 'range of emotional intensity'. This is not to say that officers do not feel emotions but that they are required to refrain from showing them in public as they must remain impartial and calm in a range of situations.

Emotions and decision-making

Some researchers have argued that the role of emotion should be incorporated into decision-making theories to assist in the explanation of behavioural consequences of the decision outcome (van Dijk and Zeelenberg 2002). Traditional decision theory (TDT) largely overlooked the role of emotion so this call makes sense. It is not true to say that it has been completely neglected (see e.g. Anderson 2003; Bechara 2004) though it still requires academic attention and it is a complex task. As we discussed in the section above, there is considerable disagreement in the literature even on a definition of emotion; much harder is the construction of a theory that can thoroughly account for the roles of emotion in decision-making. Of course, difficult does not mean impossible, nor is it a reason to abandon the task. Latterly, more has become known about emotions specifically in regard to decision-making and in this section, we shall give a brief overview of some findings that specifically relate emotion to decision-making and how they may apply in a policing environment.

It is believed that negative emotions impact on 'both how and how much people process information when making a choice' (Luce, Bettman and Payne 1997: 403). This is asserted with the finding that there is an increase in status quo bias as the individual experiences increased negative emotion (Luce 1996, cited in Luce, Bettman and Payne 1997); that is, people are more likely to stick with the status quo and avoid the decision to change things when they are experiencing negative emotion (See Chapter 10 for details on decision avoidance). Not only that, negative emotions can also lead to more narrow processing of information (Lewinsohn and Mano 1993).

Particularly pertinent is research that focuses specifically on a law enforcement environment and participants who are police officers. Ask and Granhag (in press) found that negative emotions affect investigators' judgements of crime-related information. Moreover, they distinguished between two different negative emotions. Officers who were angry showed a narrower focus and relied only on their perception of the witness who provided the information. By contrast, officers who were sad (in addition to utilising their perceptions of the witness) also took the situational variables into account before making judgements. Ask and Granhag (in press) also found differences between participants's emotional states when judging whether witness statements were consistent with the central hypothesis of an investigation. Those who were sad were more likely to take the degree of consistency into account than those who were angry. This suggests that emotional states affect the level at which information is processed; that is, angry officers relied on heuristics (see Chapter 8 for details of heuristics) whereas sad officers processed the information at a more substantive level. It is easy to see how these factors could impact on decision-making in an investigation.

The Somatic Marker Hypothesis (Bechara 2004) explicitly considers the role of emotion in decision-making. The main assumption of this theory is that emotions guide decision-making; they arise due to a previous experience (either negative or positive), producing a mark that is subsequently incorporated into decisions, and indicate which would be the more appropriate choice; in other words, emotions help an individual to focus on certain information. Within a policing context this may emerge when officers deal with two very similar cases. (Incidentally, this hypothesis has a comfortable parallel in the situation–action pattern matching of the Recognition Primed Decision-Making (RPD) model in naturalistic research. See Chapter 3 for details.) Faced with two similar cases, officers may use their knowledge of the positive and negative aspects from a previous case to inform their approach and decision-making. Specifically this could occur during the first few hours of a critical incident in which a flood of incoming information is received, and officers may use their knowledge of past events to focus often limited resources on specific leads and information. If emotions are positive at this time, this might be advantageous as Estrada, Isen and Young (1994) found that positive emotions help decision-makers to integrate information more efficiently.

Research indicates that emotions and emotional memory can determine the quality of a decision (Bechara 2004; Bechara, Damasio, Tranel and Anderson 1998). Indeed, emotional memory may guide the decision-maker at the time of the decision even if he or she does not realise it (Sayegh, Anthony and Perrewé 2004). In a policing environment this could apply to experienced senior officers. Previous incidents are likely to have elicited emotional situations and when an officer experiences a similar situation they may draw on the feelings they experienced previously to guide them in the current situation. However, if it is the case that emotional memories guide future decisions, there is a concern here; van Dijk and Zeelenberg (2002) argue that regret and disappointment are the two emotions that most commonly occur in decision-making.

Regret is primarily elicited when the individual believes that they could have done something about an event (Zeelenberg and Beattie 1997). Kahneman and Tversky (1982) found that people believed that they would feel more regret when they had done something about an event rather than when they had done nothing. However, Gilovich and Medvec (1995) believed that this was only the case in the short term and that when looking back over the longer term, it would be the opposite; that is, more regret would be felt for having done nothing. For researchers, it matters, then, when they gather data. For example, if a 10kV session is scheduled immediately an investigation is concluded, officers may be more likely to report experiencing regret when they had acted rather than when they had avoided taking action, with the reverse finding if data were gathered later on.

Connolly and Zeelenberg (2002) propose a theory called the Decision Justification Theory (DJT). In DJT, regret contains two components that are caused by decision-making. The first component is related to the evaluation of the outcome if a certain decision is made and the second component is related to feelings of self-blame. Connolly and Zeelenberg go on to say that these two components do not necessarily have to occur simultaneously. This relates to decision-making in law enforcement agencies, as a person could feel self-blame even when the outcome is good. For example, in a missing persons investigation that develops into a murder investigation, the officers may feel self-blame if they perceive that they could have done something about the event, but at the same time if they secure a conviction then the investigation would have been a success. However, had they not secured a conviction then they may have experienced a mixture of the two components.

Certainly, regret is a promising area for research within police decision-making. If one can conjure a defining image of police work, it may well be that when ordinary civilians cannot act, we simply wait for the police to arrive and do so on our behalf. Whether it is dealing with the local nuisance of noisy teenagers painting graffiti on a phone box, or venturing into the aftermath of a bomb blast to bring order to the chaos, police officers, *par excellence*, are expected to *do* something about an event. This may indicate, in accordance with Kahneman and Tversky's (1982) finding above, that police are more than usually likely to experience regret; alternatively, they may be so used to 'doing something about an event' that they are a case apart.

Regret also features prominently in relation to decision avoidance; indeed, the role of emotion generally in decision avoidance explicitly features in Anderson's (2003) integrated model; that is, he incorporates the role of emotion into more rational aspects of (non) decision-making. Decision avoidance is discussed in detail in Chapter 10, but the relevant point for the current chapter is this: for Anderson, managing emotions underpins decision avoidance. If status quo bias and omission bias do contain similar fundamental processes – for example, that negative emotions such as regret and disappointment are experienced post-decision, that individuals can anticipate negative emotion as a result of a decision, or that a negative emotion can be experienced prior to the decision – then an understanding of these emotions is imperative to understanding why individuals involved in police cases do not take action, and hence to improving the decision-making of these crucial people.

Thus, the consequences of failure and negative evaluation may cause police officers to experience fear so they may decide to take no action in order to minimise this fear. However, choosing to take no action can still lead to error, as 'mistakes are sometimes difficult to avoid and the perceived fear of the consequences may cause some officers to cover up their mistakes and failures' (Gudjonsson 1984: 236). This is not to say that officers invariably 'cover up' their mistakes but given the prominence of public inquiries and the naming and blaming that often accompanies them, it is easy to see that a blame culture is a salient feature. Hence, the fear police officers experience at the time of the decision may impact on their decision-making, and should this decision be wrong then some officers may attempt to minimise the repercussions. Further research is needed with this idea in mind but if fear of failure and negative evaluation are found to impact or impede the decision-making then, clearly, concerted efforts need to be taken to minimise them. Individuals involved in critical incidents obviously need an environment where fear of failure is at a minimum. This is another reason why high-fidelity immersive simulations are so important – mistakes and emotional responses to those mistakes can be dealt with in a safe learning environment. If accompanied by a session on knowledge of what psychological impact the delegates can expect, this can serve as a protective buffer to stress reactions and can enhance the effectiveness of decision-making (Salas and Cannon-Bowers 2001).

The theories briefly discussed here are applicable to a policing environment; however, none have explicably been tested within such a context. Critical incidents provide a unique environment for applying such perspectives, as decisions can have life-or-death consequences, occur under intense pressure, and there is the necessity to balance often conflicting aims. In this respect, the degree to which emotions in a policing context may be a separate and distinct landscape requires specialist study.

Emotions in police investigations

The study of emotions within a policing context has so far been fairly neglected yet within a policing context, emotions could affect the choice of whether to make a decision or not (action or inaction); emotions will feature in the outcome of previous or current decisions (for example, regret or pride); finally, particular emotions may arise at any time due to more general aspects of critical incident management such as lack of resources, media intrusion or the successful arrest and prosecution of a serious offender.

Officers involved in critical incidents such as a murder inquiry or child abductions are often forced to make significant decisions in complex and uncertain environments (Barrett 2005) and these environments are likely to be extremely emotional, for example, when finding the body of a missing child. Police officers constitute an atypical group of individuals in respect of the frequency with which they might be expected to experience extreme emotions, in part due to the situations they encounter (e.g. homicide, child abuse, suicide and car accidents) (Howard, Tuffin and Stephens 2000); however, the position these officers hold in society requires them to 'inhibit affective responses in emotionally charged situations' (Pogrebin and Poole 1991: 396). There is evidence that police officers view discussion of emotions as taboo (Pogrebin and Poole 1991), which may be due to an expectation that they refrain from exhibiting emotion lest it undermine their role. On the other hand, Howard, Tuffin and Stephens (2000) found that there are certain conditions under which officers do consider it acceptable to discuss emotions such as fear – as long as they refrain from doing so until the incident is over and even then it should only be discussed with those who were involved.

Police officers are required to be prepared for any eventuality even when they are faced with tragedy such as death, but maintaining composure in such situations will be made increasingly difficult when other factors such as the media and family are present. If police officers cannot openly discuss their emotions then over time it is possible that they would become more and more uncomfortable in doing so. Holding back such emotions is known to lead to long-term problems (Howard, Tuffin and Stephens 2000). Emphasising the importance of disclosing the emotions you feel, Pogrebin and Poole

(1991) found that officers actually reported that they found it a relief to be able to discuss such issues. Similarly, officers involved in 10kV debriefs, where emotional issues are more freely discussed, often report that they find the experience cathartic. This would indicate that officers want to discuss their emotions but feel that due to social or organisational factors they are unable to do so.

Emotions and critical incidents: a 10kV study

Pilot work using 10kV data (see Chapter 3 for a full description of this methodology) highlights the emotionality of critical incidents. Recall that the anonymity of 10kV technology may help to overcome possible discomfort at discussing personal, emotional issues. Although we mentioned above that officers commonly report the 10kV session itself as a positive emotional experience, to date, our research has focused on the negative emotions entailed in a critical incident.

Two coding dictionaries were devised to examine the emotional experience of a specific critical incident. The first coding dictionary enabled the examination of specific negative emotions whereas the second examined possible causes for such emotions. For the purpose of our study we defined emotions generally according to whether they were caused by the self or other agency, whether they were caused by past, present or future events, and finally by intensity of the explored emotion. (See page 197 for a list of general definitions of emotion for the case study.)

This research found that officers experience frustration, disappointment, regret, fear, sadness, helplessness, anger, annoyance and hopelessness. Our study on this particular incident has indicated that frustration and disappointment are the emotions most commonly experienced by officers. This conforms to previous research, which proposed that regret and disappointment were the emotions most prominently experienced in a decision-making environment (e.g. van Dijk and Zeelenberg 2002). It is speculative at this early descriptive pilot stage but there may be several reasons that disappointment is replicated as a common decision-making emotion but regret is replaced by frustration in a policing arena. We mentioned earlier that, when it comes to experiencing regret, police officers may be a case apart due to the frequency with which they operate in a decision environment with unusually high stakes.

The appraisal patterns of the specific emotions may also be pertinent. Van Dijk and Zeelenberg (2002) noted that disappointment is more likely when events are appraised as being beyond one's own control whereas events that generate regret are appraised thus: the individual him/herself has caused them and could have done something to alter them. It goes without saying that a murder has not been caused by the police officers charged with bringing the killer to justice; likewise, although they doubtless wish it had never happened, it is usually unlikely that there had been a realistic prospect of their being able to alter the facts. If the officers in our study appraised events thus, it is unsurprising that disappointment featured more prominently than regret.

There is another consideration. Elsewhere throughout this book, we have argued that current decision-making theories are limited because they do not consider context in a broad enough sense (traditional decision theory (TDT) does not consider context at all and naturalistic decision-making (NDM) research restricts context to the immediate field setting – see Chapter 3 for details). Organisational context may well underpin the finding in this study that frustration is one of the two most common emotions felt by officers in homicide investigations. Earlier case-based research conducted within the Centre for Critical Incident Research indicates that failing to learn lessons from previous events can be a precipitating factor in officers experiencing frustration. Further to this, many of the factors that provided the foundations for officers experiencing negative emotions were to some degree under the control of the police force. It is possible, then, that the organisational context – where officers are experienced enough to see mistakes being repeated but powerless to effect change – may form part of the appraisal pattern that leads to frustration being one of the two most commonly experienced emotions. It should be noted again that this is speculative and remains as yet an empirical question though certainly one in which further research is to be welcomed.

During the investigation[1]

The initial stage of any investigation can be critical; it can also be the point that most information is received from members of the public. Ineffective management of the initial stage and information has the potential to impact negatively on an inquiry. A sample 10kV comment was '[Due to lack of resources and press hype] *the initial days were therefore without focus, the inquiry lacked direction.*' We also illustrated this point in reference to leadership in the early stages, where effective task-oriented planning can be compromised by poor (or absent) organisational 'readiness'. If the prevailing organisational culture is one in which the force has failed to build an infrastructure that enables basic mechanisms to lock into place, then even the most robust, hardy and resilient directive leaders will struggle to bring coherence and shape to the inquiry.

Too much information brings its own problems due to the sheer volume that must be processed in order that it may be turned into a working model where lines of inquiry can be prioritised. It is daunting and there was a feeling of hopelessness among officers who felt they were faced with an impossible task: 'The feeling that we were not able to capture, process, prioritise that information and act upon [it]' and 'HOLMES 2, no matter how well staff [performed, they] could never have absorbed and assimilated the volume of information quickly enough to drive and action the large number of staff attached to the operation in the early stages'. Furthermore, many of the officers experienced a feeling of helplessness due to the lack of resources available to them. They believed that this left them ill prepared and vulnerable; however, many felt that this could have been overcome by effective planning.

Resources are a concern to police forces across the UK and senior investigating officers (SIOs) are often faced with the challenge of considering such factors when faced with a critical incident such as a homicide inquiry. This can take up valuable time in which is highlighted the fact that many police forces are struggling for funding, many have been forced to stop recruitment for the present time and are having to make difficult cutbacks. Some police forces in the UK find that when they are faced with a critical incident they do not have the necessary resources to conduct an effective investigation and must find additional personnel and so forth from outside their immediate force. However, when the expected level of assistance is not obtained from other forces this can cause a deep sense of anger. Our study found that aspects related to other forces was, in fact, the greatest factor in leading officers to experience anger. For example, one delegate stated, 'It is a disgrace that a particular force did not provide as much assistance as smaller forces. There must have been a particular agenda. It was as if someone at the top wanted us to fail.'

Due to the inherent nature of homicide investigations it is inevitable the media will take great interest. However, it is not only immensely difficult to manage the media but it also has the potential to impact on an inquiry (Crego and Alison 2004). The study presented here indicates that media intrusion caused annoyance. 'Keeping the media away from my staff' was listed as an ongoing irritation and one delegate commented, 'The case quickly came into public ownership and developed its *own persona which sometimes appeared to bear little resemblance to reality.'* This is in line with Crego and Alison (2004) who found that SIOs perceived the media as having the potential to have a high impact on an inquiry while simultaneously being immensely difficult to manage and adding further to the potential causes of distraction.

Training is an imperative component of policing; however, when faced with uncertain and novel circumstances officers can feel that lack of training let them down. In the case study presented here, officers experienced intense frustration and disappointment that the training they had was insufficient to deal with an incident of this magnitude; for example one delegate stated, *'The lack of training started at the top and worked its way down'*, again highlighting the impact of organisational context on individuals.

In this debriefing, it was found that factors within the force's control most frequently caused regret. Again, this accords with van Dijk and Zeelenberg's (2002) discussion of appraisal patterns associated with regret, namely, that events are perceived as related to self-agency as opposed to other-agency; in other words, it was within one's power to change things.

Many of the officers felt that the force was ill prepared to deal with an inquiry that was as complex as a murder investigation and one that attracted a large amount of media attention: *'It must, in my view, be accepted that the organisation was ill prepared to manage an inquiry of such a size and complexity.'* A further causal factor was that the officers believed that the force had been made aware that they were ill prepared and should have done something about this to ensure that they were not in such a position: *'If only the force had listened to him then [X] would have been dealt with differently.'*

This regret may also have been felt by the officers as their experience of policing had left them in a vulnerable position for the occurrence of a critical incident and the force should have ensured that this did not happen: *'Prior to the operation the move away from crime investigation in order to focus on community policing caused a lack of resilience in the force response.'* This is likely to become more prevalent in smaller UK police forces as many are currently moving towards a more community and neighbourhood approach to their everyday policing, thus leaving them with insufficient flexibility to deal with high-profile major crime investigations.

Not all causes of negative emotions are associated with organisational features and some are caused by the inherent nature of homicide investigations. For example, within the debriefing presented here it was found that officers experienced sadness for the family, and fear and sadness at the outcome.

Fear has been identified as an emotion that commonly occurs in the police force (Gudjonsson 1984). Connolly and Zeelenberg (2002) stated that fear was an emotion that would occur at the time that the decision was made and that sadness may occur after the event was over. On this view, sadness should perhaps have been more common than fear in this case as this 10kV session was carried out after the event. However, this was not the case; the present study showed that fear occurred slightly more frequently than sadness although many statements that contained a reference to fear did commonly refer to an earlier stage of the investigation: *'and being anxious that we were not going to find* [the victim] *in time'*. The officers in this debriefing also exhibited elements of fear towards the possibility of a similar event occurring again and whether or not they would be prepared for it, which is linked to learning lessons: *'The events that took place may happen again at any time and we must be prepared for it.'*

Conclusion

In this chapter, we discussed the difficulties associated with emotion as a research topic. Problems and issues range from taxonomies and definitions to ascribing emotion its (rightful) place in decision theory. We also drew attention to the emotion entailed in the specialised domain of critical incidents and police work and how research in this area is in its infancy.

We commented that there is currently no single perspective that can fully encapsulate the emotional impact of homicide investigations. Aspects of the debriefs captured here stress the complex and emotional world in which critical incidents and specifically homicide inquiries occur. Although limited to two case studies, this homicide investigation research showed that it was not the finding of the bodies that was a causal factor in negative emotions but factors that operate within an organisational context. This is not to say that officers involved in a case do not feel negative emotions at discovering that an investigation has moved to become a homicide inquiry but that the lasting emotional discomfort comes from frustrations at an organisational level. Furthermore, the research presented here illustrates that a full understanding of decision-making in critical incidents must consider the organisational context and the emotions experienced.

Postscript

Since the case study presented here was conducted, further homicide debriefs analysed by the Centre for Critical Incident Research indicate that lessons have been learned. Positive comments in recent debriefed cases indicate that particular strides have been made in training and also in the implementation of mutual aid arrangements where other police forces are called in to assist with extra resources and personnel.

Notes

1 Direct quotations from 10kV session are italicised throughout.

General definitions of emotion for the case study

Anger Feeling that someone else acted in an illegitimate manner. A specific emotion that is caused by something other than the self. An extreme emotion that is associated with something that has happened.

Frustration A deep sense or state of insecurity and dissatisfaction that arises from unresolved problems or unfulfilled needs. Caused by something other than the self. Associated with something that has happened or is happening. Not as extreme as anger but more extreme than a feeling of annoyance.

Annoyance A feeling caused by constant irritation by something other than the self but may also be caused by oneself. It is a general feeling that is moderate and is associated with something that has happened or is happening.

Helplessness The inability to function effectively without help. It is a precise emotion that is caused by another agency and is associated with something that has happened.

Hopelessness A feeling of despair that is felt when the individual has lost all hope or comfort or success. It is a very precise feeling that is associated with something in the future, for example, the outcome of an inquiry.

Sadness A feeling caused by a sense of lack of control and a belief that something was caused by an agency other than the self. It is a more general feeling than both helplessness and hopelessness and is related to something that has happened.

Disappointment A feeling that something that occurred during the inquiry was unexpected, immoral and caused by something beyond the individual's control. It is caused by something other than the self and is associated with something in the past.

Regret The feeling that the individual or the force could have done something about an event and that something that happened during the inquiry could have been caused or prevented by the individual. This is also associated with an event that happened in the past.

Fear A feeling of anxiety about something that may have happened. It is an emotion that is related to the future but may also be associated with 'what if?' It would also be caused by something other than the self.

References

Alison, L., Barrett, E. and Crego, J. (2005) 'Pragmatic research in criminal investigative decision making: context and process', in L. Alison (ed.), *Naturalistic decision making 7*. Cullompton: Willan Publishing.

Anderson, C. (2003) 'The psychology of doing nothing: forms of decision avoidance result from reason and emotion', *Psychological Bulletin*, 129: 139–167.

Ask, K. and Granhag, P.A. (in press) 'Hot cognition in investigative judgments: the differential influence of anger and sadness', *Law and Human Behavior*.

Barrett, E.C. (2005) 'Psychological research and police investigations: does the research meet the needs?', in L. Alison (ed.), *The forensic psychologist's casebook: psychological profiling and criminal investigation* (pp. 47–67). Cullompton: Willan Publishing.

Bechara, A. (2004) 'The role of emotion in decision making: evidence from neurological patients with orbitofrontal damage', *Brain and Cognition*, 55: 30–40.

Bechara, A., Damasio, H., Tranel, D. and Anderson, S.W. (1998) 'Dissociation of working memory from decision-making within the human prefrontal cortex', *Journal of Neuroscience*, 18: 428–37.

Connolly, T. and Zeelenberg, M. (2002) 'Regret in decision making', *Current Directions in Psychological Science*, 11(6): 212–16.

DeSteno, D., Petty, R.E., Rucker, D.D., Wegener, D.T. and Baverman, J. (2004) 'Discrete emotions and persuasion: the role of emotion-induced expectancies', *Journal of Personality and Social Psychology*, 86: 43–56.

Drodge, E.N., and Murphy, S.A. (2002) 'Interrogating emotions in police leadership', *Human Resource Development Review*, 1: 420–38.

Estrada, C.A., Isen, A.M. and Young, M.J. (1994) 'Positive effect improves creative problem solving and influences reported source of practice satisfaction in physicians', *Motivation and Emotion*, 18: 285–99.

Fischhoff, B., Gonzalez, R.M., Lerner, J.S., and Small, D.A. (2005) 'Evolving judgements of terror risks: foresight, hindsight and emotion', *Journal of Experimental Psychology; Applied*, 11: 214–139.

Fishman, D.B. (2003) 'Background to the "psycholegal lexis proposal", exploring the potential of a systematic case study database in forensic psychology', *Psychology, Public Policy and Law*, 9: 267–74.

Gilovich, T. Husted, Medvec, V. and Kahneman, D. (1998) 'Varieties of regret: a debate and partial resolution', *Psychological Review*, 105(3): 602–605.

Gudjonsson, G.H. (1984) 'Fear of "failure" and "tissue damage" in police recruits, constables, sergeants and senior officers', *Personality and Individual Differences*, 5: 233–6.

Hastie, R. (2001) 'Problems for judgement and decision making', *Annual Review of Psychology*, 52: 653–83.

Howard, C., Tuffin, K., and Stephens, C. (2000) 'Unspeakable emotion: a discursive analysis of police talk about reactions to trauma', *Journal of Language and Social Psychology*, 19: 295–314.

James, W. (1884) 'What is an emotion?', *Mind*, 9: 188–205. Retrieved 11 January 2007, from http://www.psychclassics/yorku/ca/James/emotion/htm

Kahneman, D. and Tversky, A. (1982) *Judgement under uncertainty: heuristics and biases.* Cambridge: Cambridge University Press.

Kiesler, D.J. (1983) 'The 1982 Interpersonal circle: a taxonomy for complementarity in human transactions', *Psychological Review*, 90(3): 185–214.

Lewinsohn, S. and Mano, H. (1993) 'Multi-attribute choice and effect: the influence of naturally occurring and manipulated moods on choice processes', *Journal of Behavioral Decision Making*, 6: 33–51.

Luce, M.F., Bettman, J.R. and Payne, J.W. (1997) 'Choice processing in emotionally difficult decisions', *Journal of Experimental Psychology; Learning, Memory and Cognition*, 25: 384–405.

Lucey, B.M. and Dowling, M. (2005) 'The role of feelings in the investor decision-making', *Journal of Economic Surveys*, 19: 211–27.

Plutchik, R. (1997) 'The circumplex as a general model of the structure of emotions and personality', in R. Plutchik and H.R. Conte (eds), *Circumplex models of personality and emotions* (pp. 17–46). Washington, DC: American Psychological Association.

Pogrebin, M. and Poole, E.D. (1991) 'Police and tragic events: the management of emotions', *Journal of Criminal Justice*, 19: 395–403.

Romney, D.M. and Bynner, J.M. (1997) 'Evaluating a circumplex model of personality disorders with structural equation modeling', in R. Plutchik and H.R. Conte (eds), *Circumplex models of personality and emotions* (pp. 299–325). Washington, DC: American Psychological Association.

Roseman, I.J., Antoniou, A.A. and Jose, P.E. (1996) 'Appraisal determinants of emotions: constructing a more accurate and comprehensive theory', *Cognition and Emotion*, 10: 241–77.

Russell, J.A. (1997) 'How shall an emotion be called?', in R. Plutchik and H.R. Conte (eds), *Circumplex models of personality and emotions* (pp. 205–20). Washington DC: American Psychological Association.

Russell, J.A. and Feldman-Barrett, L. (1999) 'Core affect, prototypical episodes and other things called emotion; dissecting the elephant', *Journal of Personality and Social Psychology,* 76: 805–19.

Salas, E. and Cannon-Bowers, J.A. (2001) 'The science of training: a decade of progress', *Annual Review of Psychology,* 52: 471–99.

Sayegh, L., Anthony, W.P. and Perrewe, P.L. (2004) Managerial decision-making under crisis: the role of emotion in an intuitive decision process', *Human Resource Management Review,* 14: 179–99.

Toda, M. (1980) 'Emotion and decision making', *Acta Pscyhologica,* 45: 133–55.

Van Dijk, W.W. and Zeelenberg, M. (2002) 'Investigating the appraisal patterns of regret and disappointment', *Motivation and Emotion,* 26: 321–30.

Wiggins, J.S. (1979) 'A psychological taxonomy of trait-descriptive terms: the interpersonal domain', *Journal of Personality and Social Psychology,* 37(3): 395–412.

Zeelenberg, M. and Beattie, J. (1997) 'Consequences of regret aversion 2: additional evidence for effects of feedback on decision making', *Organizational Behavior and Human Decision Processes,* 72: 63–78.

Chapter 10

Decision inertia: the impact of organisations on critical incident decision-making

Marie Eyre, Laurence Alison, Jonathan Crego and Clare McLean

Introduction

By this stage of the book, the reader is no doubt very familiar with or (perish the thought) even a little jaded by the term 'decision-making' but it is worth stopping to consider that the nomenclature itself reveals a much overlooked issue – namely, that people often *don't* make decisions (even when they ought). In this chapter, we consider two underexplored and related issues. First is the idea of decision avoidance itself; second is the impact of organisational context on decision-making (DM).[1] We argue that contemporary explanations of DM neglect the impact of organisational context and consequently fail to provide an adequate account of the decision inertia endemic in multi-agency working in critical incidents.

In support of this argument, we present results from our study into how practitioners from different organisations make (or fail to make) decisions in simulated critical incident environments. This study shows that the failure to make decisions is one of the most pervasive problems in working together in critical incidents. You may reasonably think that this is not a remarkably novel nugget of knowledge we have unearthed. After all, anyone who owns a TV or buys a newspaper could quote an example where a death might have been prevented if the relevant authorities had decided to act sooner, and public inquiries have consistently found that failing to make decisions and take action are contributory factors to tragic outcomes (e.g. Bichard on the Soham inquiry, 2004; Laming on the death of Victoria Climbié, 2003); yet it remains the (perhaps surprising) case that, despite this common knowledge, there is comparatively little research into decision avoidance or inertia.

The impact of organisational context is particularly neglected. In this respect, the study discussed in this chapter does advance knowledge in this area and thereby addresses a significant gap. Specifically, organisational structures and climates are the key elements in the emergence of this decision inertia. In this chapter, we describe these processes, relating them to the decision avoidance strategies of status quo bias, omission bias, and choice deferral (discussed below); the argument is based on our finding that practitioners experience an acute sense of accountability to their organisations, which can manifest itself as an attempt to avoid responsibility for decisions and hence post-decisional justification. This then results in decision inertia.

We do not wish to paint an overly bleak picture by suggesting that academics have ignored the phenomenon of decision avoidance completely. Anderson (2003) offers a theoretical framework and it is his original model that we extend to make explicit the impact of organisational context on DM. Anderson's original model indicated the cognitive processes that may impact an individual's decision avoidance. Here, we have incorporated the factors inherent in the broader context of the organisation and outline a path indicating how they feed into the (narrower) processes that impact an individual. Thus, we address shortcomings in current decision theory, which we argue takes too narrow a view of context, and we take the first steps in recognising and detailing the significance of organisational structure and climate on critical incident DM.

A substantial DM literature exists, and recall that in Chapter 3, we outlined two of the main approaches: Traditional Decision Theory (TDT) and Naturalistic Decision Making (NDM), with TDT suggesting that decision choices are made rationally after a thorough search of all options while NDM emphasises the heuristics, situation action-matching rules and so forth that are used in naturalistic situations. The point is this: within much of the DM literature, there is a common assumption that, in the end, a decision *will* be made. Given that there is far less research exploring how and why decisions *are not* made, we argue that this is an incomplete representation of DM in the real world; in a sense, research needs to catch up with the common-sense 'knowledge' that people tend to avoid difficult decisions.

For example, within the NDM approach, context is considered only to the extent that it impacts on the decisions people *do* make. It is not conceived of as inhibiting or preventing DM but we need to consider how the environment people work in might make them *not decide*. When we think about context, we need to conceive of it in the broadest sense as an expansive entity across space and time. Hitherto, it has been restricted, as a concept, to the immediate field in which decisions are made. As a result, the focus has been on the 'here and now' rather than the longer-term organisational, cultural and political influences; in reality, context is a multilayered phenomenon, extending much further and having a greater effect than current DM theories recognise.

In summary, NDM has certainly played an important part in developing our understanding of how context (in terms of the immediate field setting) may determine potential courses of action but we also need to recognise that context can restrict acceptable options even to the point where some may be precluded completely. In other words, it may make us *not* decide. In failing to account for this phenomenon, NDM theories fall short while TDT has long been criticised for omitting context almost entirely. Current DM theories, then, fail to offer an adequate explanation of the inertia that can pervade DM in critical incidents. Our research makes a first step towards addressing this significant gap.

Decision avoidance and organisational context

As this study shows, practitioners operate not only in the immediate contexts of practice but also within the wider sphere of their organisations. The structure of these organisations shapes the real world of practice and places limits on the DM capabilities of staff. As such, organisational infrastructure directly influences the ways in which practitioners make decisions. The fact that decisions in critical incidents are filtered through an organisational climate lens has a profound impact. It can mean that even where individuals have access to relevant information, and have the capacity to draw accurate inferences from that information, they may not commit to a decision because of the organisational climate (thus revealing the limitations of current theory). For example, a senior police officer may have to consider interviewing a potential child victim, but procrastinate or fail to commit to this decision for fear of reprisals, complaints from the child's parents or guardians and the potential ensuing media attention. This decision inertia is the outcome of the constraining effects of organisational structures on practitioners.

A key component of Anderson's model is the concept of decision avoidance, defined as 'a pattern of behaviour in which individuals seek to *avoid the responsibility* [italics added] of making a decision by delaying or choosing options they perceive to be nondecisions' (2003: 139). In a detailed review, Anderson found four decision avoidance effects: (a) status quo bias; (b) omission bias; (c) choice deferral; and (d) inaction inertia. The first three are particularly relevant here, and are discussed below in the context of our research findings.

Current study

The current study utilised a Hydra exercise to simulate a critical incident DM environment. The Hydra exercise was followed by a 10kV debrief (both described in Chapter 3) to examine how core service practitioners make decisions in multi-agency child abuse inquiries. Participants were key representatives from Health, Education, Social Services and the Police Service in a borough of a major metropolitan area. Ninety practitioners were selected and assigned to one of four child protection case simulations such that all ranks from all core services were represented in each simulation. Given that part of the reason for the process was a government review, the data are extremely sensitive. Consequently, confidentiality agreements preclude the reporting of demographic characteristics; however, the participant sample was representative of the wider core service population.

For the Hydra simulation, participants were assigned to one of four separate rooms with one room for each agency. The control team fed information about an unfolding child protection case to each agency. Participants were instructed to make decisions and work jointly in real time to protect the child. To replicate real-world conditions where practitioners work in separate agencies and/or worksites, participants could not hear discussions in other rooms. Crucially, though, the agency groups were free to communicate with each other, as they wished, throughout the simulation. The control team maintained a flow of information to each agency in response to decisions and actions. Starkly, the outcome of each simulation was further harm to the child.

A 10kV debriefing session was held after each simulation to capture participants' responses. The transcripts generated from these sessions were analysed. As a brief reminder, raw 10kV transcripts constitute free narrative statements by practitioners where they can reflect on their experiences of the (simulated) inquiry. Our content analysis consisted of extracting the most common, recurring themes from the raw 10kV output. The focus was on: 1) the difficulties in conducting child abuse inquiries; and 2) suggestions for improvement. Comments were then categorised into a form known as a coding dictionary. For example, comments that referred to what the media/public/courts would think about decisions made or avoided were categorised under the theme 'External Perceptions' – a sample comment was, 'Good news stories don't sell newspapers in the UK.' Thus, we surveyed practitioners' perceptions of the most pertinent, important issues by assessing the degree to which each one featured in their discussions (referred to below as percentage of 'coded output').

Inertia in practice

Decision and action inertia were identified as the most pervasive problems in this study of simulated critical incident decision-making, with negative comments about 'Action and follow-up/review of action' comprising 12.4 per cent of coded output concerning difficulties. Participants identified a lack of preventative work or thresholds for action that were set too high (i.e. too little, too late), a tendency to let things drift and failure to review actions, compounded by the assumption that other agencies would be making the decisions. This emerged as a key reason why the simulation exercise ended in further harm to the child. This possible diffusion of perceived responsibility or anxiety about taking responsibility for difficult decisions is discussed below in terms of the resulting model of decision avoidance. Sample comments were:

'A child was seriously injured, due to our lack of action.'

'It seems to me that a main characteristic has been a lack of focused decisive action.'

'Difficult to get other agencies, Police/SSD [Social Services Department] to act on identified concerns.'

'I am frustrated by other agencies not wanting to take positive actions.'

'A common issue in real life.'

'In particular it is concerning that this case was allowed to drift substantially.'

'The agencies responsible for promoting his well-being have failed him (and his siblings) by not acting on information which was available.'

'Risks were identified very clearly but there was no preventative work.'

'Services only provided to the family at points of crisis.'

'[In real life,] unfortunately, this is too often the case.'

'Are they [thresholds] set too late in the chain of events to trigger prevention?'

'Police and Social Services did not carry through the decision to do a home visit.'

'We made many correct decisions but did not check that they had been implemented.'

'I feel that I had a role in ensuring that things should have been done and carried out within my own agency and I didn't check.'

'Willingness to accept agencies were taking actions without being pro-active in finding out what was going on.'

These findings refute Traditional Decision Theory's assumption that, armed with all the relevant information, the decision-maker will face no further difficulty in making a choice and taking action. Rather, as this study shows, practitioners involved in multi-agency child protection cases frequently fail to make choices about future action, even when they possess a relatively detailed and comprehensive picture. This suggests that context plays an important role in DM.

Inertia in theory: omission and status quo biases

For Anderson (2003), rationality does have a part to play in DM (as TDT theories would suggest) but emotion is also a significant influence and, as human beings, we seek to regulate emotions and reduce uncomfortable or dissonant feelings. Two of the decision avoidant effects identified by Anderson are: 1) The status quo bias, 'a decision-maker's inflated preference for the current state of affairs' (2003: 143); and 2) The omission bias, 'an inflated preference for options that do not require action' (2003: 143). Both concepts have potential explanatory power to help to understand the decision inertia found in our study.

Omission bias

If a decision-maker anticipates regret or blame (by mentally simulating the outcome), he or she will experience negative emotion during the DM process and is, thus, biased to avoid (*omit*) the decision. Avoiding the decision will minimise uncomfortable feelings or negative emotion felt *during* the DM process while the individual is imagining the blame or regret that might be felt *in the future*, post-decision (e.g. Inman and Zeelenberg 2002; Riis and Schwarz 2000). In short, if you don't want to worry about being blamed for a decision, don't decide.

Anderson explains an individual's cognitive processes but we argue that the organisational context is also a factor. Anxiety about anticipated blame or regret does not come from nowhere. In concrete terms, if an individual is employed within a sector that has undergone public shaming and blaming (for example, social workers subjected to public criticism for: (a) taking a child into care; or (b) not taking a child into care), it would be relatively easy to mentally simulate one's name across the front of the tabloids. In other words, anticipated blame may be a highly salient feature.

Status quo bias

Also highly salient for us all is what's normal – the status quo. We can all mentally simulate how deviating from the normal state of affairs – the status quo – could engender dissonant feelings. Imagine deciding to burst into song as you enter a packed lecture theatre. Regardless of whether you have the voice of an angel or are tone deaf, it's simply not 'normal' behaviour. You may anticipate some regret but, in this silly example, the decision consequences are no greater than mere personal embarrassment. Where it is an organisational norm to keep families together whenever possible, this 'status quo' will be a powerful influence on a practitioner who considers deviating from it as he or she thinks about the decision to remove a child from the family. Hence, people are biased towards sticking with the status quo and avoiding a decision and, again, we argue that the context plays a part. It goes without saying that, in the child protection scenario, the consequences of a decision error for the child, family and professionals concerned are far greater than the straightforward embarrassment of singing in an inappropriate setting.

Status quo and omission biases appear to share underlying causes, with evidence showing that negative emotion *anticipated* as a result of a decision, negative emotion *experienced* prior to making the choice, and regret *experienced* post-decision, can be reduced by selecting either of these decision avoidant options. To make matters more difficult, all of this is compounded by a well-established DM tendency to weigh potential losses more heavily than potential gains of the same amount; that is, losing £100 brings more hurt than gaining £100 brings joy.

The underlying theory suggests that individuals tend to anticipate more potential regret as a result of actions than as a result of inactions, and therefore elect to take no action. For example, Ritov and Baron (1990) found that regret influenced the inaction of participants who declined a vaccination. Rationally, there was more chance of dying if you were unprotected and caught the disease; there was less chance of dying from the side effects of the vaccination but humans are not as rational as TDT originally suggested; participants still took no action. Anderson (2003) argues that status quo and omission options result in lower levels of perceived responsibility. There is some disagreement between researchers about whether responsibility is essential for regret (e.g. Simonson 1992) but it is nevertheless possible to explain Ritov and Baron's findings thus: Do nothing; less regret will accrue for something you haven't done than for something you have – despite the (strictly rational) probability of your dying having increased. Individuals, then, are posited to select these avoidant options to reduce their perceived responsibility and so, in turn, reduce their anticipated negative emotion and post-decisional regret.

Inertia in theory: conflict theory and the trade-off avoidance hypothesis

Choice deferral occurs when an individual selects not to choose for the time being – it is 'decision avoidance characterized by postponing a decision or refusing to select an option' (Anderson 2003: 144). Degree of conflict among different options affects choice deferral, although several theories have been advanced as to why this is so. There is evidence to suggest that two of these are applicable in critical incident DM: conflict theory and the trade-off avoidance hypothesis.

Conflict theory

Conflict theory posits that decision-makers desire justifications for the choices they make. It argues that conflict among options increases the difficulty of justifying the selection of one particular option. Consequently, people prefer those options that reduce their responsibility for the decision, for example, choice deferral. In our study, participants' identification of a pervasive 'blame culture' in critical incident environments gives weight to the utility of status quo and omission biases and conflict theory in explaining decision inertia. Difficulties relating to blame, avoidance of responsibility, and lack of honesty were the subject of 9.4 per cent of coded comment concerning difficulties. A tendency to criticise and blame other agencies for poor outcomes was frequently highlighted as pervasive in both the simulation and in real-life multi-agency child abuse inquiries.

In terms of Anderson's model, the factors of anticipated regret and blame can explain the reluctance of individuals to take responsibility and admit mistakes. However, the source of these factors must also be considered (i.e. the broader context that we have incorporated into the extended model) and the political culture was clearly salient for these participants, as is evident from the comments below. The tendency to distrust other agencies shows the difficulties in perceiving everyone as collaborating towards the same end goal (as they ought to have done); in short, this shows the impact of the organisational context on DM.

'The exercise gave the impression that a blame culture still exists amongst professionals from different agencies.'

'Whilst everyone was blaming the other, the child was in more danger.'

'People blame other agencies or attack other agencies to defend themselves.'

'No one admitted to failure of their procedures and duties.'

'No one is admitting "We got it wrong."'

'Although we all sing the song of children's welfare being paramount, when in a real-life situation, individual professionals tend to focus at protecting their backs first.'

'Covering ones back is a feature unfortunately.'

'By the time this review is taking place on legal advice each agency may be far too defensive to get to the truth of what in fact did or did not happen in this case.'

'There is no honesty as this leads to blame and people are victimised.'

'Interagency dishonesty.'

'We are also in need of trust and honesty within organisations.'

'Politics will limit multi-agency working.'

'As it stands, Working Together[2] is something we sometimes pretend to do, because we know it is what is required, and it can feel like a political game.'

Given this 'blame culture', it follows logically that the prospect of justifying a course of action will, in line with conflict theory, weigh significantly in practitioners' minds. As practitioners are aware, justifications may have to be made to two different audiences: (a) those external to their organisation, for example in the course of a public enquiry and (b) those within their organisation. Practitioners, however, will be much more concerned with (b) because, whereas external justification is merely a possibility, intra-organisation justification will definitely be required.

Consistent with this, the social contingency model of judgement and choice argues that, among the information that decision-makers consider, 'Subjective estimates of the reactions of those to whom they are accountable will be prominent' (Tetlock 1997: 663) or, in plainer English, people will worry what the boss might say. Furthermore, the nature of these reactions is likely to be determined by the degree of fit between the decision and organisational policies and procedures; consequently, these are significant considerations for practitioners as they contemplate decision options. Yet, as this study shows, policies and procedures can sometimes hinder DM. It is difficult even to select let alone justify an option if policy is not clear – 3.8 per cent of coded comment concerning difficulties highlighted this issue. Some found policies too complicated; others were concerned that existing policies and procedures were not comprehensive enough to be useful in complex cases. This is unsurprising as critical incidents, by definition, are atypical events but there are two points to be made here: 1) In theoretical terms, it reveals the limitation of NDM theories, which rely on situation/action-matching decision rules (Lipshitz 1994); that is, NDM does not account for how decisions are made in unique situations; and 2) In real-world terms, practitioners find themselves operating within legislative or policy frameworks that do not provide the means to deal effectively with the complexity they face.

Some features of a complex situation are unlikely to have been incorporated into any procedural 'guide'. Put simply, even policy planners with great foresight are unlikely to include what should be done in situation Z if situation Z has never occurred before. Note that we are not arguing that they should try. On the evidence of this study, overly prescriptive policies can restrict the autonomy of professionals who need to tailor decisions to a very specific situation. It is beyond the scope of this chapter to discuss the issue in detail and is, necessarily, a question for future research to explore the optimal balance between enabling and constraining policies in critical incident management. The straightforward point here is that organisational policies and procedures affect DM, (manifested in this study as decision avoidance) – hence, this context is incorporated into our extended DM model. Sample comments were:

'The necessity to ensure professional competence, whilst very important in itself, allows us to become too rigid to react to fluid and completely unique circumstances.'

'Procedures/standard operating procedures (SOP) do not describe the complexity of the incidents being dealt with.'

'The protocols and policies need to be clearer and simpler.'

'The processes seemed to paralyse me.'

'The professionals genuinely cared and wanted to do a good job but were let down possibly by poor systems or poor structures.'

'I do worry about my agency's performance indicators possibly having a detrimental effect on my ability to provide a service which genuinely seeks to protect children.'

'Some of those decisions made outside the Child Protection Meeting are because of laid down procedures that must happen in any investigation.'

'The constraints on people in their working life often hinders the ideal.'

In particular, the current legislative distinction between children in need and children at risk was singled out for criticism, being described as *'one that does not work well in favour of children'* and as *'actually putting children in danger of being overlooked and not provided with the safeguarding they deserve'*. Yet despite its perceived detrimental impact, practitioners have no choice but to operate within an organisational context of which this distinction forms an integral part. Again, it supports the argument that we need to look beyond the immediate environment in which decisions are made to the broader legislative, political and cultural context in which practitioners must operate.

Organisational structures can, therefore, frustrate practitioners, generating negative emotions such as fear, anxiety and despair through the imposition of legislation, policies or procedures that can be restrictive, inadequate or overly complex; that is, procedures that fail to support practitioners in the field. These emotions are likely to be heightened by the fact that, despite this lack of support, practitioners remain accountable to their organisations and are therefore bound to these flawed procedures. Anticipated regret emerges from this sense of accountability, as does anticipated blame. The outcome is a powerful desire to avoid responsibility for the decision and thereby reduce the degree of blame that may be ascribed to them for any potential negative outcome. Given the relationship between perceived responsibility and status quo and omission biases, together with the fact that individuals associate less wrongdoing with non-action than with action (e.g. Ritov and Baron 1990, 1995), this desire is often fulfilled through decision avoidance. When this course is taken, even by a single practitioner, the result is often complete inertia, since a unanimous plan of action cannot be agreed.

The features that incline towards decision avoidance, which we have discussed above, are features of any single agency. The picture is even more complicated in multi-agency collaborations; that is, the impact that these difficulties have on DM is multiplied in a multi-agency context, because the differing policies and procedures of several organisations can often produce further conflict. This effect was evident in this study, with lack of joined-up thinking and co-operation emerging as a key difficulty. Comments coded under this category made up 9.1 per cent of output concerning difficulties, with comments referring to different agendas, experiences and failure to collaborate effectively:

'Each agency basically operates to its own agenda.'

'Each agency has different agendas which frustrates the other.'

'The significance of particular events isn't always recognised in the same way by the different agencies.'

'Frustrations: other agencies getting on with their own thing – not really taking on board concerns expressed/overriding others/not giving other professionals credit for their opinion.'

'How often do we consider ourselves to be the only worker involved forgetting to look outside?'

'If you want to feel isolation, try being a social worker or police officer in this sort of situation!'

'What concerns me most is that we don't understand each others perspectives and we get stuck in our own agency's perspectives.'

'The first issue that strikes me was the absence of true joined-up thinking between the agencies.'

'I am frustrated when agencies take decisions that compromise decisions made in formal Child Protection Meetings.'

These themes highlight the overwhelming significance of organisations in the multi-agency process. The structure and climate of practitioners' 'home' organisations defines their behaviour within the multi-agency context, and consequently has an enormous impact on DM. Thus, the findings from this study clearly demonstrate that the context of critical incident DM extends far beyond the immediate case, and is firmly shaped by organisational structures. This ties in with the principles of conflict theory, the social contingency model of judgement and choice, and Anderson's proposed concepts of anticipated blame and regret.[3] Ultimately, when presented with conflicting options – none of which can be easily justified to their 'home' organisations – practitioners will seek to reduce their responsibility for the choice through deferral, omission or status quo biases (Anderson 2003). Again, this decision avoidance, even when carried through by only one practitioner in the group, will often result in complete inertia, since a plan cannot be agreed and implemented in the absence of total consensus.

Trade-off avoidance hypothesis

The trade-off avoidance hypothesis focuses on the relative values of decision options; it posits that when individuals are faced with options that have highly valued attributes, they will choose to avoid decisions in order to reduce the negative emotions stimulated by having to make such difficult choices. In other words, it is easy to choose between something highly valued versus something worthless. When someone has to choose between very good versus really good, they'll avoid the decision. This process, it is argued, may operate either on its own or simultaneously with that proposed by conflict theory. This theory has empirical support. Research has found that people often experience negative emotion when they are faced with a choice among options that put different values at odds (e.g. Luce *et al.* 1997; Luce, Bettman and Payne 2001). Furthermore, studies have shown an association between experiencing intense negative emotion and deferring decisions; people choose instead to acquire more information and then spend more time analysing that information (Luce 1998; Luce *et al.* 1997). The most information-acquisitive behaviour in these studies occurred in contexts where there was both a high level of conflict among options and a high level of experienced negative emotion. In the current study, information searches were frequent yet, as a result of poor communication and information-sharing practices, these searches were often overly time-consuming and, thus, were a key factor in decision inertia. Comments highlighting general poor communication between organisations comprised 6 per cent of coded output concerning difficulties that may have contributed to the ultimate failure to protect the child from further harm:

'Why did health ... discharge the child without informing the agencies involved?'

'Poor communication between school and other agencies involved.'

'Communication initially between all agencies could have been better.'

'Inter-agency communication was poor.'

'Appears still a lack of communication between all agencies has resulted in the circumstances unfolding as they did.'

A further 4.8 per cent of coded comment referred to general difficulties in information sharing, again attributed to issues such as lack of knowledge about policies or procedures but this time on an inter-agency level; incompatible systems and lack of trust between agencies was also a perceived difficulty:

'Not enough info from police or SS [Social Services] disseminated.'

'Education were aware of a history of non-attendance which wasn't shared with partner agencies.'

'Information was not available at the right time, i.e. info was there but failed to reach the right people at the right time.'

'Who to share information with?'

'Not knowing the other agencies abilities to find out information and what information.'

'The inconsistent distribution of information was frustrating but this reflects the real world!'

'Often, working across agencies, systems don't talk.'

'Was there enough trust and confidence between agencies to support full disclosure?'

'Inter-agency dishonesty – keeping control of the info (tell one agency enough to keep them on side or to give them the work).'

This highlights the extent of the impact of organisational structure and climate on multi-agency DM. Fear of being held accountable in one's own organisation can restrict information sharing with other organisations; this in turn is instrumental in effecting inertia.

These difficulties culminated in significant time delays and lengthy consultation processes – these were highlighted as problematic by 4.6 per cent of comment concerning difficulties. For example:

'We were unable to obtain the necessary information in time, many were requested but failed to materialise.'

'Substantial delay in the receipt of new information led to perception of lack of action.'

'Information requested was very slow in coming back.'

'It seems to take so much longer to get things done when you need to consult.'

The overall picture is one of complete inertia in which organisational structures and climates play an important role. This is consistent with the trade-off avoidance hypothesis, which posits that the primary source of negative emotion to be reduced 'is the process of making compromises (trade-offs) between options on attributes that are highly valued' (Anderson 2003: 145). It is the structure and climate of practitioners' 'home' organisations that determine many of the attributes they will value highly in the DM context. Accountability, through the prospect of post-decisional justification, likely increases the negative emotion being experienced, as practitioners search for valid reasons to value one attribute of organisational importance more highly than another. This often translates into a time-consuming search for further information, plagued by delays and poor practice; thus, decision avoidance results.

The impact on multi-agency teamwork

Critical incident decisions are usually made within teams, often comprised of practitioners from a number of different agencies. Teamwork is entirely dependent upon the behaviours of these team members. In shaping these behaviours, organisational structure and climate thus have a substantial impact on teamwork and, consequently, on team DM. For example, having a shared mental model is an important factor in effective teamwork; however, practitioners in multi-agency teams inevitably, although not necessarily consciously, incorporate features of their 'home' organisation into their mental models. This applies both to how practitioners understand the situation, and to the options by which they believe it might be best addressed.

As well as differences in the historical development and functions of different organisations at the broadest level, different perspectives may be apparent in the smallest operational details; for example, a manager who told practitioners to 'Check the history of the case' might discover very different documents landing on his/her desk: a record of past convictions from a police officer, family background information from a social worker, school attendance and behaviour information from an education welfare officer, while the health practitioner has indicated which injuries, jabs, or illnesses the child has had. Of course, when functioning effectively, this multi-agency collaboration would give a case manager a comprehensive picture for assessment purposes but given that 'what usually surfaces is a strong adherence to one's individual professional perspective' (Furniss 1991: 160), achievement of a shared mental model conducive to effective teamwork is delayed and possibly obstructed.

Team situational awareness is another significant factor in teamwork; it is achieved when information is gathered and exchanged earlier by team members, when plans are made farther in advance (Orasanu

1994), and when information is successfully shared between team members (Lipshitz *et al.* 2001). As this study shows, information sharing, communication and planning in the multi-agency arena often suffer as a result of organisational structures and climates. A mutual distrust pervades organisations, and instils in practitioners a reluctance to communicate and share information across agency boundaries, and a reluctance to make plans, for fear of being held to account within their 'home' organisations. Further, practitioners often selectively filter information to each another as they seek to avoid responsibility for decisions, and attempt to leave them for others to make. The outcome of these processes is often complete inertia; as consultation becomes increasingly time-consuming and complex, teamwork and DM are significantly impeded.

A model of decision avoidance

Anderson (2003) has pulled together the antecedent emotions described in this discussion, and incorporated them into a rational–emotional model of decision avoidance. This model allows for the fact that organisational structures and climates are instrumental in outcomes of decision avoidance. However, it does not make these relationships explicit. Thus, as it stands, it does not completely fill the gap left by major theories such as TDT and NDM. Rather, it provides a framework upon which the 'domino effect' of organisations on practitioners' DM in a multi-agency team setting can be fleshed out and understood in its entirety. In Figure 10.1, we suggest such an extension to the model (2003: 142), depicting the described impact of organisational climate on practitioners attempting to make decisions.

Avoiding decision avoidance? Looking for the positives

Recognition of the potential for negative outcomes generated by decision and action inertia was evident among the practitioners who took part in this study. Notably, this was complemented by a clear desire to overcome the antecedents of decision avoidance – 552 comments suggested improvements to working practices geared towards achieving this goal. Three key themes emerged, each divided into two sub-themes:

Table 10.1 Practitioners' perceptions of existing problems in child abuse inquiries

Category	Frequency
Action and follow-up/review of actions	75
Blame, responsibility/accountability and lack of honesty	57
Lack of joined-up thinking and co-operation	55
Decision-making and interpretation of information	40
General poor communication between agencies	36
General difficulties regarding the sharing of information	29
Length of time to consult, communicate and/or share information	28
Failure to include/consider child	27
Difficulties regarding policies/procedures/targets	23
Failure to learn from past incidents and/or mistakes	18
Difficulties involving leadership	16
Lack of involvement of key professionals	16
Poor-quality records and/or referrals	14
Failure to include family in process	12
Difficulties with interaction with family	12
Ambiguity and/or unclear meaning of shared information and/or referrals	11
High staff turnover	10
Constraints/barriers/resources	10
Roles and responsibilities	10
Data protection and/or confidentiality concerns	10
Complacency	9
Quantity of meetings	9
Overemphasis on cultural issues	8
Language	8
Failure to consider culture	7
External perceptions	7
Shortage of financial resources	7
Staff support and/or supervision	7
Shortage of skilled/experienced staff	7
Thresholds	6
Volume of information and overcomprehensiveness	6
Approach/decision-making	5
Failure to include and/or consider community in process	3
Poor communication within agencies	3
Failure to listen to frontline workers	2
Rationale for decisions not properly explained	1
Failure to challenge practice	1

I Accountability: learning lessons and sharing responsibility

(i) Improve review processes and learn from mistakes
Practitioners most frequently suggested improvements in review processes and learning from mistakes as ways to work together and respond to critical incidents more effectively. Comments in this category comprised 8.7 per cent of total coded output suggesting improvements; they referred to the need to learn from experience and to strive to improve even where practice is already effective by fostering a climate where constructive criticism, mutual monitoring and reciprocal quality assurance are encouraged.

> *'Blame is not the issue but moving on, learning and implementing those lessons must be.'*

> *'We have to look at where things went wrong. If we don't learn and improve things then it is a useless exercise in my view.'*

> *'We should always be looking to improve even where things went well.'*

> *'I think Part 8s[4] are sometimes more damaging than helpful, the way they are sometimes conducted. We must look at alternative ways of reviewing'* – with the aim of *'[e]stablishing an environment conducive to open exploration of actions taken and not taken.'*

> *'I think we should quality assure each other as agencies.'*

> *'We should all be encouraged to ask more "why" questions of each other.'*

> *'The biggest benefit to come from working closely with other agencies is when challenges are made.'*

> *'We must not hesitate to criticise where appropriate, but it has to be constructive.'*

(ii) Responsibility and commitment to improvement
Suggestions relating to responsibility and commitment to improvement were the subject of 5.4 per cent of the coded comment concerning strategies for improvement, and referred to owning and sharing responsibility for decisions and mistakes and the need for a commitment to improvement:

> *'Accepting that we share the same responsibility rather than dumping it on any one agency!'*

'Accepting responsibility for your actions, saying sorry ... vital.'

'Committing yourself to improving your practice [is] vital.'

'I will in future organise a conference if I am concern [sic] and not assume that another agency will do it.'

2 Information: records, sharing and communication

(i) Speed, clarity and understanding

Comments referring to the improvement of communication and information sharing through greater speed, and enhanced clarity and understanding comprised 7.6 per cent of coded comment suggesting improvements. Practitioners placed a strong emphasis on the importance of effective communication and information sharing, with a notable emphasis on the fact that different agencies' perspectives and boundaries must be transcended to facilitate communication, thus highlighting the importance of organisational context:

'Need to accept that while we do not always agree I would rather have the information.'

'We also need to ensure other agencies understand the reason for our request and so understand the urgency.'

'We need not only to present the information but offer an explanation/ interpretation of the impact of the information on the situation and plan from the presenting agency's viewpoint.'

'Is the language issue more about understanding each others language?'

'There is something about sharing a common approach to risk so that if information is requested it can be prioritised appropriately: what needs to be shared immediately, what can wait a little.'

'But can we put ourselves in other people's shoes – do we make enough effort to "understand" what they are trying to convey?'

(ii) Improve record keeping

The importance of good record keeping was widely agreed upon by practitioners, and was the subject of 4.9 per cent of coded comment suggesting improvements. Suggestions included the need for all agencies to keep comprehensive, contemporaneous records. The need for a central database and common methods of recording information across agencies was also highlighted; this supports our argument that different organisational contexts and procedures can impede collaboration and effective DM. Participants also suggested the use of pro formas to support accurate records and a clear overview system to manage the information:

'Importance of adequate recording' – in response: 'Very important – if it isn't in the notes it didn't happen.'

'That the case is recorded properly including dates and times etc.'

'Clearly timed communication which is recorded.'

'Documentation and capturing corridor conversations' – re recording these: 'We have to try, only by striving for the ideal can we improve.'

'Contemporaneous recording would have enabled a better understanding of the status of the [simulation] case.'

'The need for contemporaneous notes.'

'If all agencies involved with children all kept an overview of case file information ...'

'A shorthand overview such as on the IRT [Identification, Referral and Tracking] will help.'

'Perhaps pro-forma forms could be used to help staff keep better records so that in the event of another crisis it is easier to have a time-line and chronology' – in response: 'Interesting idea ... I support this proposal.'

'The need for [sic] central database.'

'Uniform file structure etc. to help them manage and absorb the information.'

'Common documentation where possible.'

3 Interpositional knowledge, co-operation and building relationships

(i) Building relationships, sharing and learning
Practitioners stressed both the need for and a commitment to genuine partnership working to improve multi-agency inquiries. Learning from other professionals/agencies and sharing one's own experiences were identified as key ways by which practitioners could work together more effectively and evolve good practice. Suggestions included a shared focus and networking with professionals in other

areas, again, implying the difficulties caused by barriers between different organisations:

'This [saving lives] will only happen when we work together collectively.'

'What matters to me is the child and the way we work together in a truly multi-agency context.'

'I want more time to get into the heads of other agencies.'

'Being willing to work together on issues – not just saying it's now over to you.'

'The most important element for me of working with other agencies is to learn from other professionals' experience, also to share my experiences.'

'The thing that excites me most about multi-agency working in CP [child protection] is the potential for a synchronised evolvement of good (i.e. genuinely effective) practice.'

'I find it of great benefit that colleagues from other agencies bring their concerns to me.'

'When a good relationship is developed then we do a better job.'

'The need for inter-agency networking – say, quarterly – to establish good partnership working.'

'Personal knowledge of different professionals can help to achieve success.'

'Face-to-face interaction.'

'A shared focus despite differing outcomes.'

'Shared understanding of our joint outcomes.'

(ii) Understanding others' roles, responsibilities and systems
A strong emphasis was placed on the importance of understanding other professionals and agencies. Specifically, a need for greater interpositional knowledge (knowledge of the tasks performed by others) was identified. Highlighted as particularly important to achieve were increased understanding of other agencies' systems and approaches and the roles, responsibilities and constraints within which other professionals work. Again, we may infer the impact of organisational context in impeding effective collaboration:

'An absolute knowledge/awareness/understanding explosion across the agencies about the agencies.'

'An appreciation of other agencies' methods of decision-making.'

'We need to understand the role of other agencies.'

'Being clear about the strengths and limitations of each other's roles.'

'There needs to be a greater understanding of each other's ... restrictions.'

'In an investigation other agencies need to realise that police need to fully investigate by speaking to victims.'

'Understanding the complexities of policing and social working when driven by legal constraints.'

'Better understanding needed of systems in place in other departments.'

Yet, while agreement on the need for understanding in these areas was widespread, and acceptance of the responsibility for such understanding was expressed – *'It's up to us as learning people to continue with our learning'* – few practitioners suggested ways in which this could be achieved in practice. Some ideas were put forward referring to building knowledge and understanding across agency boundaries; however, they were not discussed in depth or widely commented upon by practitioners:

'It is a must to have regular joint forums, formal and informal to look at the world of others.'

'The need for in-borough regular service meetings to . . . [understand] roles and responsibilities of each agency.'

'Learn about them, spend an hour a week at their offices.'

'Explaining the thresholds.'

Moving forward

These suggestions for improvement correspond to the key difficulties in critical incident decision-making identified in this study – inertia, blame, difficulties in communication and information sharing, and lack of co-operation among agencies. They are aimed towards altering the organisational climates within which practitioners operate, and consequently towards reducing the negative emotion and conflict that these can give rise to in decision situations. Ultimately, their implementation may therefore serve to tackle decision avoidance effectively through 'freeing' practitioners to make decisions.

Conclusion

Decision theory has overlooked the possibility that organisational structures and climates play an important role in decision-making. This shortcoming has arisen both from omission of the influence of contextual factors, for example in TDT, and from an insufficient view of context as the immediate field setting only, such as in NDM. Rather than constituting the context, the immediate field setting is simply the arena in which a range of competing forces are played out. These forces, and thus DM processes, can only be completely understood by recognising that context is an expansive entity, incorporating practitioners, organisations, and wider social and political systems. Such forces interact dynamically, the structure and climate of each influencing and shaping each other. Politicians legislate to create the broad context in which public sector employees must work. Organisations' policies and procedures are powerful communicators of the status quo to practitioners. Reciprocally, professionals lead and shape their agencies via the development of new strategies; even the decisions, decision errors or decision avoidance of individuals can be powerful enough to alter the political, cultural and legislative landscape over the long term. Consider the impact of the Stephen Lawrence inquiry (Macpherson 1999).

In this chapter, we have called for the necessary expansion of decision theory to recognise and incorporate these effects. Organisations have an overwhelming impact on DM and, in the multi-agency arena in particular, can often be the forces behind decision avoidance. Differences in organisational structures and climates result in differences in the way practitioners perceive both situations and potential actions. This in turn generates conflict in the multi-agency setting: a shared mental model cannot be agreed upon, and no response option presents which is acceptable to all organisations. For the individual, the accountability of practitioners to their 'home' organisations causes them to experience negative emotions in these situations. Anticipated blame and regret can weigh heavily in their thoughts. As demonstrated, this often has a detrimental impact

Earlier antecedents   Antecedents   Decision

Emotional   Avoidance   Outcomes

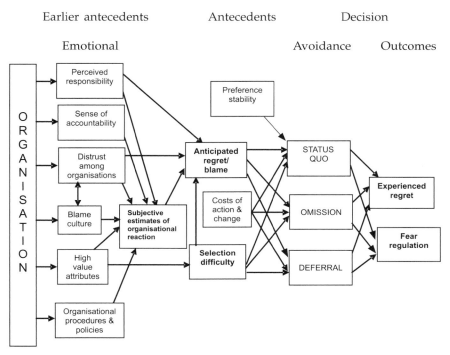

Figure 10.1. An extension of Anderson's (2003) rational–emotional model of decision avoidance, presented in the form of a path diagram. As in Anderson's diagram, bold text indicates emotional influences.

on information sharing and communication, resulting in a time-consuming consultation process. The overarching effect, however, is the desire that practitioners experience to reduce their responsibility for the decision and, if possible, to avoid it altogether. This desire is realised by practitioners through implementing a decision avoidance strategy, such as status quo maintenance, action omission, or choice deferral; the ultimate outcome is inertia.

We have presented below, in Figure 10.1, an extension to Anderson's rational–emotional model of decision avoidance, indicating the impact of the organisation. Hitherto, the model made a valuable contribution to our understanding of the cognitive processes within an individual that may cause decision avoidance but none of us exists in a social vacuum. The simplest decision – to have a pint, say – will be influenced by the wishes of others with whom we may wish to drink – one friend likes traditional pubs, another insists on a happy hour bar serving garish cocktails complete with umbrellas and sparklers; either could increase your anticipated regret and make you avoid the decision, depending, of course, on your own preferences. Likewise, professionals – in any organisation – rarely make decisions alone. No decision is devoid of context so the context must be considered. In a political culture that increasingly promotes 'joined-up thinking', where practitioners are expected to collaborate across agencies, this context is especially pertinent.

We have incorporated into Anderson's original model various factors gleaned from this study highlighting the blame culture in which organisations exist and how this may be manifested as distrust between organisations. Similarly, differing organisational procedures and priorities may contribute to the selection difficulty when contemplating a decision. Participants in this study revealed their lack of interpositional knowledge about colleagues in other agencies. They also displayed a keen sense of accountability. When they are expected to act in relative ignorance of the priorities and procedures of agencies other than their 'home' organisation, making a subjective estimate of organisational reactions is extraordinarily difficult. In concrete terms, it is easy to see how an individual would be anxious if he or she anticipates being held responsible for a decision when they have limited knowledge of, say, the legislative constraints of other agencies. Small wonder that they seek to pass the decision on to others and inertia occurs – those others have similarly imperfect knowledge.

This study showed that information sharing and communication is problematic but it would be trite to draw the simplistic conclusion that it's merely 'the old communication problem'. Rather, this study has taken the first steps in gathering valid data from practitioners who bring with them extensive real-life experience of the contexts in which they work. In the resulting extension to Anderson's (2003) model, we have presented a path diagram from the broadest organisational context to the emotional and rational factors that may cause decision avoidance in an individual. Future research should build on the work discussed here, beginning with an exploration of the impact of organisations in a range of multi-agency DM arenas, and a test implementation of the strategies for improvement suggested in this study. Understanding these relationships, and investigating the effects of wider social and political systems on these organisations, and subsequently on DM, will bolster the field of decision theory, and, potentially in time, decision-making itself. Edwards and Fasolo claim that, 'Decisions are defined by their stakes' (2001: 582). Given that the stakes in this arena concern the life or death of children, there are few more important tasks.

Notes

1 For the sake of brevity, the term 'decision-making' and its abbreviation 'DM' refer interchangeably to decisions that *are* made as well as to decisions that *are not* made (i.e. decision avoidance).

2 This comment refers to the 1999 government document 'Working Together to Safeguard Children', which sets out how all agencies (e.g. health, education, police, social services, probation etc.) should work together to promote children's welfare and protect them from abuse and neglect. It sits within the broader legislative framework of the 1989 Children Act and the 1950 European Convention on Human Rights.

3 Although, notably, Anderson argues that deferral is less clearly associated with decreased blame than status quo or omission options.

4 A 'Part 8 Review' refers to Chapter 8 of the Department of Health document 'Working Together to Safeguard Children' (1999). Such reviews are conducted by Area Child Protection Committees. They are convened in the event that a child has died or sustained life-threatening injuries or serious and permanent impairment of health and development or been subjected to serious sexual abuse and the case gives rise to concerns about inter-agency working. They aim to establish what lessons may be learned.

References

Alison, L.J., West, A. and Goodwill, A. (2004) 'The academic and the practitioner: pragmatists' views of offender profiling', *Psychology and Public Policy*, 10: 71–101.

Anderson, C.J. (2003) 'The psychology of doing nothing: forms of decision avoidance result from reason and emotion', *Psychological Bulletin*, 129: 139–67.

Beach, L.R. (1997) *The psychology of decision making: people in organizations*. Thousand Oaks, CA: Sage Publications.

Bernoulli, D. (1738) 'Specimen theoriae novae de mensura sortis [Exposition of a new theory of the measurement of risk]. *Commentarii Academiae Scientrum Imperialis Petropolitanae*, 5: 175–92.

Bichard, M. (2004) The Bichard inquiry report. London: The Stationery Office. Available: [online] http://www.bichardinquiry.org.uk/report [accessed February 2006].

Cannon-Bowers, J.A., Salas, E. and Converse, S. (1993) 'Shared mental models in expert team decision making', in N.J. Castellen (ed.), *Individual and group decision making: Current Issues* (pp. 221–46). Hillsdale, NJ: Erlbaum.

Cohen, M.S., Freeman, J.T. and Thompson, B. (1998) 'Critical thinking skills in tactical decision making: a model and a training strategy', in J.A. Cannon-Bowers and E. Salas (eds), *Decision making under stress: emerging themes and applications* (pp. 161–9). Aldershot: Ashgate.

Connolly, T. and Beach, L.R. (2000) 'The theory of image theory: an examination of the central conceptual structure', in T. Connolly, H.R. Arkes and K.R. Hammond (eds), *Judgment and decision making: an interdisciplinary reader* (pp. 755–65). Cambridge: Cambridge University Press.

Crego, J. (2002) *10,000 volts for critical incident managers.* Police Training College, England, November, 2002.

Crego, J. and Alison, L.J. (2004) 'Control and legacy as functions of perceived criticality in major incidents', *Journal of Investigative Psychology and Offender Profiling,* 1: 207–25.

Crego, J. and Harris, C. (2002) 'Training decision-making by team based simulation', in R. Flin and K. Arbuthnot (eds), *Incident command: tales from the hot seat* (pp. 258–69). Aldershot: Ashgate.

Department of Health, Home Office, Department for Education and Employment (1999) Working together to safeguard children: a guide to inter-agency working to safeguard and promote the welfare of children. Available: [online] http://www.dh.gov.uk/assetroot/04/07/58/24/04075824.pdf [accessed September 2006].

Edwards, W. and Fasolo, B. (2001) 'Decision technology', *Annual Review of Psychology, 52:* 581–606.

Fishman, D.B. (1999) *The case for pragmatic psychology.* New York: New York University Press.

Furniss, T. (1991) *The multi-professional handbook of child sexual abuse.* London: Routledge.

Inman, J. and Zeelenberg, M. (2002) 'Regret in repeat purchase versus switching decisions: the attenuating role of decision justifiability', *Journal of Consumer Research,* 29: 116–28.

Klein, G.A. (1998) *Sources of power: how people make decisions.* Cambridge, MA: MIT Press.

Klein, G.A., Orasanu, J., Calderwood, R. and Zsambok, C.E. (1993) *Decision making in action: models and methods.* Norwood, CT: Ablex.

Laming. H. (2003) The Victoria Climbié inquiry. Report of an inquiry by Lord Laming. London: The Stationery Office. Available [online]: http:/www.victoria-climbie-inquiry.org.uk/finreport/finreport.htm [accessed March 2006].

Lipshitz, R. (1994) 'Decision making in three modes', *Journal for the Theory of Social Behaviour,* 24: 47–66.

Lipshitz, R. (1997) 'Coping with uncertainty: beyond the reduce, quantify and plug heuristic', in R. Flin, E. Salas, M. Strub and L. Martin (eds), *Decision making under stress: emerging themes and applications* (pp. 149–60). Aldershot: Ashgate.

Lipshitz, R. and Strauss, O. (1997) 'Coping with uncertainty: a naturalistic decision making analysis', *Organizational Behavior and Human Decision Processes,* 69: 149–63.

Lipshitz, R., Klein, G., Orasanu, J. and Salas, E. (2001) 'Taking stock of naturalistic decision making', *Journal of Behavioral Decision Making,* 14: 331–52.

Luce, M.F. (1998) Choosing to avoid: coping with negatively emotion-laden consumer decisions', *Journal of Consumer Research*, 24: 409–33.

Luce, M.F., Bettman, J.R. and Payne, J.W. (1997) 'Choice processing in emotionally difficult decisions', *Journal of Experimental Psychology: Learning, Memory and Cognition*, 23: 384–405.

Luce, M.F., Bettman, J.R. and Payne, J.W. (2001) 'Emotional decisions: tradeoff difficulty and coping in consumer choice', *Monographs of the Journal of Consumer Research*, 1.

Macpherson, W. (1999) The Stephen Lawrence inquiry. Report of an inquiry by Sir William Macpherson of Cluny. London: HMSO. Available [online]: http://www.archive.official-documents.co.uk/document/cm42/4262/4262/htm [accessed March 2006].

Orasanu, J. (1994) 'Shared problem models and flight crew performance', in N. Johnston, N. Mcdonald and R. Fuller (eds), *Aviation psychology in practice* (pp. 255–85). Aldershot: Ashgate.

Orasanu, J. (1997) 'Stress and naturalistic decision making: strengthening the weak links', in J.A. Cannon-Bowers, and E. Salas (eds), *Decision making under stress: emerging themes and applications* (pp. 49–160). Aldershot: Ashgate.

Pennington, N. and Hastie, R. (1997) 'Explanation-based decision making: effects of memory structure on judgment', in W.M. Goldstein and R.M. Hogarth (eds), *Research on judgment and decision making: currents, connections and controversies* (pp. 454–81). Cambridge: Cambridge University Press.

Riis, J. and Schwarz, N. (2000, November) *Status quo selection increases with consecutive emotionally difficult decisions*. Poster presented at the meeting of the Society for Judgment and Decision Making, New Orleans, LA.

Ritov, I. and Baron, J. (1990) 'Reluctance to vaccinate: omission bias and ambiguity', *Journal of Behavioral Decision Making*, 3: 263–77.

Ritov, I. and Baron, J. (1995) 'Outcome knowledge, regret and omission bias', *Organizational Behavior and Human Decision Processes*, 64: 119–27.

Salas, E., Prince, C., Baker, D.P. and Shrestha, L. (1995) 'Situation awareness in team performance: implications for measurement and training', *Human Factors*, 37: 123–36.

Savage, L.J. (1954) *The foundations of statistics*. New York: Wiley.

Simonson, I. (1992) 'The influence of anticipating regret and responsibility on purchase decisions', *Journal of Consumer Research*, 19: 105–18.

Tetlock, P.E. (1997) 'An alternative metaphor in the study of judgment and choice: people as politicians', in W.M. Goldstein and R.M. Hogarth (eds) *Research on judgment and decision making: currents, connections and controversies* (pp. 657–80). Cambridge: Cambridge University Press.

Volpe, C.E., Cannon-Bowers, J.A., Salas, E. and Spector, P. (1996) 'The impact of cross training on team functioning', *Human Factors*, 38: 87–100.

Appendix A

Existing Problems

A Multi-agency working
I Communication and information sharing
1 *Length of time to consult, communicate and/or share information*
Failure to respond promptly to requests for information or to referrals; delays in receiving information; failure to chase up requested information or referrals when no response was received or there was a delay in response; process of consultation, e.g. organising strategy meetings and/or case conferences, was overly time-consuming; urgency for/need for information not made clear in requests.

2 *Data protection and/or confidentiality concerns*
Concerns about data protection issues and/or confidentiality adversely affected information sharing; lack of confidence and/or lack of clear guidance about when information can be shared.

3 *Ambiguity and/or lack of clarity in the meaning of shared information and/or referrals*
Shared information was ambiguous/open to misinterpretation/difficult to interpret/unclear/misleading; concerns were not made clear/explicit; inconsistency in information.

4 *Poor-quality records and/or referrals*
Records/referrals incomplete, i.e. incidents/conversations not recorded; records/referrals inaccurate; records/correspondence/referrals not clearly dated; poor note taking; flimsy reports; records missing, including missing minutes.

5 *Volume of information and overcomprehensiveness*
Too much information; agencies focused too much on obtaining further information; overcomprehensiveness of referrals.

6 *General difficulties regarding the sharing of information*
Difficulties regarding the sharing of information not elsewhere categorised. Ineffective information sharing; not enough information shared; information shared in an *ad hoc* manner; information, intentionally or unintentionally, not made available to all relevant agencies and/or personnel; flow of information restricted and/or controlled.

7 *Poor communication within agencies*
Staff from the same organisation communicated poorly with each other.

8 *General poor communication between agencies*
Poor communication between agencies not elsewhere categorised. Lack of early communication; distance between agencies hindering communication; difficulty in contacting staff in other agencies.

II Other agencies
9 *Roles and responsibilities*
Failure to understand the roles and responsibilities of other agencies; need for greater understanding of the roles and responsibilities of other agencies.

10 *Constraints/barriers/resources*
Failure to understand the constraints, legal and otherwise, and barriers that other agencies operate under; need for greater understanding of the constraints, legal and otherwise, and barriers that other agencies operate under; differences between agencies in prioritisation and use of resources.

11 *Language*
Failure to understand the language and/or terminology used by other agencies; need for greater understanding of the language and/or terminology used by other agencies; different language and/or terminology used by agencies.

12 *Approach/decision-making*
Failure to understand the approach taken by other agencies and/or their decision-making processes; need for greater understanding of the approach taken by other agencies and/or their decision-making processes; differences between agencies' approaches and/or their decision-making processes; lack of agreed consistent practice.

13 *Thresholds*
Failure to understand other agencies' thresholds of concern and/or action; need for greater understanding of other agencies' thresholds of concern and/or action; differences between agencies' thresholds of concern and/or action.

14 *Lack of joined-up thinking and co-operation*
General lack of multi-agency working; agencies/professionals isolated; agencies failing to co-operate with one another; differences between agencies' agendas and/or priorities; agencies continuing 'to do their own thing'; agencies not taking on board concerns expressed by other agencies; overriding others; failure to consider alternative views; difficulties caused by different/conflicting interpretations of events/information; disagreements.

III Decision-making; action; accountability and responsibility

15 *Quantity of meetings*

Too many meetings are held; there is too much talking/discussion.

16 *Decision-making and interpretation of information*

Decisions made without all the facts/without gathering all the information; decisions based on or affected by presumptions or assumptions; failure to interpret information appropriately; failure to pull information together; failure to 'put puzzle pieces together'; failure to understand and/or weight risk; failure to recognise/identify warning signals early; failure to identify main issues early.

17 *Action and follow-up/review of actions*

Lack of preventative work; action too late/only at crisis point; thresholds for intervention too high; failure to act promptly on information; lack of action or not enough action; letting cases drift; failure to put agreed plans into action; failure to check agreed plans were put into action; failure to review actions/practice.

18 *Lack of involvement of key professionals*

Key people not attending strategy/planning meetings; people with authority and/or ability to make decisions not attending strategy/ planning meetings; lack of consultation; key people not involved in decision-making/planning process.

19 *Difficulties involving leadership*

Lack of clarity around leadership, including both leadership of single agencies and leadership of the multi-agency process; failure to identify lead agency in multi-agency process; reluctance and/or failure to take lead/control/initiative/responsibility in an inquiry.

20 *Blame, responsibility/accountability and lack of honesty*

Blaming other agencies; back covering; politics; unnecessary or unhelpful criticism; failure to accept responsibility or accountability when mistakes are made and/or things go wrong; lack of honesty; diffusion of responsibility; lack of clarity about accountability between agencies. NB: this does not include statements blaming other agencies, but rather statements identifying the blaming of other agencies as a difficulty in multi-agency working.

21 *Difficulties involving policies/procedures/targets*

Time-consuming, lengthy policies/procedures; adverse effect of performance indicators on responses/actions, for example slowing, constraining; complex/unclear policies/procedures; procedures do not capture complexity of child protection work.

22 *Complacency*
Complacency; lack of contingency planning (failure to consider 'what if?' possibilities); lack of proactivity.

23 *Failure to learn from past incidents and/or mistakes*
Lack of reflection; lessons not learned; practices not changed in light of past incidents and/or mistakes.

24 *Failure to challenge practice*
Failure to challenge practice of other professionals and/or agencies.

25 *Rationale for decisions not properly explained*
Rationale for decisions unclear/not properly explained; lack of transparency in process.

IV Management, staff, supervision and resources

26 *High staff turnover*
High turnover of staff; no consistent allocated keyworker; constant change in personnel.

27 *Shortage of skilled/experienced/permanent staff*
Shortage of skilled staff; lack of 24-hour availability of staff; junior staff allocated complex cases; high levels of temporary or locum staff.

28 *Staff support and/or supervision*
Staff do not receive and/or are not confident of receiving adequate support and/or supervision from their managers and/or organisations; staff feel overwhelmed.

29 *Failure to listen to frontline workers*
Policymakers and/or managers do not listen to the ideas of frontline workers.

30 *Shortage of financial resources*

B General

31 *External perceptions*
Concern about what the media/public/courts/public inquiries will say/think about decisions made and/or actions taken and/or not taken; stigma attached to agencies; media do not report successes; 'Good news stories don't sell newspapers in the UK.'

32 *Failure to include/consider the child*
Focus not always on the child; child not included in the process; child's needs not considered; failure to speak to child (at all or away from parent); best interests of child did not come first.

33 *Difficulties with interaction with family*
Excess focus on any one member of the family; excess focus on and/or attention given to parents; actions affected by fear of offending parents/fear of interfering/fear of infringing parents' rights/sympathy

to parents/wanting to keep open mind; failure to consider family as a system; failure to consider impact of one family member's behaviour on the others.

34 *Failure to include family in process*

Failure to look at wider support needs of family; failure to consider family's input.

35 *Failure to consider culture*

Failure to consider cultural issues; failure to consider language issues; failure to consider impact of culture on access and engagement with services.

36 *Overemphasis on cultural issues*

Overemphasis/consideration of cultural issues; consideration of cultural issues rather than child welfare issues; consideration of cultural issues at expense of child safety.

37 *Failure to consider and/or include community in process*

Failure to consider views and/or concerns of community; failure to consider impact of community on child and/or family; failure to include community agencies in process.

Appendix B

Suggested improvements

General

1 *Create multi-agency teams/a common agency*
Create multi-agency/inter-agency teams; develop a new agency to address all issues under one roof; a common agency; co-location (common, shared premises).

2 *Lead agency*
Establish lead agency early/from outset; have clear leadership; ensure all agencies know who lead agency is; named key worker/case worker; flexibility for lead to change; base lead agency on priority issues.

3 *Improving procedures*
Change system; establish shared procedures; clear processes; follow procedures; work from bottom up; structure multi-agency working in role and responsibility of each agency; universal set of child welfare priorities; improved recruitment procedures/systems; clearly structured multi-agency approach; develop consistent practice across local authorities; establish joint working procedures; legislation to make practitioners attend strategic/ordinary meetings; have clear thresholds for intervention.

4 *Improving record keeping*
Contemporaneous recording; importance of adequate record keeping; include dates and times; record all information and communications (including corridor conversations); retain overview of information; uniform file structure/common documentation; use of pro formas; time-line, chronology; importance of good notes; shared, central database.

5 *Maintain focus on children*
Focus on child; children's needs must be priority; best interest of child first; protection of children must be priority; less focus on needs of adults; keep child at centre of practice; focus on best outcome for child, not best outcome for agency.

6 *Include children*
Children's voices should be heard; children should be represented; speak to children and ascertain their views, wishes, feelings; work with children; consult children; seek children's views about joint working; empower children; enable children to participate in process; include input of children; involve children in Chapter 8 process.

7 *Parents/families*
Enable parents to participate in process; empower families; include input of families; don't be intimidated by parents/families and therefore fail to take action; adults must have investment in changing; work with families; sometimes make decisions for parents; enable parents to feel supported, not shamed and judged; involve parents in Chapter 8 process.

Specific
Improving communication and information sharing
8 *Develop common language*
Develop a common language/a core shorthand.
9 *Technology*
Use technology to overcome time delays.
10 *Duty/responsibility and protocols/procedures*
Develop clearer channels of communication; understand responsibilities and duty to share/disclose information; shared responsibility to communicate/share information; develop processes/protocols/ legislation/positive guidance/corporate responsibility re information sharing; confidence in info sharing.
11 *Speed, clarity and understanding*
Need to disseminate information quickly and effectively; make sure communication is clear; ensure what we're saying is being understood; make effort to understand information that is being conveyed; interpret facts correctly; check information; seek clarification; clearly timed communication; offer interpretation of information; understand significance of info; grade info correctly; make clear reason for request; ensure urgency is understood; set info in context.
12 *Regular meetings*
Hold regular multi-agency meetings to exchange information; update regularly; communicate outside crisis situations; develop good relationships at senior level.
13 *Commitment and inclusion*
Involve all agencies in information-gathering process; hold meaningful discussions with partner agencies; talk to all agencies; provide all agencies/professionals with information; willingness to share information; include community/voluntary agencies; full involvement of relevant staff; recognise all agencies have a role to play; ensure relevant people invited to strategy meetings.

Staff, training and resources
14 *Resources, staff numbers and staff availability*
Need more trained staff; 24-hour availability of staff; need enough experienced staff; need more resources.
15 *Training*
Joint training; training using Hydra; ensure child protection training is undertaken; monitor staff training; need to be more expert at risk assessing; inter-agency training; single agency training.
16 *Quality and attitude*
Can-do mentality; ambition and passion; committed; drive; professionalism; belief; sincere; proactive; need good-quality staff; genuine interest in well-being of children and families; commitment to working together; skilled and experienced; strive for ideal; willing to go extra mile; ability to work with partner agencies; commitment to children; professional distance; understanding; empathy.
17 *Working conditions and motivation*
Better pay; time to think; incentives.
18 *Managers and supervision*
Support staff; listen to workers' ideas; have clear lines of accountability within agencies; appraisal; regular supervision; provide support, guidance and advice; clear management and supervision; commitment at senior level to inter-agency work; deal with performance issues in supportive, developmental, effective manner; managers able to take difficult decisions; managers should be aware of investigations from early stages; take action against serious professional issues; managers to ensure implementation of plans/actions agreed.

Blame, responsibility/accountability and trust
19 *Eradicate blame and defensiveness*
Stop apportioning blame; stop complaining; move away from defensiveness; avoid blame culture; eliminate blame culture.
20 *Responsibility and commitment to improvement*
Take responsibility for enhancing practice; take responsibility for doing what is best for child; take ownership; accept responsibility; apologise; admit to mistakes; commit to improvement; implement lessons learned; agencies should take equal responsibility for action or inaction; recognise responsibility to raise concerns; shared responsibility for risk management; don't pass buck; equal ownership of joint decisions; responsibility to attend meetings; shared responsibility and accountability.
21 *Trust, honesty and confidence*
Trust between agencies; trust others to do their job; need honesty

within and between agencies; need transparency; trust others to work in best interests of child; openness and honesty; confidence that each agency will complete tasks assigned to them; get to know colleagues in other areas and build up trust.

Actions and decision-making

22 *Improve decision-making*

Better decisions made when all agencies take responsibility; need to make decisions; need to have clear rationale/explanations for decisions; need more strategic thinking.

23 *Improve planning and actions*

Action decisions earlier; take protective measures; identify key issues early; prioritise responses; focus on preventative work; trace root cause; don't sit and wait; take immediate protective/investigative actions; use and analyse available info; formulate plans; be proactive; recognise multi-agency intervention is an ongoing process; engage children/families before need issues become harm issues.

24 *Improve review processes and learn from mistakes*

Honestly review practice; learn from mistakes; learn from training events; continual review; question and reflect; agencies should quality assure each other; be prepared to challenge each other; constructive criticism; quarterly reviews; monitor though joint agency meetings; ask 'why' questions; exploration actions taken and not taken; review actions on time-effective basis; build review into action plans; don't assume actions are being taken; look at alternative ways of reviewing; look to improve even when things go well.

25 *Acknowledge good practice*

Give positive feedback; multi-agency commendation process; research what is working; celebrate and praise good practice/decisions.

Interpositional knowledge, co-operation and building relationships

26 *Understanding others' roles, responsibilities and systems*

Understand roles and responsibilities of others; cross-agency understanding; understand systems in other departments; understand other agencies'/professionals' constraints; understand barriers; spend time in each other's offices; joint forums; explaining thresholds.

27 *Understanding each others' perspectives/issues*

Understand others' perspectives; think about other agencies' issues; put ourselves in other peoples' shoes; know opinion of others; respect others' perspectives; open mind to views of others.

28 *Building relationships, sharing and learning*
Share experiences; learn from others' experiences; shared professionalism and shared focus; share frustrations; evolve good practice; agreed and shared outcomes that are achievable; listen; dialogue; meet regularly; networking; face-to-face interaction.

Table 10.2 Practitioners' suggestions for improving working together

Category	Frequency
Improve review processes and learn from mistakes	48
Speed, clarity and understanding (of communication/ information)	42
Building relationships, sharing and learning	37
Responsibility and commitment to improvement	30
Understanding others' roles, responsibilities and systems	29
Quality and attitude of staff	29
Improving record keeping	27
Parents/families	26
Managers and supervision	25
Commitment and inclusion	23
Improving procedures	21
Include children	20
Maintain focus on children	19
Improve planning and actions	18
Training	18
Understanding each others' perspectives/issues	17
Trust, honesty and confidence	17
Duty/responsibility and protocols/procedures	17
Eradicate blame and defensiveness	16
Lead agency	13
Improve decision-making	12
Create multi-agency teams/a common agency	12
Acknowledge good practice	9
Resources, staff numbers and staff availability	8
Develop common language	8
Regular meetings	7
Working conditions and motivation	2
Technology	2

Index

Note: The letter 'f' after a page reference denotes a figure and the letter 't' denotes a table.